SHALOM ON THE RANGE

A Roundup of Recipes and
Jewish Traditions from Colorado Kitchens

Friends of Shalom Park
Denver, Colorado

PROFESSIONAL CREDITS

Illustrations
Rick Biederman

Photographs
Front Cover: Stock Imagery, Inc.
Mt. Audubon in the Indian Peaks Range of Colorado

Back Cover: Courtesy of Denver Buffalo Company

Divider Page Mountains: Norton Singer, Photographer
Maroon Bells, Aspen, Colorado

Thank you to the galleries and museums that so graciously
allowed us to photograph their unique and historical stoves:

Cover stove: Preusser Gallery, Taos, New Mexico
Arvada Center for the Arts and Humanities
Byers-Evans House
Colorado Historical Society
Cripple Creek District Museum
Grant Humphreys Mansion
Molly Brown House
It's a Victor Thing, Victor, Colorado
On A Ledge, Manitou Springs, Colorado
William Ohs Kitchens

Nutritional analysis - *Master Cook II, 1994, Arion*

Proceeds from the sale of **SHALOM ON THE RANGE** will be used to fund special projects to further enhance the quality of life for the residents of Shalom Park.
Shalom Park is a Jewish continuum-of-care organization providing residential health and social services to the elderly and their families.
**Additional copies of SHALOM ON THE RANGE may be obtained
by sending $24.95 plus $5.50 for shipping and handling for the first copy,
$2.00 for shipping and handling each additional copy to the same address to:
Shalom Park, 14800 East Belleview Drive, Aurora, CO 80015
Colorado residents please add $1.80 sales tax for each book.**

LCCCN #97 - 060380
ISBN 0-9656849-0-3

First Printing, 5,000 copies, 1997
Second Printing, 4,000 copies, 1998
Third Printing, 3,000 copies, 2001

Printed in the USA by
WIMMER
The Wimmer Companies
Memphis
1-800-548-2537

TABLE OF CONTENTS

FOREWORD

by Rabbi Daniel Goldberger

Jewish Dietary Laws

Dear Readers,

In an effort to be helpful, the cookbook committee has included an overview of the major reasons for practicing kashrut. (This is the Hebrew term for the dietary laws, coming from the root word kosher, which means "ritually proper or fit".) The Torah ("Five Books of Moses") which contains the original commandments of these laws gives only one reason for them — that they are of Divine origin and are part of the Holiness Code which the Torah prescribes for all aspects of life.

Jewish scholars over the centuries have suggested a variety of additional reasons which have been meaningful for those who seek a deeper understanding of these unusual laws. They include the following, which are not given in order of importance.

Jewish survival requires a number of practices which are different and separate from those practiced by other faiths or cultures. Having a unique assortment of eating practices has proven to be one important factor of continuity in the struggle for survival over the centuries.

Ensuring the perpetuation of institutions, practices and beliefs of the Jewish faith requires continual reminders of one's identity. Eating is done on a regular basis regardless of circumstances. Recalling admonitions of what can or cannot be eaten serves as a daily reminder of our particular identity in cultures that often are oriented to assimilation and loss of identity.

Others have pointed out that these laws are national/ethnic manifestations of Jewish civilization in the same way that other practices (e.g. Sabbath, holidays, prayers) are followed, not necessarily because of religious belief, but because they are part of a historical totality of Jewishness.

A profound reason is that food laws afford an opportunity to sanctify the ordinary. Time can become routine, but the Sabbath and holidays elevate these specific moments in time to a higher level. Food can be taken for granted. Observance of dietary laws raises the physical act of eating to an interaction between the sacred and the ordinary.

Another possibility is developing a sense of discipline. If a person is keenly aware of the permitted and the forbidden in one's dietary habits, he or she may transfer this to the choices in the moral and ethical areas of life.

These are some of the more compelling reasons that have been suggested by major Jewish thinkers. There are other approaches that are beyond the limitations of this introduction. Readers will note that the usual popular explanations of hygiene and health are not included in my listing. Those reasons were undoubtedly crucial at an earlier time in Jewish history. Today, they may or may not be significant. Space does not permit this discussion.

In observing dietary laws, matter and spirit are intertwined. We know today that food has a powerful effectiveness and must be good for the soul as well as for the body!

Let us hope that the use of these kosher recipes will result not only in delicious and appealing treats for the body, but will also contribute, with an understanding of the reasons given above, to the perpetuation of the force of the Jewish spirit in our individual and collective lives.

PREFACE

Why a cookbook? Because cooking is so near and dear to the Jewish heart. Because for Jewish people food means sharing, and love, and nurturing and hospitality. And because great Colorado Jewish cooks tested and tasted delicious recipes collected from over 400 Shalom Park supporters. More than 140 community volunteers — mothers, daughters, and granddaughters — rolled up their sleeves in the kitchen and cooked. We've double kitchen-tested every recipe, carefully assembling a collection of recipes that blends contemporary dishes you can cook every day and classic recipes passed down from generation to generation. We've reduced fat without sacrificing flavor and introduced buffalo, adding a bit of that special spice of life we enjoy in the Rockies. All recipes are adjusted for preparation a mile high, at 5,280 feet. At lower altitude, recipes may need less liquid, shorter cooking times and more leavening.

All the recipes in this book are kosher. They don't mix meat and milk, nor do they include shellfish or pork. They are labeled *meat, dairy* and *pareve* (neutral) to assist you with meal planning. If you want more information on kosher cooking than this book provides, please contact the rabbi of your choice.

Jewish cooking isn't just *schmaltz* and *kishka*. It can be delicious and healthy and still follow Jewish dietary laws. In fact, you don't even have to be Jewish to enjoy making these recipes. You'll learn a little of our tradition by reading about Shabbat and the history of major holidays that are associated with special foods and festive meals. We hope this book will be part of your everyday life, giving you inspiration in the kitchen, while providing a resource for celebrating our Jewish heritage and traditions. We also hope that our fond recollections will bring back cherished memories of *your own family's* tastes and traditions.

Shalom Park

"The past we inherit, the future we create."

The need for a Jewish nursing home was first recognized in 1917 by Bella Mintz, one of Denver, Colorado's first advocates for the elderly. Together with a group of dedicated women, Bella Mintz formed the Beth Israel Hospital and Home Society to raise funds for a new home to be located in Denver. A spirited and dynamic visionary, Bella campaigned coast-to-coast to enlist financial support. It wasn't until Isadore Rude donated land and Leopold Guldman donated $50,000 to start construction that the dream became a reality. **Beth Israel Hospital and Home for the Aged** finally opened its doors in December 1923, its mission to care for the poor and infirm.

Beth Israel's services expanded over the years until, in 1983, the Allied Jewish Federation commissioned a study of Denver's projected long-term needs. The study showed that the Jewish population in Denver was moving Southeast, creating a physical distance between Beth Israel residents and their families that was difficult to bridge. The need for a new facility in a new location, with an eye toward the future, was indicated. Community leaders responded to this need; and through their diligent and dedicated efforts, a site was purchased and construction began on a new campus to be named **Beth Israel at Shalom Park**.

Part of a planned 34.5 acre continuum-of-care campus, the new state-of-the-art long term care and skilled nursing facility opened in 1992 for 135 residents. Just as in the original facility, Beth Israel at Shalom Park accepts Medicare, private payment and, out of a commitment to serve all who need care, reserves up to 60% of its beds for Medicaid-eligible residents.

6

The Patio Homes and Apartments at Shalom Park opened in September 1996, offering a variety of independent and assisted living options. All of the cottages and apartments have been designed for aging in place and are fully adaptable to meet special needs and physical limitations.

Shalom Park's success is largely due to the high level of involvement, commitment, and support extended by the Denver community. A dedicated Board of Trustees and a legion of volunteers offer their time and talents. Members of the community enjoy participating in activities and holding meetings on the campus.

A vital community resource offering outstanding services for the elderly and their families, Shalom Park is the culmination of the dream and vision of Beth Israel's founders, a nationally-recognized residential health and social service organization that is considered a leader in its field.

"The times have changed, but the spirit remains the same."

FRIENDS OF SHALOM PARK

When the Beth Israel Nursing Home moved from the west side of Denver to its magnificent new home southeast of Denver, it sought to recreate its auxiliary and embrace the many new friends made in the new location. Creating a cookbook brought together volunteers of all ages and levels of observance. This project offered an opportunity for those who wanted to support Shalom Park to step forward. It was a project around which to begin a new "family" — *Friends of Shalom Park.*

Bringing the community together was a significant goal of this project. A wealth of skills and expertise were focused on one purpose — to enhance Shalom Park's state-of-the-art care and programming for the elderly. Proceeds from the sale of **SHALOM ON THE RANGE** will contribute to the *exceptional view of life* enjoyed by our parents at Shalom Park, a community's treasure that was more than ten years in the making. Thus, a couple of years invested in the nurturing of a cookbook didn't seem like much to ask.

We want to thank all of the people who so generously contributed their energy and ideas and helped in one way or another to bring **SHALOM ON THE RANGE** from concept to success.

This is our gift to you! The *Friends of Shalom Park* hope you enjoy this collection of recipes from some of Colorado's best Jewish cooks.

This book is dedicated

to our mothers and fathers,

to our children and grandchildren,

and to our spouses,

without whose support this work would not have been possible.

COOKBOOK COMMITTEE

Honorary Chairperson
Essie Perlmutter

Chairperson
Noreen Stillman

Editors
Carol Singer
Marion Galant

Recipe Coordinator
Jackie Frazin

Testing Coordinators
Sharon Ripps
Sherrie Zeppelin

Art Directors
Arlene Galchinsky
Sheila Rudofsky

Marketing
Artis Roslyn Silverman

Treasurer
Sherry Stark

Secretary
Barbara Lipkin

Judaic Writer
Sue Hochstadt

Judaic Advisor
Rabbi Daniel Goldberger

Cookbook Advisor
Joanie Hartman

Nutritionist
Robyn Naiman

Art Committee
Arlene Kaufman Levine
Janice Rosen
Ethel Mendel
Roberta Volin
Marion Galant

Marketing Committee
Ellen Beller
Karen Frankel
Lee Kay
Cynthia Kutner
Sally Loeb
Lou Ann May
Stephanie Milzer
Sharon Ripps
Bonnie Saliman
Ellen Selig
Lisa Taussig
Vicki Trachten-Schwartz
Fran Yeddis

A Special Thank You to

Diane Amdur, *Johnston Wells Public Relations*
Board of Trustees of Shalom Park

and to the following individuals and companies:

Bob Adelstein
Roz Ash
Carole Cantor
Sharon Cooper
Denver Buffalo Company
Adele Gelfand
Marion Goldstein
Blanche Greenberg
Sheryl Gurrentz
Junior League of Denver

Sue Krems
Jennifer Ledden
Ruth Leisenring
Le Petit Gourmet Catering
Marilyn Mishkin
Will McFarlane
Lyn Munger
Neiman Marcus
Joanne Pepper
Libby Printz

Earl Roper
Hindi Roseman
Libby Rosen
Betty Shaer
Wesley Stark
Stillman Photographics
Strings Restaurant
Tattered Cover Bookstore
Abe Wagner

Section Heads

Appetizers
Carol Paderski

Brunch
Vicki Eskanos

Breads
Marilyn Hyman

Soups and Salads
Sherry Stark

Meat
Lil Speyer
Jean Olshansky
Jackie Frazin

Poultry
Ketsie Klausner

Fish
Cindy Ustun

Pasta and Grains
Andrea Stillman

Vegetables
Robyn Naiman

Desserts
Cathy Neistat
Marilyn Snyder
Peggy Stone

Traditional
Goldie Shapiro

We are grateful to the Shalom Park staff for their support of this project.

COOKBOOK RECIPE TESTERS

The Friends of Shalom Park gratefully acknowledge the energy and dedicated efforts of the men and women who tested and perfected the recipes in this book. We are immensely grateful for their commitment and cooking skills.

Appetizers
Carol Paderski – *Chair*
Geegee Brunschwig
Diane Cohn
Heidi Dudley
Helen Finklestein
Bill Goldberg
Roselyn Kark
Judy Kippur
Francine Koller
Jody Lipsitz
Joyce Perlmutter
Jamie Roll
Cindy Ustun
Barbara Zall

Brunch
Vicki Eskanos – *Chair*
Jackie Cooper
Jodi Cooper
Carol Hein
Lucy Joseph*
Hedy Monheit
Kim Monheit
Marci Rivkin
Barbara Silverman

Breads and Muffins
Marilyn Hyman – *Chair*
Lieba Alpert
Myrna Engbar
Linda Goodman
Judy Howard
Diana Kaplan
Carole Rich

Soups and Salads
Sherry Stark – *Chair*
Renee Brilliant
Carol Brooks
Janet Frank
Sue Goldberg
Dean Goss
Susie Kamlet
Cathryn Lutz
Richard Lutz
Susan McKinney
Bonnie Merenstein
Maxine Miller
Roberta Sanders
Susan Siegel
Sherry Tenenbaum
Elaine Tinter

Meats
Jackie Frazin – *Co-Chair*
Jean Olshansky – *Co-Chair*
Lil Speyer – *Co-Chair*
Susie Currie
Karen Frankel
Ruth Goodman
Lisa Jacobs
Ruth Kahn
Mitzi Kurtz
Shirley Leff
Mona Pasternack
Joanne Pepper
Sharon Ripps
Libby Rosen
Jan Wayne
Sherrie Zeppelin

Poultry
Ketsie Klausner – *Chair*
Bobbie Carr
Sheila Cohen
Vicki Dansky
Phyllis Goodman
Hyla Greinetz
Carol Karsh
Pearl Neiman
Peggy Pepper
Charlotte Rubin
Gerard Rudofsky
Joyce Sachter
Bonnie Saliman
Elaine Soy
Janet Yabrove

Fish
Cindy Ustun – *Chair*
Dana Burding
Cheryl Cohen
Heidi Dudley
Anna Fine
JoAnn Fleischman
Margie Gershtenson
Diane Marks
Renee Reckler

Pasta and Grains
Andrea Stillman – *Chair*
Sheri Brummett
Alison R. Cooper
Jodi Eisen
Jamie Idelberg
Nancy Kaufman

Laurie Morris
Ilene Rosen
Traci Sidon
Shelley Siegel
Lori Weiner
Debra Weinstein

Vegetables
Robyn Naiman – *Chair*
Carla Bartell
Jodi Capps
Berdine Clumpus
Ellen Finer
Sherri Goldstein
Cynthia Kutner
Peggy Mayer
Bonnie Saliman

Desserts
Cathy Neistat – *Co-Chair*
Marilyn Snyder – *Co-Chair*
Peggy Stone – *Co-Chair*
Sandy Burg
Linda Carney
Lisa Feld
Galit Gottlieb
Linda Kernis
Karen Niernberg
Barbara Rodak
Cece Siegel
Leslie Simon
Lori Snyder
Reesa Webb

Traditional
Goldie Shapiro – *Chair*
Barbara Cohen
Estelle Klein
Rebecca Klein
Raeann Lampert
Carol Laycob
Barbara Lipkin
Leslea Mutnick
Robyn Mutnick
Rae Ann Negreann
Barbara Pluss
Helen Pringle

* Of blessed memory

COOKBOOK CONTRIBUTORS

The Friends of Shalom Park thank all of the cooks and storytellers who generously contributed their treasured recipes and food memories to this book. We regret that we were unable to include all of the recipes and stories which were submitted due to space limitations. We also hope that we have not inadvertently overlooked any contributors.

Wilma Aaron
Robert Adelstein
Andrea Allen
Lieba Alpert
Sarah Alterman
Barbara Amdur
Diane Amdur
Lynne Anagast
Sharlene Ancell
Anne Gottlieb Angerman
Zisan Anter
Risa Aqua
Diane Arave
Elaine Asarch
Carolyn Auerbach
Suzanne Z. Barkin
Carla Bartell
Micki Belstock
Liza Berkoff
Mary Beth Berkoff
Karla Berman
Dubby Bernstein
Michael Biales
Sue Biales
Dorothy Bittan
Deena Blank
Betsy Block
Marilyn Bogan
JoAnn Boss
Judy Bowman
Gayle Boxer
Amy Boymel
Richard H. Brice
Karen Briggs
Renee Brilliant
Carol Brooks
Meraly Brown
Rose Brown
Carol Z. Bruce
Geegee Brunschwig
Joan Bub
Sandy Burg
Iolene Burstein
Arlene Bushbach
Joan Byrne
Beth Caffey
Carole Cantor
Bobbi Carr
Adessa Catchman
Sugar Chalus
Barbara Cohen
Cece Cohen
Cheryl Cohen

Harold J. Cohen
Herb Cohen
Jim Cohen
Harold Cohen
Leah Cohen*
Marty Cohen
Amy Cohn
Diane Cohn
Karen Cole
Midge Colman
Sherry Conner
Lisa Cook
Alison Reckler Cooper
Cami Cooper
Jackie Cooper
Jodi Cooper
Ann Cornfeld
Jan Cramer
Noel Cunningham
Vicki Perlmutter Dansky
Gladys Decker
Denver Buffalo Co.
  Restaurant
Arlene Devorkin
Barry Dolin
Becky Dolin
Jodi Boxer Dinkin
Wendy Rifkin Dorband
Dorothy Dorsey
Sandra Dorsey
Sylvie Drake
Helen Drazen
Heidi Dudley
Nellie Mae Duman
Jodi Eisen
Dee Emeson
Myrna Engbar
Shirley Engbar
Renee Engel
Charlene Engleberg
Craig Eskanos
Josephine Eskanos
Vicki Eskanos
Marsha Feur
Elyse Fieldman
Helen Finkelstein
Arlene Fishman*
Joanne Fleischman
Deanna Fox
Elizabeth Fox
Shirley Frances
Janet Frank
Linda Frank

Molly Frank
Karen Frankel
Elise Franklin
Shirley Franklin
Jackie Frazin
Anita Fricklas
Jan Friedland
Mary Ellen Friedland
Ada Friedman
Berdie Friedman
Lisa Binswanger Friedman
Susan Frisch
Corinne Fronko
Barbara Fruitman
Marion Galant
Arlene Galchinsky
Sarah Galchinsky
Sally Gardenswartz
Stacy Gardner
Martin Garelick
Nancy Gart
Adele Gelfand
Betty Gelt
Sarah Whiton Gelt
Judie Gershaw
Margie Gershtenson
Toby Ginsburg
Barbara Glick
Dorothy Goldberg
Ida Goldberger
Nancy Goldin
Dorothy Goldstein
Zelda Goldstein
Berta Goodman
Linda Goodman
Nancy Goodman
Ruth Goodman
Adele Gordon
Fran Gottlieb
Galit Pinsky Gottlieb
Stan Gottlieb
Barbara Gray
Goldie Greenblatt
Zelda Greene
Rachel Greenholtz
Gussie Greenstein
Lorraine Greenstein
Sally Greer
Marsha Greiner
Hyla Greinetz
Jessie Grommet*
Renee Gross
Rose Gvirtz

Bonnie Gwozdecky
Elka Haligman
Joanie Hartman
Cathy Heins
Martha Helstien
Esther Henken
Dorothy Hirschfeld
Diane Hochstadt
Sue Hochstadt
Miriam Hoffman
Elizabeth Holtze
Judy Howard
Meryl Howell
Barbara Hubler
Dee Hunter
Sere Hunter
Gloria Husney
Ellen Hutt
Marilyn Hyman
Jamie Idelberg
Donna Ilacqua
Carole Jacobs
Meryl Jacobs
Phyllis Jacobs
Robyn Jacobs
Leslie Jjarks
Mary Joannou
Lucy Joseph*
Wendy Judd
Sylvia Drake Jurras
Shirley Justman
Ruth Kahn
Susie Kamlet
Leon Kanowitz
Rae Kanowitz
Diana Kaplan
Deanne Kapnick
Roselyn Kark
Shellie Kark
Betty Karsh
Carol Karsh
Sally Karsh
Eileen Katz
Norma Katz
Rosalee Katz
Mollie Katzen
Linda Kernis
Phyllis Kipper
Judy Kippur
Ketsie Klausner
Estelle Klein
Mimi Klein
Francene Koller

Gloria Kris
Marcia Kuperstein
Mitzi Kurtz
Anne Kushner
Cynthia Kutner
Fran Kutner
Karen LaMar
Adele Lambert
Raeann Lampert
Miriam Landau
Carol Laycob
Le Petit Gourmet
Jennifer Ledden
Shirley Leff
Legends Park Restaurant
Ita Leitner
Edra Levi
Carolyn Salzer Levin
Judy Levin
Renae Dechter Levin
Helen Levitch
Sarah Lew
Jackie Lewin
Elaine Lintes
Barbara Lipkin
Jody Lipsitz
Susan Look
Charlene Loup
Ellen Wilner Lozow
Dorothy Lumerman
Aaron Lutz
Catherine Lutz
Richard Lutz
Sue Maguire
Isabel Make
Frieda Marcus
Lois Margolin
Lorrie Margolin
Diane Marks
Helene Martin
Diane Martinez
Kay Martley
Colette Mattatia
Joanie McCallie
Carolyn McElfatrick
Susan McKinney
Minnie Meisler
Florence Melnick
Shirley Melnick
Bonnie Merenstein
Bev Michaels
Maxine Miller
Meg Miller
Pat Miller
Sue Miller
Wendy Engbar Miller
Elaine Millman
Jeanie Milofsky
Marilyn Mishkin
Michelle Mittler
Hedy Monheit
Kim Monheit
Gail Mordka

Amy Morris
Rita Morris
Joyce Moskowitz
Leslea Mutnick
Robyn Naiman
Celia Nathenson
Rae Ann Negreann
Barbara Neider
Pearl Neiman
Cathy Neistat
Simone Chaya Nemon
Shirlee Nickow
Karen Niernberg
Gail Okner
Beverly Olesky
Sydney Olesky
Vicki Bluma Olesky
Marilyn Ogrin
Jean Olshansky
Marjorie Ostrov
Jan Paddock
Carol Paderski
Mona Pasternack
Donna Mae Paul
David Pells
Gertrude Pepper
Joanne Pepper
Marilyn Pepper
Alice Perl
Essie Perlmutter
Joyce Perlmutter
Joyce Persky
Ruth Peter
Bobbie Pinkert
Ina Pinkncy
Alisa Pluss
Barbara Pluss
Zoni Pluss
Helene Pollock
Helen Pomerantz
Fern Primack
Helen Pringle
Libby Printz
Phyllis Behrens Pritcher
Adele Pritzker
Renee Reckler
Ida Reisman
Florence Rest
Carole Rich
Rose Richtel
Estelle Rifkin
Sharon Ripps
Marci Rivkin
Barbara Rodak
Jamie Roll
David Root
Berdie Rosen
Erica Rosen
Florence H. Rosen
Ilene Rosen
Libby Rosen
Genny Rosenberg
Miriam Ross

Patti Ross
Michael Roth
Jill Rothery
Beth Rubin
Charlotte Rubin
Lynn Rubin
Sylvia Ruda
Gerard Rudofsky
Lee Rudofsky
Sheila Rudofsky
Leslie Ruttedge
Joyce Sachter
Sandra Salar
Bess Saliman
Bonnie Saliman
Sue Schafer
Eileen Schechter
Susie Scher
Ellen Selig
Betty Shaer
Cindy Shaiman
Andi Shainberg
Goldie Shapiro
Karen Shapiro
Betty Sharoff
Bernice Sharp
Shellie Sheanen
Litamae Sher
Lottie Sher
Cheryl Sherer
Eleanor Shidler
Arlene Shwayder
Traci Sidon
Susan Siegel
Sandra Silver
Artis Silverman
Barbara Silverman
Susie Silverstein
Carolyn Simon
Harriet Simon
Leslie Simon
Carol Singer
Lenny Singer
Harriet Sklar
Sherma Sloan
Pam Smith
Tecla Smith
Lori Snyder
Marilyn Snyder
Mary Soffen
Lil Speyer
Ruth Springer
Ann Stanley*
Ruth Stark
Sherry Stark
Nancy Steiner
Marilyn Stepnek
Andrea Stillman
Julie Stillman
Noreen Stillman
Peggy Stone
Irma Strear
Rama Strod

Sandy Sukin
Beverly Sunshine
Donna Supinger
Clara Swartz
Joan Swartz
Linda B. Swartz
Susan Swartz
Peggy Tarbox
Alva Tauger
Gloria Taussig
Lisa Taussig
Sherry Tenenbaum
Cheryl Thaemert
Jack Thaler
Lois Thikoll
Elaine Tinter
Mary Troyer
Lucille Turner
Ida Uchill
Cindy Ustun
Roz VanHauten
Bernadette Vanya
Joan Vehik
Gert Friedman Waldman
Nan Waldman
Sharon Waldman
Merrily Wallach
Janet Warren
Joan Warton
Jenny Wasko
Jan Wayne
Phil Wayne
Reesa Webb
Kathie Weber
Lola Weiner
Lori Weiner
Marlene Weiner
Debra Weinstein
Faye Weinstein
Larry Weiss
Enid Wenner
Susan Wetstein
Jennifer Wickman
Linda Willis
Sandra Wittow
Liz Wolfson
Fran Wolpo
Joan Worton
Jill Wright
Janet Yabrove
Shirley Yoelin
Barbara Zall
Diane Zelinger
Louise Zelinger
Deanie Zelkin
Jeff Zelkin
Kristopher Zelkin
Sherrie Zeppelin
Fanny Zerobnick
Mira Zevin

Of Blessed Memory

11

BLESSINGS

Pronunciation Guide to Transliterated Hebrew (Sephardic)

a .... as in 'papa' or 'father' (long)	u .... as in 'pull' (short) or 'rule' (long)
e .... as in 'get' or 'the' (sheva)	ai .... as in 'aisle'
ee ...... as in 'free'	oi .... as in 'boil'
eh ...... as in 'get' (used only at the end of a word)	ei .... as in 'veil'
i .... as in 'bit' (short) or 'machine' (long)	g .... as in 'get' (hard 'g')
o .... as in 'over'	ch ...... as in Scottish 'loch' or German 'ach'

Chanukah Blessings

Ba-ruch a-ta, A-do-nai E-lo-hei-nu,
me-lech ha-o-lam, a-sher ki-de-sha-nu
be-mits-vo-tav, ve-tsi-va-nu
le-had-lik neir shel Chan-u-ka.

You are blessed, Lord our God,
Sovereign of the world,
who has sanctified us with your commandments
and has commanded us to kindle the Chanukah
    lights.

Ba-ruch a-ta, A-do-nai E-lo-hei-nu,
me-lech ha-o-lam, she-a-sa ni-sim
la-a-vo-tei-nu ba-ya-mim ha-heim
ba-ze-man ha-zeh.

You are blessed, Lord our God,
Sovereign of the world,
who wrought miracles for our ancestors
in those days at this season.

The following blessing is also recited on the first night of Chanukah.

*Blessing for the Beginning of Every Holiday

Ba-ruch a-ta, A-do-nai E-lo-hei-nu,
me-lech ha-o-lam, she-he-che-ya-nu
ve-ki-ye-ma-nu ve-hi-gi-ya-nu
la-ze-man ha-zeh.

You are blessed, Lord our God,
Sovereign of the world,
who has kept us alive, who has sustained us,
and enabled us to reach this occasion.

Blessing After Kindling Shabbat Candles

Ba-ruch a-ta, A-do-nai E-lo-hei-nu,
me-lech ha-o-lam, a-sher ki-de-sha-nu
be-mits-vo-tav, ve-tsi-va-nu
le-had-lik neir shel Shabbat.

You are blessed, Lord our God,
Sovereign of the world,
who made us holy with your commandments
and commanded us to kindle lights for Sabbath.

Blessing Over Wine

Ba-ruch a-ta, A-do-nai E-lo-hei-nu,
me-lech ha-o-lam,
bo-ray pree ha-ga-fen.

You are blessed, Lord our God,
Sovereign of the world,
Creator of the fruit of the vine.

Blessing Over Bread

Ba-ruch a-ta, A-do-nai E-lo-hei-nu,
me-lech ha-o-lam,
ha-motzi le-chem min ha-a-retz.

You are blessed, Lord our God,
Sovereign of the world,
who brings forth bread from the earth.

Blessing After the Lighting of Holiday Candles (*other than Chanukah*)

Ba-ruch a-ta, A-do-nai E-lo-hei-nu,
me-lech ho-o-lam, a-sher ki-de-sha-nu
be-mits-vo-tav, ve-tsi-va-nu
le-had-lik neir shel yom tov.

You are blessed, Lord our God,
Sovereign of the world,
who made us holy with your commandments
and commanded us to kindle lights for the
    festival.

SHABBAT

The Midrash relates that the challah of Sarah, our foremother, was unique. From her mind and heart, and through her fingertips, she'd knead with intention — imbuing her challah with spiritual sustenance so that all who ate felt satisfied the entire week.

Today, women still focus their minds on their challah when they knead, filling up the dough with their own spirituality — to be shared with family and guests.

HAFRASHAT CHALLAH (SEPARATING CHALLAH)

One of the oldest Jewish laws commanded that when one prepared dough it was required that a part of the dough should be given as a gift to the Kohain, the Priest. This was called "taking challah". Since we no longer give a part of the dough to any of the present day members of the Kohain family, it is required that when dough is prepared for challah or bread, that a portion shall be taken and burned, simply as a symbol and a reminder of that ancient practice of giving a gift to G-d's representative, the Priest. The prayer for taking challah is as follows:

> *"Boruch ato adonoy elohaynu melech ha-olom a-sher kidshonu b'mitvosov v'tzivonu l'haf-rish challah."*

> *"Blessed art Thou, Our G-d and G-d of our Fathers, who hast sanctified us with His Commandments, and has given us the commandment for the separation of the Challah."*

The prayer said before eating challah or bread is as follows:

> *"Boruch ato adonoy eloheynu melech ha-olom ha-motzi lechem meen ho-oretz."*

> *"Blessed art Thou, our G-d and G-d of our Fathers, who brings bread forth from the earth."*

It is appropriate to use two challahs on the Sabbath table and the holiday table as a reminder of the time when our ancestors were wandering in the wilderness, after the exodus from Egypt, and would collect a double portion of manna on Friday to provide for their tables both for Friday and for the Sabbath.

After a meal there is a long blessing which is called "benchen." After eating any other food, there is also a blessing which is called "brocho achrono."

SILVER MEDAL WINNER   GOLD MEDAL WINNER

BARON
HERZOG

California

Award

Winning

Wines

for

Every

Occasion.

JEWISH HOLIDAYS

JEWISH HOLIDAYS — INTRODUCTION

Jews throughout the world observe different customs and traditions. The observances described in this book reflect traditional Ashkenazic (Middle and Eastern European) Jewish practices. This book is not intended to be a guide for Jewish observances. Rather it offers a taste of the Jewish heritage for those with an appetite to learn.

In this cookbook, you will find information about major Jewish observances, along with menu suggestions for each holiday. Recipes reflecting the diversity of the Denver area Jewish community are included for most of the dishes mentioned.

There are two significant forms of pronunciation of the Hebrew text among Jewish people — Ashkenazic (Middle and Eastern European) and Sephardic (Spanish-North African). The English transliteration of the blessings in this book reflect the Sephardic form, which is prevalent in Israel today.

SHABBAT

The Sabbath is one of the first observances celebrated by our people, dating back to the days of the Exodus. It may be one of the greatest contributions our ancestors have shared with the world, as the Jews were the first people to dedicate one day each week to rest. From the Hebrew word Shabbat, to "rest," the Sabbath is a time to spend with family and friends in thought, prayer, celebration and festivity. It is a time to rest, both physically and mentally, and to pause from our preoccupation with daily, mundane affairs.

As the busy work week draws to a close, Jewish families eagerly prepare for Shabbat. The general, everyday clutter is set aside; the table is set with our best dishes and silver-ware; and we cook and bake our favorite foods which may vary depending on nationality and tradition. Special foods make this day different from the other days of the week. Shabbat begins at sundown on Friday with the lighting and blessing of the candles (which often includes a special prayer asking for the well-being of all Israel), blessing the children, and blessings over the wine and two challahs (braided egg bread).

One traditional Shabbat food that is universal is the challah, which can be prepared nowadays very quickly in a bread machine but, almost as easily, by hand. The custom of having two loaves of challah on the Sabbath and holidays comes, historically, from the double portion of manna gathered by Jews on Fridays when, for forty years, they wandered and lived in the desert on their journey to the land of Israel. The aroma of challah baking in your oven will surely be one of your family's treasured memories.

The Sabbath ends at sundown Saturday with the Havdalah ceremony. We light the braided multi-wick candle in gratitude for the distinction between light and darkness; smell the fragrance of mixed spices, including cinnamon, cloves, and nutmeg, which remind us of the hopes we have for a sweet week ahead; and drink from our wine cup as a sign of joy for the coming of the new week.

Traditional Shabbat foods are chopped liver, chicken soup with matzo balls, gefilte fish, potato kugel and roasted chicken. According to tradition, lighting or extinguishing a fire on the Sabbath is forbidden, so a traditional meal of "cholent," which consists of meat, potatoes, beans and barley, is placed in a slow oven or crockpot before sundown on Friday to be eaten for Shabbat lunch.

SUGGESTED MENUS

Shabbat — *All menus should include ceremonial wine
and Honey Twist Challah*

*Chopped Liver, p. 33
Divine Salad, p. 104
Challah Stuffed Chicken Breasts, p. 155
Rosemary Green Beans with Hazelnuts, p. 215
Apple Glazed Carrots, p. 212
Plenty O' Pecans, p. 246
Elegant Baked Pears, p. 264*

———

*Oriental Spinach Salad, p. 105, or
Kettle Potato and Leek Soup, p. 99
Grilled Halibut with Lemon Basil Vinaigrette, p. 163
Orzo and Toasted Barley Pilaf, p. 205
Boulder Broccoli Casserole, p. 211
Coconut Lemon Ice Cream Pie, p. 242, or
Denver Chocolate Cake, p. 231*

———

*Spinach Mushroom Roll Ups, p. 54
Salad Mexicana, p. 105
Herb Crusted Rack of Lamb, p. 143
Red Rocks Potatoes, p. 225
Sautéed Leeks and Asparagus, p. 211
Palisade Fall Fruit Salad, p. 121
Crunchy Mandel Bread, p. 256*

ROSH HASHANAH

Rosh Hashanah is the Jewish New Year. It is also called the Day of Judgment and the Day of Remembrance. Along with Yom Kippur, Rosh Hashanah is known as one of the most solemn of the religious observances because these days are given over to prayer and introspection, while the other Jewish holy days either celebrate great historic events or are a celebration of the various harvest seasons. As the holiday at the head of the year, Rosh Hashanah sets a pattern. Tradition says that what people do on Rosh Hashanah they will do the remainder of the year. Although it is a thoughtful and insightful day, it is not a sad day. This season is approached with happiness because we hope the holiday will be the beginning of an even better year than the one just ended.

During this season it is customary for Jewish families to eat sweet foods. Fresh apples dipped in honey are traditional as a symbol for a good and sweet year. Sour and bitter foods are usually avoided during this holiday. Nuts are also avoided because the numerical value of the word "nut" in Hebrew has the same numerical value as the Hebrew word for "sin."

The challah loaves that are braided for Shabbat are formed into a round shape to remind us of continuity. The dough is filled with raisins to symbolize the sweetness in life for which we pray. Fish is often served as a symbol of fertility and as "brain food."

New seasonal fruits such as pomegranates and persimmons, which are grown in Israel, are also eaten. Pomegranates are said to contain 613 seeds, of special significance since there are 613 commandments in the Torah. It is fun, after the holiday meal has been eaten, for the pomegranates to be peeled, divided into sections, and the seeds counted. (Don't forget to account for the ones that get eaten during the counting, or smashed by the knife; and, remember bibs for the little ones, because pomegranate juice stains.)

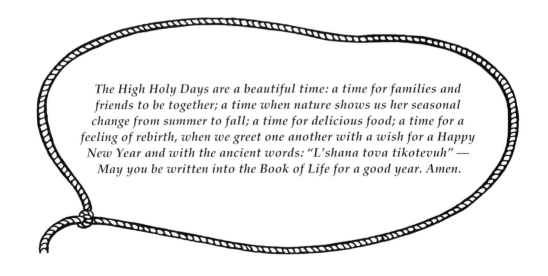

The High Holy Days are a beautiful time: a time for families and friends to be together; a time when nature shows us her seasonal change from summer to fall; a time for delicious food; a time for a feeling of rebirth, when we greet one another with a wish for a Happy New Year and with the ancient words: "L'shana tova tikotevuh" — May you be written into the Book of Life for a good year. Amen.

SUGGESTED MENUS

Rosh Hashanah — *apples & honey, wine & challah would be served with all menus. A fresh fruit plate goes with all desserts.*

Homemade Gefilte Fish, p. 35, with Horseradish, p. 37
Basic Chicken Soup, p. 93, with Mama's Matzo Balls, p. 95
Plum Creek Turkey Breast, p. 161
Columbine Cranberry Chutney, p. 122
Pecan Crumble Sweet Potatoes, p. 219, or
Mashed Potatoes and Butternut Squash, p. 221
Balsamic Vinegar Glazed Vegetables, p. 226
Honey Cake, p. 233, Festive Mandel Bread, p. 255
Cherry Vishnik Cordial, p. 256

Quick and Easy Gefilte Fish, p. 36, with Horseradish, p. 37
Grandma's Secret Chicken Soup. p. 94, with Mama's Matzo Balls, p. 95
Haimisheh Brisket, p. 130
Potato Kugel, p. 223, with Applesauce
Vegetarian Kishka, p. 190
Drunken Tzimmes, p. 274, or Classic Carrot Ring, p. 212
Steamed Broccoli, with Orange Sauce, p. 227
Pireshkes, p. 262, or Taiglach, p. 257
Quick and Easy Brownies, p. 245
Stretch Dough Strudel, p. 260

Strawberry Spinach Salad, p. 106
Chilled Poached Salmon with Cucumber Sauce, p. 171
Upside Down Kugel, p. 202
Eggplant Oriental, p. 110
Holiday Rugelach, p. 254
Swiss Tartlettes, p. 249
Chocolate Strudel, p. 246

The Best Mock Chopped Liver, p. 33
French Vegetable Soup, p. 100
Vegetarian Cabbage Rolls, p. 192
Kasha with Varnishkes, p. 204
Stuffed Acorn Squash, p. 217
Wild West Raspberry Brownies, p. 244
Fludin, p. 258

YOM KIPPUR

Ten days after Rosh Hashanah is Yom Kippur, the Day of Atonement. On this holy day we confess our past sins and sincerely repent. Unique to Judaism is the concept that if one has done an injustice to a fellow human being, he or she must seek that person's forgiveness before asking forgiveness from God. Judaism teaches us that if we are truly sorry for our misdeeds, we will be forgiven. It is customary to fast (no food or drink) on this awe-inspiring day because self-imposed abstinence from all pleasures of the body leaves our spirit free for prayer and introspection.

To prepare for the 25-hour fast, many Jews prefer to eat bland foods such as boiled chicken and rice that are not salty or spicy. Others have found comfort from a full stomach derived by eating a heartier meal, such as steak with baked potato and salad. If you are a heavy coffee or cola drinker, it is a good idea to taper off a week or so before the fast to avoid the physical unpleasantness caused by withdrawal from caffeine.

At some synagogues, congregants break the fast together, eating fruit and sweets to restore ourselves physically, and exchanging good wishes for well-being as we leave for home and the beginning of the new year. Sometimes family and friends come together to enjoy a festive meal. Some families enjoy a simple brunch-type menu with bagels, lox, eggs, and fruit; and some prefer a more dinner-type fare with soup, a main course, side dishes, and dessert.

Whether meat or dairy, simple or lavish, the meal is usually prepared in advance of the holiday, to require only warming before it is served to a hungry family returning home from synagogue services after the first stars are seen in the sky.

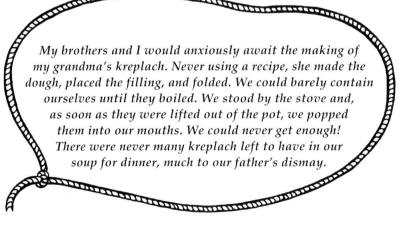

My brothers and I would anxiously await the making of my grandma's kreplach. Never using a recipe, she made the dough, placed the filling, and folded. We could barely contain ourselves until they boiled. We stood by the stove and, as soon as they were lifted out of the pot, we popped them into our mouths. We could never get enough! There were never many kreplach left to have in our soup for dinner, much to our father's dismay.

SUGGESTED MENUS

Yom Kippur

Erev Yom Kippur

Basic Chicken Soup, p. 93, with Kreplach, p. 95
Your Favorite Salad with Basic Vinaigrette, p. 106
Shabbat Roast Chicken, p. 147
Almond Rice, p. 207
Tzimmes, p. 273
High Country Herbed Peas, p. 216
Stretch Dough Strudel, p. 260
Poppy Seed Mandel Bread, p. 257

————

Break-The-Fast

Apple Chopped Herring, p. 44
Lox Pizza, p. 53
Cheese Blintzes, p. 59
Silver Peak Salad Niçoise, p. 119
Fresh Vegetables, with Yogurt Dressing and Dip, p. 107
Sour Cream Schnecken, p. 252, or Company Cheese Braids, p. 250

————

Lox Spread, p. 67
Smoked Whitefish Spread, p. 41
Bagels
Your Favorite Tuna Salad
Upside Down Kugel, p. 202
Ute Spinach Pie, p. 54
Bubbie's Babka, p. 78
Awesome Blueberry Muffins, p. 88

SUKKOT

Sukkot occurs two weeks after Rosh Hashanah. There are practical similarities between Sukkot and the American holiday of Thanksgiving — both give thanks for a bountiful harvest. Celebrated in the synagogue as well as the home, Sukkot is a festive time to celebrate the harvest season and to pray for fruitful harvests to come. The word "sukkah" means booth, referring to the temporary shelters where our ancestors dwelled when they left Egypt and wandered and lived for forty years in the wilderness before entering Israel.

Today, to commemorate this joyous holiday, a family will often build its own sukkah, decorate it with colorful fall fruits and vegetables, and cover it with a roof of bamboo or evergreen branches through which the full moon and stars can be seen. It is customary to share our bounty with friends and especially to include those people who do not have their own sukkah.

The last day of the fall holiday season is Simchat Torah. This is a day of great rejoicing which marks the completion of the cycle of reading the Torah and the immediate beginning of a new cycle of reading. As the Torah scrolls are carried by happy celebrants around the synagogue, children carry small flags, singing and dancing as they follow the Torahs.

Casseroles, stuffed cabbage, chili, and hearty soups, easily carried from kitchen to sukkah, are perfect for this holiday. Fresh fruits and vegetables of the season add to the joy of the autumn harvest celebration as do the traditional round challah loaves, or little challah rolls for variation.

SUGGESTED MENUS

Sukkot

Chopped Eggplant Dip, p. 37
Red Rocks Rye Bread, p. 73
Stuffed Cabbage, p. 135
Mashed Potatoes
Green Beans, with Leadville Lemon Zing!, p. 227
Pueblo Pecan Pie, p. 237

———

Bubbie's Fricassee, p. 134
Stuffed Breast of Veal with Wild Rice, p. 145
Awesome Asparagus, p. 211
Joseph's Coat Vegetable Salad, p. 109
Crusty French Bread, p. 73
Elegant Baked Pears, p. 264

———

Cherry Creek Bruschetta, p. 45
Salmon Stuffed Portobello Mushrooms with Spinach and Cheese, p. 179
Middle Eastern Couscous, p. 206
Onion Focaccia, p. 77
Peachy Custard Pie, p. 238

———

Heavenly Hummus, p. 38
Ratatouille Tart, p. 185, or Vail Valley Vegetable Strudel, p. 186
Sunshine Salad, p. 112
Dried Tomato-Basil Bread, p. 75
Italian Parmesan Bread, p. 75
Telluride Apple Pie, p. 241

CHANUKAH

Although, religiously, Chanukah is considered a minor holiday, the fact is that this holiday commemorates what might historically be the first recorded battle for freedom of religion. Twenty-two hundred years ago, Judah Maccabee and his army recaptured the Temple from the Syrians. In order to rededicate the holy Temple, they needed to rekindle the ner tamid (perpetual lamp). There was only enough oil to burn for one day, yet miraculously the oil lasted for eight full days and nights until more sacramental oil could be made.

This eight-day festival is a wonderful opportunity to celebrate and join together with family and friends. The focus of the holiday is the lighting of the menorah, or chanukiyah, a candle holder used only during Chanukah. This eight branched candle holder has an additional place for one special candle (called the shamash) used to light the other candles. Some families light only one menorah, some light a menorah for each member of the family, and some have many menorahs and light them all!

After sundown on each day of the holiday, the shamash is used to light an additional candle so that by the eighth night the entire menorah is ablaze. The candles are placed in the menorah from right to left (as you are looking at it) and lit from left to right. It is a lovely custom to place the lighted menorahs in windows so that they can be seen from the outside. In this way passers-by can be reminded of the great miracle that happened to the Jewish people. Blessings over the candles are recited, Chanukah songs such as "Rock of Ages" ("Maoz Tzur") are sung, and a few games of spin the draydel (a four-sided top) are played.

Because of the significance of oil on this holiday, it has become traditional to serve foods cooked in or made with oil such as latkes (potato pancakes) and sufganiyot (jelly-filled doughnuts).

Chanukah is such a fine time for the family. The candles in the menorah glow warmly, the potato latkes just barely make it from skillet to table, the children are having a difficult time trying to decide which of their gifts to open, and there is a warm feeling in the house. When my children were small, we decorated our house with homemade art. We made candleholders out of white Styrofoam for tall, blue tapers for the table, and mobiles out of silver or colored paper in the shapes of Stars of David and draydels and menorahs. We would tape a candy treat on each mobile (Chanukah gelt, lollipops or wrapped candy) and hang them all over the house as our gifts to children who came to visit us during the holiday.

SUGGESTED MENUS

Chanukah

Herring Cacciatore, p. 44
Glazed Corned Beef, p. 145, or Tantalizing Tongue, p. 146
Potato Latkes, p. 223, with Applesauce
Roundup Baked Pumpkin, p. 218
Pawnee Pear Cake, p. 232

———

Tangy Redstone Cole Slaw, p. 108
Colorado Barbecued Brisket, p. 131
Potato Latkes, p. 223, with Applesauce
Spinach with Roasted Garlic Butter, p. 216
Grandma's Chocolate Zucchini Bread, p. 87

———

Spinach Borscht, p. 97, or Creamy Cucumber Soup, p. 97
Salmon Pecan, p. 173
Zucchini Potato Latkes, p. 278
Summer Squash Soufflé, p. 218
Timber Creek Rolls, p. 81
Bonanza Butter Cookies (Chanukah Cookies), p. 247

PURIM

The historic saga of Purim dates back about 2500 years ago when King Ahasuerus reigned over Persia. We celebrate as we recall the amazing story of an evil man named Haman who bribed the King to issue a decree of death for all Jews. A pious Jew named Mordechai and his wise and beautiful niece named Esther managed to convince the King of Haman's wickedness, and they thwarted the evil decree. The King fell in love with Esther and made her Queen, good triumphed over evil, and everyone (except Haman) lived happily ever after. No wonder everyone loves Purim.

To celebrate the carnival-like festival of Purim, children (and grownups who are young at heart) dress in costumes and go to the synagogue to listen to the Megillah (biblical scroll) of Esther.

In the synagogue, we listen patiently to hear the name of the evil Haman mentioned so that we can wave our noisemakers, called "greggers," and stamp our feet to symbolically blot out the name of this wicked man.

Gifts and food baskets called Mishloach Manot, which children can help prepare, are exchanged with relatives and friends. Items such as hamantashen (three cornered pastries recalling the three pointed hat worn by Haman), cakes, cookies, small bottles of wine, and candy can be included in the baskets. This holiday is celebrated with parties including singing, dancing, feasting, and drinking.

It is customary to give charity and send food to the less fortunate to ensure that they are able to join in the celebration as well, for Purim bids each Jew to have courage and hope. On this holiday all of us are reminded that every "Haman," every wicked person, in the present and future must and can be overcome.

SUGGESTED MENUS

Purim

Simcha Nuts, p. 50
Savory Salmon Quiche, p. 55, or Four Cheese Quiche, p. 55
Orzo Salad, p. 114
Fresh Fruit
Lemon Blueberry Bread, p. 65
Hamantashen, p. 251, Pireshkes, p. 262,
Orange Kiss-Me Cake, p. 65, Melt-In-Your-Mouth Crescent Cookies, p. 247

———

Oven Beef Barley Soup, p. 102
Five-Spice Orange-Glazed Chicken, p. 152, or Wild Tequila Chicken, p. 153
Front Range Rice, p. 208
A Dilly of a Carrot, p. 213
Sourdough-Like Beer Bread, p. 77
Fruita Hot Fruit Compote, p. 120
Hamantashen, p. 251, Poppy Seed Mandel Bread, p. 257
Cherry Vishnik Cordial, p. 256

PASSOVER (PESACH)

Passover is not only an eight day spring agricultural festival; as the Passover Seder (ceremonial meal) reminds us, it is the historic commemoration of Jewish freedom from Egyptian bondage.

To prepare for Passover (Pesach), we begin making shopping lists and devising menu plans right after the holiday of Purim. A thorough cleaning of the house, particularly the kitchen, becomes a labor of love and a religious obligation. When it comes to work and preparation, Passover is the most demanding holiday. Everything is changed from the everyday — dishes, pots, and utensils which are used year-round are stored away temporarily, and those which are used only at Pesach are brought out and readied for use. Refrigerator shelves are lined, counter tops are covered, and the oven and range burners are turned to their hottest to eliminate any sign of chametz (leavened food) such as flour, rice, wheat, barley, oats, lentils, beans, peas, millet, maize, and corn. No leavened food may be eaten throughout the eight days of Passover.

Finally, the eve of Passover arrives. On the first two nights of the festival, at home celebrations called Seders, we read from the Haggadah (the narrative read just for this holiday): "All those who are hungry, let them come and eat." As we sit around the table joined by family, friends, and others from the community who may not have a Seder of their own, we retell the story and are instructed to imagine that each of us is experiencing the Exodus.

Specific foods, such as the roasted shank bone, roasted egg, greens, horseradish, romaine, an apple-nut mixture called charoset, and matzo which are symbolic of our oppression and road to freedom, are displayed and eaten. We read from the Haggadah, drink four cups of wine (or grape juice), and answer the traditional four questions which begin, "Why is this night different from all other nights?" These questions are asked by the youngest Jewish person present.

Set before the leader are three matzos which represent the three branches of the Jewish people: Cohen, Levi, and Yisrael. During the Seder, the middle matzo is broken into two pieces; the larger part, called the afikoman (dessert), is reserved for the conclusion of the meal. The afikoman is covered and set aside for the children to hold until after the meal is served. In order for the Seder to continue, the leader must have the afikoman to serve as dessert. The children (who have waited the entire evening for this part) are promised a special gift for the return of the afikoman, and the Seder is concluded, ending with many songs.

Traditional foods for this holiday include gefilte fish, chicken soup with matzo balls, poultry with matzo stuffing, and sponge cake. Don't forget the custom of serving new fruits and vegetables which are plentiful during this season. This is one holiday when you can really enjoy being creative and know that everyone at your table will appreciate the fruits of your labor.

SUGGESTED MENUS

Passover

Charoset, p. 271, or Sephardic Charoset, p. 271
Grandma's Secret Chicken Soup, p. 94
Mama's Matzo Balls, p. 95, Passover Soup Noodles, p. 272
Quick and Easy Gefilte Fish, p. 36, with Horseradish, p. 37
Passover Chicken with Farfel, p. 272
Passover Meatless Tzimmes, p. 273
Awesome Asparagus, p. 211
Sunlight Strawberry Rhubarb Sauce, p. 122
Sponge Cake or Jelly Roll with Lemon Filling, p. 283, and Fresh Berries
Passover Mandel "Bread", p. 288
Cake-Like Passover Brownies, p. 287
Fresh Fruit

———

Charoset, p. 271
Basic Chicken Soup, p. 93, with Mama's Matzo Balls, p. 95
Chopped Liver, p. 33
Redstone Rib Roast with Watercress Sauce, p. 138
Anytime Potatoes, p. 221
Pineapple Matzo Kugel, p. 276
Passover Broccoli Soufflé, p. 277
Chocolate Chunk Macaroons, p. 290, Matzo Brittle, p. 291
Cocoa Passover Cake, p. 284
Fresh Fruit

———

Entrée Variations:

Haimisheh Brisket, p. 130
Mom's Gedempte Pot Roast with Fruit, p. 133
Shabbat Roast Chicken, p. 147
Mountain Mushroom Chicken, p. 148
Apricot Cornish Hens, p. 159

SHAVUOT

As in Biblical days, the exact date of Shavuot is determined by counting seven weeks from the second day of Passover. This holiday celebrates the summer harvest festival, recalling the time of the giving of the Torah to Moses and the Jewish people after he led them out of Egypt. In the time of the Temple, at this season, the Jews brought the first of their crops of barley, wheat, grapes, figs, olive oil, dates, and pomegranates to Jerusalem. Today, the holiday serves as a reminder of the social obligations of all people to each other. As Passover marks the birthday of Jewish nationhood, Shavuot is the birthday of the Jewish religion. The receiving of the Torah is a tie that binds the Jewish people together throughout the generations.

There is a legend that, prior to Shavuot, there was no kashrut. The laws given that day through Moses included that of making meat kosher. When the children of Israel returned to their tents, there was no time to prepare any meat dishes, so a quick dairy meal was prepared. This custom has been handed down from generation to generation; today, meals including cheese blintzes (filled, folded pancakes), beet borscht (soup) with sour cream, and cheesecake are served on the eve of Shavuot or when the family returns home from the synagogue service. An alternative tradition links dairy foods to the land of "milk and honey" and to the nourishing (milk and honey) words of the Torah.

SUGGESTED MENUS

Shavout

Avocado Delight, p. 62
Almond Crusted Trout, p. 162
Creamy Angel Hair Pasta, p. 200
Aspen Apricot Scones, p. 84, or Herb-Olive Oil Scones, p. 83
Caponata with Pine Nuts, p. 214
Chocolate Turtle Pie, p. 236, or Low-Fat New York Cheesecake, p. 235

Beet Borscht, p. 96
Cheese Blintzes, p. 59, and Salmon Blintzes, p. 60
Ute Spinach Pie, p. 54
Sliced Fresh Tomatoes
Wilderness Raspberry Squares, p. 66
Anna Banana Bread, p. 86
Strawberry Delight, p. 67

PAREVE FOOD PREPARATION

Many of the recipes in this cookbook were tested as dairy dishes. However, in kosher meal planning, it is often necessary to substitute *pareve* ingredients for either *dairy* (milk), or *meat* ingredients.

You can usually substitute pareve margarine or solid white shortening for butter in a recipe. Or if you prefer, you can substitute oil for the butter or a combination of oil plus margarine or shortening.

The following ingredients are commonly used substitutes for **dairy**:

◆ For pareve baking, when a recipe calls for 1 cup of milk, substitute 1 cup water and 2 tablespoons pareve shortening, or 1 cup of potato water (water in which potatoes have been boiled).

◆ Use pareve chocolate chips.

◆ Use pareve non-dairy liquid creamer instead of milk or cream.

◆ Substitute pareve non-dairy whipped topping for whipped cream.

◆ For recipes other than baked goods, substitute water, fruit juice, black coffee, canned vegetable broth, or the water from cooked vegetables for milk.

◆ To make a pareve "cream sauce," add potato starch, pareve fat, and liquid to the desired consistency.

In place of **chicken or meat stock**, substitute pareve beef- or chicken-*flavored* broth.

A
P
P
E
T
I
Z
E
R
S

APPETIZER INDEX

CHOPPED LIVER

Meat Traditional

1 pound chicken livers
salt and pepper
1 large onion, chopped
2 teaspoons plus 1 tablespoon oil or
schmaltz, divided
3 hard boiled eggs

Variation: Well-trimmed calf or beef liver may be substituted for chicken livers. Increase oil as needed when combining ingredients.

✦ Wash, trim and salt chicken livers. Place on broiler rack and broil until brown on both sides, turning once. Sauté onion in 2 teaspoons oil until tender and translucent, but not browned.

✦ Meat grinder method: Put liver, onions and eggs through grinder. Place in a bowl and add remaining oil. Mix well. Season to taste with salt and pepper.

✦ Food processor method: Process liver, onion and eggs until well mixed, but do not overprocess. Remove from processor to a bowl. Add remaining oil and mix well. Season to taste with salt and pepper.

THE BEST MOCK CHOPPED LIVER

Pareve Traditional

1 pound fresh mushrooms, washed
and blotted dry with paper towel
2 large onions, chopped
1 tablespoon pareve margarine
1½ tablespoons olive oil
3 hard boiled eggs
¼ pound walnuts
1 teaspoon salt
pepper to taste
parsley

✦ Sauté mushrooms and onions in margarine and olive oil in a large skillet until golden. Remove from heat and cool. Place mushrooms, onions and remaining ingredients, except parsley, in food processor. Pulse several times until mixture is smooth. Remove to serving bowl and chill before serving. Garnish with parsley and serve with challah.

✦ Yields 3½ cups.

SICILIAN EGGPLANT DIP

`Pareve` `Lighter`

1 (1 pound) eggplant
2 tablespoons olive oil
½ cup chopped onion
1 teaspoon minced garlic
1 (14½ ounce) can Italian stewed
   tomatoes
¼ cup dry red wine
2 tablespoons red wine vinegar
2 tablespoons capers, drained
1 tablespoon lemon juice
⅛ teaspoon salt
⅛ teaspoon pepper
1 baguette loaf
olive oil
thyme sprigs, optional
1 cup sliced ripe olives, optional
¼ cup toasted pine nuts, optional

✦ Peel eggplant and chop in ¼-inch cubes. Heat olive oil in a large skillet. Add eggplant, onion, and garlic and sauté over medium-high heat until tender, about 10 minutes, stirring occasionally. Add tomatoes, wine, vinegar, capers, lemon juice, salt and pepper. Bring to a boil, then reduce heat, and simmer, uncovered, for ten minutes, or until liquid evaporates. Remove from heat and cool slightly. Cover and refrigerate.

✦ Slice baguette and brush cut sides of each slice with olive oil. Arrange in a single layer on baking pan and broil a few inches from heat for 2 to 3 minutes, turning once.

✦ Garnish dip with thyme, olives or pine nuts, if desired. Serve with baguette toast.

✦ Yields 4 cups.

✦ Nutritional information per serving

Calories: 145.9	Saturated Fat: 0.6g	Calories from Fat: 22.2%
Protein: 4.1g	Dietary Fiber: 2.5g	Calories from Carbohydrate: ... 66.5%
Carbohydrate: 24.0g	Sodium: 295mg	Calories from Protein: 11.3%
Cholesterol: 0mg	Total Fat: 3.6g	

✦ **Rendered Chicken Fat (Schmaltz)**
fat and skin from chicken
1 medium onion, diced
dash of salt
Cut fat and skin into small pieces. Place in skillet over low heat and cook, stirring often, until fat has melted. Add onion and sauté until onion browns and skin crisps. Add salt. Remove from heat and cool. Strain into glass jars and refrigerate or freeze.
Hint: The onions and skin make a good nosh, or they can be added to chopped liver or mashed potatoes.

HOMEMADE GEFILTE FISH

5 pounds fish filet (carp, buffalo, whitefish, and pike), mixed to taste, heads and bones reserved
3 medium yellow onions
10 eggs
1 tablespoon kosher salt
2 teaspoons pepper
2 tablespoons sugar
½ cup matzo meal
1 cup cold water

Broth:
3 onions
3 large carrots
4 stalks celery
salt, pepper and sugar

Note: Whitefish and pike are milder than buffalo and carp.

✦ Have your fishmonger remove heads and bones from enough fish to net 5 pounds of fish filet. Rinse thoroughly and reserve heads and bones for broth. Grind fish and onion. Place in a large bowl and add eggs, seasonings and matzo meal. Gradually add water. Combine thoroughly. Add more seasoning and water if needed. Knead mixture until firm enough to form oval balls 2½ inches in diameter.

✦ For broth, place reserved fish heads and bones in a large stockpot. Add vegetables and half-fill with water. Add seasonings to taste. Bring water to a boil. Drop balls into boiling broth. Return broth to a boil, reduce heat to medium and cook for about 4 hours. Correct seasonings and add additional water as needed. Remove fish from broth and cool. Serve with horseradish and challah.

✦ **Nutritional information per serving**

Calories: 176.8	Saturated Fat: 1.2g	Calories from Fat: 21.8%
Protein: 29.4g	Dietary Fiber: 0.4g	Calories from Carbohydrate: 8.8%
Carbohydrate: 3.7g	Sodium: 470mg	Calories from Protein: 69.4%
Cholesterol: 194mg	Total Fat: 4.1g	

Imagine my delight to come home from school to a new family pet—a huge fish swimming in our one and only bathtub. "For me?" I squealed! "How wonderful. I'll feed it and love it!" (Pets, needless to say, were a luxury in a family of six children.) My mom looked pained when she told me grandma would kill it on Friday morning for the gefilte fish for our Shabbat dinner. I cried, but to no avail. That Shabbat, I wouldn't touch the fish.

MOTHER'S GEFILTE FISH

1 medium onion, finely chopped
2 carrots, cut into thin rounds
1 teaspoon freshly ground black
  pepper, to taste
2 teaspoons paprika, to taste
1 tablespoon vegetable oil
1 tablespoon sugar
2 jars gefilte fish, whitefish only
  (8 pieces per jar), undrained

Note: Can be made 1 day ahead.

✦ Place onion, carrots, pepper and paprika in a medium saucepan with a lid. Add water to cover and bring to a boil. Reduce heat to simmer, cover, and cook for 1 hour. Add oil and sugar and continue simmering for another 30 minutes, covered. Add fish with liquid, cover, and continue cooking on a low simmer for an additional 2 hours. Remove lid, increase heat and boil approximately 30 minutes more, or until liquid is reduced and thickened. Serve hot or cold with horseradish and fish gravy.

I remember when I was a child, the lake at Rude Park was stocked with carp. I would go with my mother to the park to buy our fish for the Sabbath or the holidays. We would take them home and put them in a tub until it was time to prepare them.

QUICK AND EASY GEFILTE FISH

2 (27 ounce) cans traditional
  European-style gefilte fish, drained
  and liquid reserved
1 onion, chopped
2 carrots, sliced
1 tablespoon vegetable oil
1 tablespoon sugar
salt and pepper
paprika

✦ Place reserved liquid in a saucepan. Add onion, carrots, oil, sugar, and salt and pepper to taste. Bring to a boil. Add fish and sprinkle with paprika. Return to a boil, reduce heat and simmer 1½ hours, basting frequently. Cool and serve.

HORSERADISH

Pareve | Traditional

1 large horseradish root, peeled and
  cut into pieces
2 large beets, peeled and quartered
⅔ cup white vinegar
2 heaping tablespoons sugar, or more
  to taste
dash salt
¼ to ½ cup water

✦ Shred horseradish in food processor. Remove from work bowl. Shred beets in processor. Return horseradish to work bowl and add remaining ingredients. Pulse several times. Gradually add water, as needed, to reach a fine consistency. Place in a glass jar, cover and refrigerate.

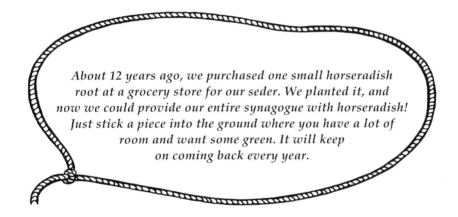

About 12 years ago, we purchased one small horseradish root at a grocery store for our seder. We planted it, and now we could provide our entire synagogue with horseradish! Just stick a piece into the ground where you have a lot of room and want some green. It will keep on coming back every year.

CHOPPED EGGPLANT

Pareve

2 medium eggplants
2 medium onions, sliced
2 cloves garlic, sliced
2 green bell peppers, seeded and
  sliced
1 jalapeño pepper, seeded and sliced
4 tablespoons olive oil
2 teaspoons white vinegar
salt and pepper

*Note: This will keep in refrigerator for up
to a week, but should not be frozen.*

✦ Pierce eggplants with a sharp knife in several places. Bake at 350° for 40 minutes, or until soft. Remove from oven and cool. Sauté onion, garlic, bell pepper and jalapeño pepper in olive oil until soft. When eggplant is cool enough to handle, peel and cut into 2-inch pieces. Put in food processor along with sautéed ingredients. Pulse 3 or 4 times, until mixture is smooth, but not overprocessed. Place in a bowl and stir in vinegar. Season with salt and pepper to taste. Refrigerate. Serve with fresh challah or crackers.
✦ 12 servings.

HEAVENLY HUMMUS

1 (15 ounce) can garbanzo beans,
   drained and liquid reserved
¼ cup sesame tahini
2 cloves garlic
2 tablespoons extra virgin olive oil
juice of 1 lemon
1 teaspoon ground cumin
dash of hot pepper sauce
1 tablespoon plum vinegar, optional

✦ Combine all ingredients, except reserved liquid, in food processor. Process until smooth. Add enough reserved liquid to reach desired consistency. Adjust seasonings to taste. Serve as a dip with vegetables, chips or pita bread.

✦ 6 to 8 servings.

ROASTED GARLIC AND SUN-DRIED TOMATO SPREAD

2 large heads garlic
1 teaspoon olive oil
1 (8-ounce) package cream cheese,
   softened
3 ounces feta cheese, crumbled
1 tablespoon chopped fresh oregano
2 ounces sun-dried tomatoes in oil,
   drained and chopped
½ cup chopped walnuts

Note: A different spread with savory ingredients.

✦ Trim top quarter of garlic heads to expose cloves. Arrange in the center of a large piece of aluminum foil. Drizzle with olive oil and seal in foil. Bake in preheated 450° oven for about 45 minutes, or until very tender. Remove from oven and let stand until cool enough to handle. Remove skin and place roasted garlic in food processor. Pulse until smooth. Add remaining ingredients and pulse several times, until well blended, but not overprocessed. Cover and chill for at least two hours or overnight. Serve at room temperature with water crackers.

✦ 8 servings.

MIDDLE EASTERN LAMB MEATBALLS

Meat

⅓ cup minced onion
1 large clove garlic, minced
1½ teaspoons olive oil
½ teaspoon dried mint
½ teaspoon salt
¼ teaspoon ground allspice
pinch of cinnamon
1 pound ground lamb
1 cup fine bread crumbs
¼ cup currants, covered in warm
   water and soaked for 30 minutes
1 egg
¼ cup black sesame seeds
¼ cup white sesame seeds
mint jelly

✦ Sauté onion and garlic in olive oil in a skillet until softened. Transfer to a bowl and stir in mint, salt, allspice, and cinnamon. Add lamb, bread crumbs, drained currants and egg. Mix well and form into ½-inch balls. Roll half of meatballs in black sesame seeds, and remaining in white sesame seeds. Bake in preheated 450° oven for 8 to 10 minutes, or until browned. Serve with mint jelly.
✦ Yields 32 (½-inch) meatballs.

CHICKEN SATAY WITH PEANUT SAUCE

Meat

2 pounds skinless, boneless chicken
   breasts
4 teaspoons grated fresh ginger
4 cloves garlic, minced
2 tablespoons curry powder
2 tablespoons coriander powder
1 cup coconut milk
1 teaspoon fish sauce
bamboo skewers, soaked in water

Peanut Sauce:
1½ cups coconut milk
1½ tablespoons red curry paste
1 tablespoon sugar
2 tablespoons peanut butter
1 tablespoon lemon or tamarind juice
1 teaspoon fish sauce

Hint: Light coconut milk may be substituted for regular in the marinade, but not in the Peanut Sauce.
Note: Sauce keeps well in refrigerator and may be made several days in advance.

✦ For Chicken: Cut chicken into 1-inch strips. Combine ginger, garlic, curry powder and coriander to make a paste. Brush chicken with paste and place in a shallow pan. Combine coconut milk and fish sauce. Pour over chicken and marinate for at least 2 hours, turning occasionally. Thread chicken on skewers. Grill or broil until done, turning once during cooking. Serve with Peanut Sauce.
✦ For Sauce: Heat coconut milk until boiling. Reduce heat to medium, add curry paste and stir until blended. Add remaining ingredients and stir to combine. Serve hot or at room temperature.
✦ 10 servings.

WANNA WONTON

2 cups minced onion
⅓ cup plus 1 tablespoon vegetable oil, divided
1 teaspoon minced garlic
4 mushrooms, finely diced
3 cups thinly sliced green onions
1 teaspoon grated fresh ginger
1 pound ground turkey
2 tablespoons soy sauce
1 tablespoon sesame oil
⅛ teaspoon chili oil
salt and pepper
1 (1 pound) package wonton wrappers
2 egg whites, lightly beaten with 1 teaspoon water

East-West Sauce:
½ teaspoon dry mustard
4 teaspoons hot water
4 tablespoons ketchup
4 teaspoons sake
4 teaspoons soy sauce
4 teaspoons Worcestershire sauce
4 teaspoons sugar
4 teaspoons white vinegar
½ teaspoon ground allspice
dash of ground cloves

Hint: To make in advance, freeze un-cooked wontons on cookie sheets. When frozen, transfer to plastic bags. Fry while still frozen, increasing cooking time as needed.

✦ Sauté onion in 1 tablespoon oil in large skillet over medium heat until golden. Add garlic, mushrooms, green onions and ginger. Sauté an additional minute. Add turkey and separate into fine pieces while it cooks. Add soy sauce, sesame oil, chili oil and salt and pepper to taste. Continue cooking until most of moisture has evaporated. Remove from heat, transfer to a bowl and cool.

✦ When filling has cooled, place one wrapper at an angle on a sheet of waxed paper. Put 1 teaspoon filling on the corner nearest you. Fold corner over filling and roll toward center, leaving ½ inch of opposite corner unrolled. Lightly moisten this corner with the egg wash. Bring both ends together to form a triangle. Pinch tightly to seal. Place on a cookie sheet and continue with remaining wrappers. Cover each layer of wontons with waxed paper. Top last layer with a damp towel and refrigerate until ready to cook.

✦ Heat remaining oil in a medium skillet over high heat. Fry a few wontons at a time, turning frequently. Cook until golden brown, about 3 minutes. Remove to a cookie sheet lined with paper towels. When drained, place in preheated 300° oven to keep warm while cooking remaining wontons. Serve hot with East-West Sauce.

✦ Place mustard in a saucepan. Add hot water and blend thoroughly. Stir in remaining ingredients and heat through. Serve with wontons.

✦ Yields 60 wontons.

SMOKED WHITEFISH SPREAD

¾ pound smoked whitefish, skinned and boned
1 (8 ounce) package cream cheese, softened
2 tablespoons unsalted butter, softened
1 tablespoon grated onion
3 tablespoons horseradish, drained
dash of hot paprika
¼ teaspoon dill seed

✦ Flake fish into a bowl. Add cream cheese, butter and onion and stir until smooth. Add horseradish and combine thoroughly. Place in a shallow serving bowl and sprinkle with paprika and dill seed. Serve with crackers, mini bagels or party rye.
✦ 12 servings.

ALPINE MARINATED GOAT CHEESE

1 (12 ounce) log goat cheese
½ cup extra virgin olive oil
1½ teaspoons dried chervil
1½ teaspoons dried thyme
1 teaspoon crushed dried rosemary
2 medium cloves garlic, peeled and pressed
sun-dried tomatoes, optional
roasted red peppers, optional

Hint: Save any crumbled cheese for use in your next green salad, along with any extra marinade.

✦ Slice cheese into ½-inch rounds with a very sharp knife dipped in hot water between each slice. Place on a shallow serving platter. Whisk together olive oil, herbs and garlic. Spoon over cheese. Refrigerate, covered, for at least several hours, but preferably 8. Return to room temperature before serving, basting with marinade occasionally. Garnish with sun-dried tomatoes or roasted red pepper, if desired. Serve with water crackers or thinly sliced French bread.
✦ 10 servings.

✦ Melba toast, low-fat crackers and rice cakes make exceptionally low-fat bases for your hors d'oeuvres.

GOAT CHEESE AND ROASTED GARLIC IN PHYLLO

Dairy

6 large cloves garlic, unpeeled
1 tablespoon olive oil
11 ounces goat cheese, room
   temperature
2 tablespoons sliced fresh basil
4 sheets phyllo dough
¼ cup butter, melted
6 tablespoons bread crumbs, divided

Note: Garlic can be roasted several days in advance. The phyllo rolls can be assembled one day ahead, wrapped tightly with plastic wrap and refrigerated until ready to bake.

✦ Cut tops off garlic cloves. Drizzle with olive oil and wrap in aluminum foil. Bake in preheated 375° oven until very tender, about 45 minutes. Remove from foil and cool. When able to handle, peel and mash to a paste in a medium bowl. Crumble in goat cheese and basil and stir until smooth.

✦ Place one phyllo sheet with long side parallel to edge of work surface. Brush the right half with butter. Fold unbuttered half over buttered half and brush again with butter. Sprinkle with 1½ tablespoons bread crumbs. Spoon one-quarter of goat cheese mixture along bottom edge, leaving a border on each side. Fold short sides in. Fold long edge over and roll up. Place seam side down on a heavy baking sheet which has been coated with non-stick vegetable spray. Brush with butter. Repeat with remaining phyllo sheets. Bake in preheated 375° oven for 15 minutes, or until golden. Remove from oven and cut into 2-inch slices with a serrated knife. Serve immediately.

PHYLLO PIZZA

Dairy

4 ounces feta cheese, crumbled
2 tablespoons extra virgin olive oil
1 tablespoon chopped fresh oregano
½ teaspoon freshly ground pepper
8 sheets phyllo dough
¼ cup melted butter or olive oil
3 large plum tomatoes, sliced
½ cup very thinly sliced red onion

✦ Toss feta with olive oil, oregano and pepper in a small bowl. Arrange 1 sheet phyllo on greased cookie sheet or jelly roll pan. Brush lightly with butter or olive oil. Layer with remaining phyllo, buttering each sheet. Arrange tomato slices on top and sprinkle with cheese mixture. Top with onion. Bake in preheated 375° oven for 20 minutes, or until golden brown on edges and flaky. Cut with kitchen scissors into 2½-inch squares. Serve warm or at room temperature.
✦ 24 squares.

GREEK OLIVE SPREAD

Pareve

1 pound pitted Kalamata olives
¼ cup plus 1½ tablespoons olive oil

✦ Process olives and oil in food processor until chopped but not puréed. Serve as a dip with French or Italian bread.
✦ Yields ½ cup.

MARINATED OLIVES

Pareve

3 cups brine-cured mixed olives
  (Kalamata, mixed country), drained
3 tablespoons olive oil
1½ tablespoons minced fresh
  rosemary
1½ tablespoons minced fresh thyme
1 tablespoon marinated artichoke oil,
  optional
2 cloves garlic, thinly sliced
1 teaspoon fresh lemon zest
½ teaspoon crushed dried fennel
¼ teaspoon crushed red pepper flakes

✦ Place all ingredients in a container with a tight lid. Refrigerate and shake occasionally. Marinate for 24 hours and up to 1 week. Serve at room temperature with a hearty crusty bread.
✦ 12 servings.

Note: Great with antipasto salad.

HERRING CACCIATORE Pareve

1 (12 ounce) jar herring in wine sauce,
  drained and sauce reserved
2 stalks celery, diced
1 large green pepper, seeded and diced
1 large tomato, chopped
½ cup diced red onion
1 (16 ounce) can artichoke hearts,
  drained and chopped
1 (12 ounce) bottle chili sauce
1 (2¼ ounce) can sliced black olives,
  drained

✦ Cut each piece of herring into quarters. Add ¼ cup reserved herring sauce and remaining ingredients. Mix well. Cover and marinate in refrigerator overnight. Serve with party rye or your favorite crackers.
✦ 10 to 12 servings.

*Note: Keeps well in refrigerator for up to a
  week.*

APPLE CHOPPED HERRING Pareve Traditional

1 (12 ounce) jar herring and onions
  in wine sauce
2 hard boiled eggs, chopped
1 Granny Smith apple, chopped
1 tablespoon plus 1 teaspoon sugar

✦ Drain herring and onions and reserve sauce. Chop herring and onion and combine with remaining ingredients. Add enough reserved sauce to moisten. Serve with fresh challah or ayer kichel.
✦ 8 servings.

*Note: Can be made several hours before
  and refrigerated. Keeps well for up
  to 4 days.*

HERRING SURPRISE Dairy

1 (2 pound) jar pickled herring in
  wine vinegar
1 (16 ounce) carton sour cream
1⅓ cups minced red onion
1 (15 ounce) can whole cranberry
  sauce
dried cranberries, optional

✦ Drain herring and discard onion. Chop herring finely and combine with remaining ingredients. Refrigerate until ready to serve. Garnish with dried cranberries, if desired.

*Note: This is great for Break-the-Fast or
  brunch. It can be prepared ahead and
  frozen.*

44

CHERRY CREEK BRUSCHETTA

Dairy

½ cup olive oil, divided
1 clove garlic, minced
1 baguette loaf
½ pound Roma tomatoes, seeded and diced
½ cup minced celery
4 ounces feta cheese, crumbled
¼ cup minced red onion
2 tablespoons minced Italian parsley
2 tablespoons balsamic vinegar
1 tablespoon chopped fresh basil
salt and pepper
fresh basil for garnish, optional

✦ Combine ¼ cup olive oil and garlic. Slice baguette into 1-inch slices. Brush with olive oil mixture and place on cookie sheet. Bake in preheated 350° oven until toasted, about 10 minutes. Combine remaining olive oil with remaining ingredients. Spread over baguette toasts and arrange on a platter garnished with fresh basil, if desired. Serve warm or cold.

✦ Try reducing the amount of cheese in your recipes to trim calories while preserving texture and flavor.

SPINACH AND SUN-DRIED TOMATO BRUSCHETTA

Dairy

¼ cup olive oil
2 cloves garlic, minced
1 baguette loaf
1 (10 ounce) package frozen chopped spinach, thawed and drained well
4 ounces shredded asiago cheese
2 ounces sun-dried tomatoes in oil, drained and chopped

✦ Combine olive oil and garlic. Slice baguette into ½-inch slices. Brush with olive oil mixture. Place bread on cookie sheet. Combine spinach, cheese and sun-dried tomatoes and mix well. Spread over bread. Bake in preheated 350° oven until cheese is melted, about 10 minutes. Serve immediately.
✦ Yields 20 bruschetta.

VEGETARIAN NORI ROLLS

carrots, spinach, zucchini, or
   asparagus, lightly steamed and cut
   into strips or small pieces
4 nori (seaweed) sheets, toasted in a
   350° oven 30 seconds
4 cups sushi rice (see recipe below)
4 (¼-inch) strips cucumber
avocado
red bell pepper
watercress
pickled daikon radish
wasabi powder, mixed with a few
   drops of hot water to make a thick
   paste
pickled ginger

✦ Place a sheet of nori, shiny side down on a bamboo mat. Dip fingers in water and spread a thin layer of sushi rice evenly over nori, leaving a ¼-inch border on top edge of sheet. Lightly press rice into nori. Place a strip of cucumber across center of rice one-third up from bottom edge. Arrange a colorful selection of vegetables on either side of cucumber, making thin lines adjacent to each other. Lightly press vegetables into rice. Position mat so that filling is closest to you. Put thumbs under mat and begin rolling end of nori nearest you, rolling tightly. Peel mat back gradually as you roll. When completely rolled, place seam side down and squeeze with mat to seal seam. Remove roll to a cutting surface, seam side down. Slice with a sharp knife into 1-inch thick rounds. Turn cut side up and arrange on serving platter. Serve with wasabi paste and pickled ginger.
✦ 6 servings.

SUSHI RICE

2 cups kokuro rose rice
2¼ cups water
pinch of salt
¼ cup brown rice vinegar
1 tablespoon sugar
   or 1 teaspoon mirin

✦ Rinse rice in several changes of cold water until water runs clear. Combine rice, water and salt in a heavy saucepan. Bring to a boil over high heat. Cover and reduce heat. Simmer over low heat for 20 minutes. Remove from heat and allow to sit covered for 10 minutes. Combine vinegar and sugar in a small saucepan and bring to a boil. Remove from heat. Turn rice into a wide shallow wooden bowl and sprinkle with vinegar mixture. Toss rice with a spoon and, at the same time, fan with a folded piece of paper until rice is cooled. This makes the rice glisten. Use immediately or cover with damp kitchen towel and leave at room temperature for up to 1 hour.

ZUCCHINI BLINIS

3 large zucchini, grated and drained
   well
2 large eggs, lightly beaten
3 tablespoons flour
2 tablespoons grated Parmesan cheese
1½ teaspoons chopped fresh chives
½ teaspoon chopped parsley
¼ teaspoon garlic powder
salt and pepper
vegetable oil
caviar, optional
sour cream, optional
finely chopped onion, optional

✦ Combine zucchini, eggs, flour, Parmesan and seasonings. Heat 2 tablespoons oil in a large skillet. Drop batter in skillet by tablespoonfuls to form small pancakes. Brown lightly on each side. Serve hot or cold with caviar, sour cream and onion, if desired.
✦ 12 servings.

Note: To serve as a vegetable, increase size of pancakes.
Hint: May be prepared several hours in advance and reheated in a 350° oven.

SMOKED SALMON QUESADILLAS

4 (10-inch) flour tortillas
5 ounces goat cheese, softened
¼ pound smoked salmon
¼ cup minced green onion
1½ tablespoons fresh dill or 1½
   teaspoons dried
capers, optional

✦ Spread half of each tortilla with one-fourth of goat cheese. Top with one-fourth of salmon, onions and dill. Sprinkle with capers, if desired. Fold tortillas in half and place on cookie sheet. Bake in preheated 500° oven for 5 minutes or until heated through and crisp. Cut in wedges to serve.
✦ 10 servings.

Note: Great instead of bread with a spinach salad or as a main course salad for a luncheon.

COLORADO QUESADILLAS

Papaya Salsa:
1½ cups diced peeled papaya
¼ cup chopped fresh cilantro
3 tablespoons minced red onion
3 tablespoons fresh lime juice

Quesadillas:
4 ounces goat cheese, crumbled
¼ cup bottled roasted red bell
  peppers, drained and chopped
3 ounces cream cheese, softened
1 teaspoon minced, seeded jalapeño
  pepper
6 (8-inch) flour tortillas
cilantro sprigs, optional

Variation: Fresh peaches or mangos can be substituted for papaya.
Note: Light cream cheese may be used.

✦ For salsa, combine all ingredients in a bowl and stir well. Cover and chill.
✦ For quesadillas, combine goat cheese, roasted peppers, cream cheese and jalapeño in a bowl and stir well. Spread 2 tablespoons cheese mixture over each tortilla and fold in half. Place on a nonstick baking sheet. Brown under broiler, turning once. Cut each quesadilla into two wedges. Arrange on a platter and top each with ¼ cup salsa. Garnish with cilantro, if desired.
✦ 12 servings

LONGHORN CASHEW LOG

1 pound longhorn or cheddar cheese
6 ounces cream cheese, softened
1 cup chopped cashew nuts
2 cloves garlic, minced
paprika

Hint: Do not substitute reduced fat cheeses.

✦ Place cheese in food processor and pulse several times until crumbled. Add cream cheese and process until smooth. Add cashews and garlic and pulse for a few seconds. Place mixture in a bowl and chill until firm enough to handle. Sprinkle a layer of paprika on a sheet of waxed paper. Divide cheese mixture in half. Form each half into a log and roll in paprika until covered. Wrap in plastic wrap and chill for several hours, or overnight. Serve with your favorite crackers and wine.
✦ 10 servings.

MEXICAN STUFFED CHEESE   `Dairy`

1 (2 pound) round of longhorn colby
   cheese
1 (15 ounce) can refried black beans
1 (4 ounce) can diced green chiles
1 medium tomato, seeded and
   chopped
2 large cloves garlic, minced
¼ teaspoon oregano
¼ teaspoon coriander
¼ teaspoon hot pepper sauce
5 corn tortillas
vegetable oil
tortilla chips
sour cream, chopped green onions,
   tomatoes, cilantro, and avocado,
   optional

*Hint: Can be prepared early in the day and
baked just before serving.*

✦ Hollow out cheese using a serrated knife and spoon, leaving a shell about ½-inch thick. Reserve scooped out cheese. Combine beans, green chiles, tomato, garlic, oregano, coriander and hot pepper sauce in a medium saucepan. Cook until heated through. Remove from heat. Pour ¼ inch of oil into a large skillet. Cook tortillas one at a time for a few seconds only. Drain and pat dry. Line a 10-inch deep dish pie plate with overlapping tortillas. Place cheese shell in center and fill with bean mixture. Cover with reserved cheese. Bake in preheated 375° oven for 45 minutes. Serve warm with tortilla chips. Garnish with sour cream, green onions, tomatoes, cilantro and/or avocado, if desired.

*At a kitchen shower, my new mother-in-law
to be told me, "Don't worry about burning anything.
Stanley thinks that's the way it should be."*

SPICED MIXED NUTS   `Pareve`

2 tablespoons vegetable oil
2 teaspoons chili powder
¼ teaspoon cayenne pepper
2½ cups mixed raw whole almonds,
   cashews, pecans and peanuts
2 tablespoons sugar
1 teaspoon salt

*Note: Can be made 5 days ahead. Cover
and store at room temperature.*

✦ Heat oil in a small saucepan over medium heat. Add chili powder and cayenne and stir until aromatic, about 15 seconds. Place nuts in a large bowl and cover with hot oil. Add sugar and salt and stir to blend. Transfer to baking pan and bake in preheated 300° oven for 20 minutes, stirring occasionally, until toasted. Serve warm or at room temperature.

SIMCHA NUTS

1 egg white
1 tablespoon butter or pareve
   margarine, melted
½ teaspoon vanilla
1 pound pecan halves (3½ cups)
½ cup sugar
1 teaspoon cinnamon
¼ teaspoon salt

Note: These make a great gift!

✦ Beat egg white in a large bowl with a whisk until foamy. Fold in melted butter and vanilla. Add nuts and coat completely. Combine sugar, cinnamon and salt. Fold into nuts and stir to coat. Spread nuts in a single layer on a jelly roll pan lined with foil and coated with non-stick vegetable spray. Bake in preheated 250° oven for 25 minutes. Stir nuts, then continue baking until very crisp and dry, about 20 more minutes.

✿ See Pareve Food Preparation, page 30

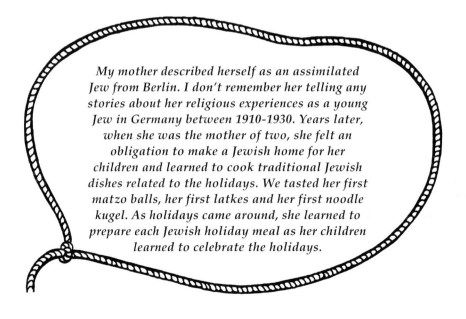

My mother described herself as an assimilated Jew from Berlin. I don't remember her telling any stories about her religious experiences as a young Jew in Germany between 1910-1930. Years later, when she was the mother of two, she felt an obligation to make a Jewish home for her children and learned to cook traditional Jewish dishes related to the holidays. We tasted her first matzo balls, her first latkes and her first noodle kugel. As holidays came around, she learned to prepare each Jewish holiday meal as her children learned to celebrate the holidays.

BRUNCH

BRUNCH INDEX

LOX PIZZA

1 package active dry yeast
1 teaspoon sugar
⅞ cup warm (110°) water
½ cup fresh chopped chives
2¼ cups plus 1 tablespoon flour
¼ teaspoon salt
2½ tablespoons olive oil, divided
1 tablespoon cornmeal
1 (8 ounce) package cream cheese, softened
½ pound lox tidbits
1 medium red onion, thinly sliced
1 large tomato, thinly sliced
½ cup capers, optional
1 tablespoon chopped parsley

Hint: Make individual size pizzas to serve as an appetizer.

✦ Stir yeast, sugar and warm water together in a small bowl. Let stand until foamy, about 10 minutes. Chop chives in the work bowl of a food processor. Add flour and salt. With processor running, add yeast mixture and process a few seconds. Add 1 tablespoon olive oil. Process until dough forms a ball at the side of the bowl, then process for 30 to 40 seconds more. Transfer dough to a bowl that has been rubbed with 1 tablespoon olive oil. Turn dough so that all sides are coated with oil. Cover with a damp towel and let rise in a warm, draft free place for 1 hour, or until dough has doubled in size. Roll and stretch dough on a lightly floured surface to a 12-inch circle. Lightly grease pizza pan with remaining olive oil and sprinkle with cornmeal. Place dough on pan and trim edges. Bake in preheated 425° oven on bottom shelf for 10 minutes. Combine cream cheese and lox. Spread over warm pizza crust. Arrange onion and tomato slices on top. Sprinkle with capers, if desired. Garnish with parsley. Serve immediately.
✦ 12 servings.

SEA STRATA

7 slices white bread
½ pound mushrooms, sliced
¼ cup sliced green onions
1 tablespoon margarine
½ pound imitation seafood
6 eggs
2¾ cups milk
½ teaspoon salt
¼ teaspoon cayenne pepper
1 teaspoon dry mustard
2 tablespoons dry sherry or dry white wine
10 ounces cheddar cheese, shredded

✦ Trim crust from bread and cube. Spread in bottom of a greased 9 x 13-inch pan. Sauté mushrooms and onion in margarine in a large skillet over medium-high heat until soft. Spoon over bread cubes. Top with imitation seafood. Combine eggs, milk, salt, cayenne and mustard. Add sherry. Pour over all and sprinkle with cheese. Cover and refrigerate overnight. Bake in preheated 350° oven for 50 to 55 minutes, or until set.
✦ 6 servings.

SPINACH MUSHROOM ROLL UPS

1 medium onion, chopped
5 tablespoons pareve margarine, divided
½ pound mushrooms, sliced
1 tablespoon flour
½ teaspoon hot pepper sauce
½ teaspoon nutmeg
2 teaspoons lemon juice
1 (10 ounce) package frozen spinach, thawed and well drained
salt and pepper to taste
1 (17¼ ounce) box frozen puff pastry, thawed
¼ cup chopped oil packed sun-dried tomatoes, drained

Hint: *To make ahead, place uncooked slices on baking sheets and freeze until hard. Store in plastic bags. Thaw before baking.*

✦ Sauté onion in 3 tablespoons margarine just until it starts to soften. Add mushrooms and sauté until soft but not brown. Add remaining margarine. When it has melted, add flour, hot pepper sauce, nutmeg, lemon juice and salt and pepper to taste. Cook and stir until flour is blended. Add spinach and mix well. Adjust seasonings. Allow mixture to cool. Unfold one pastry sheet. Spread half of spinach mixture evenly over pastry. Sprinkle with half of sun-dried tomatoes. Roll up pastry jelly roll style and pinch seam to seal. Repeat with remaining pastry sheet. Cut into ½-inch pieces and place one inch apart on baking sheet coated with nonstick vegetable spray. Bake in preheated 425° oven for 10 to 15 minutes, or until golden brown.
✦ Serves 12.

UTE SPINACH PIE

1 (17¼ ounce) package frozen puff pastry
6 eggs
1 (3 ounce) package cream cheese, softened
2 tablespoons chopped green onion
¼ cup shredded cheddar cheese
1 tablespoon chopped parsley
1 teaspoon garlic powder
salt
2 (10 ounce) packages frozen chopped spinach, thawed and drained
1 tomato, sliced
¼ cup Parmesan cheese

Variation: *To make individual pies to serve as appetizers, cut pastry into rounds with a cookie cutter. Arrange in muffin tins and fill ⅔ full. Elegant and easy.*

✦ Thaw one pastry according to package directions. Reserve remaining pastry for future use. Roll out thawed pastry and place in 10-inch pie plate, trimming and fluting edges. Beat eggs in mixer. Add cream cheese and beat until smooth. Add green onion, cheddar cheese, parsley, garlic powder and salt to taste. Stir in spinach and pour into prepared crust. Bake in preheated 375° oven for 30 minutes. Top with tomato slices and Parmesan cheese and bake an additional 5 minutes.
✦ 8 servings.

FOUR CHEESE QUICHE

1 stick butter
1 cup flour
2 tablespoons water
pinch of salt
8 ounces cheddar cheese, shredded,
   divided
4 ounces Swiss cheese, shredded
4 ounces mozzarella cheese, shredded
4 ounces Monterey Jack cheese,
   shredded
2 eggs
1 cup half and half
1 (4 ounce) can chopped green chiles,
   drained
¼ teaspoon cayenne pepper

✦ Knead butter, flour, water and salt together to form a soft ball. Place in a greased 9-inch round quiche pan. Pat onto bottom and up sides of pan. Combine half of cheddar cheese with remaining cheeses and sprinkle in quiche shell. Beat eggs well. Add half and half, chiles and cayenne. Mix well and pour over cheese. Bake in preheated 350° oven for 45 minutes. Remove from oven and let stand for 2 hours. Reheat before serving for 20 minutes at 350°. Sprinkle with remaining cheddar cheese and heat until melted. Serve immediately.

✦ 10 servings.

B
R
U
N
C
H

SAVORY SALMON QUICHE

3 eggs, slightly beaten
1 cup sour cream
½ teaspoon Worcestershire sauce
¾ teaspoon salt
1 cup coarsely grated Swiss cheese
1 (14¾ ounce) can pink salmon,
   drained, boned and skinned
1 medium red bell pepper, seeded and
   chopped
1 8 or 9-inch unbaked pie shell
1 (3 ounce) can onion rings

✦ Preheat oven to 350°. Combine eggs, sour cream, Worcestershire sauce, salt, cheese, salmon and red pepper; blend well. Pour into pie shell and bake for 50 minutes. Top with onion rings and bake an additional 10 minutes, or until onion rings are brown and crispy.

✦ 8 servings.

BREAKFAST BURRITOS

Dairy Lighter

6 medium red potatoes, diced and
  cooked
2 medium onions, chopped
butter or margarine
salt and pepper
3 eggs, beaten
9 flour tortillas
chunky salsa
1 (12 ounce) can vegetarian green chile
1 (8 ounce) package grated sharp
  cheddar cheese

✦ Sauté potatoes and onion in a large skillet in butter over medium heat until browned. Season with salt and pepper to taste. Scramble eggs in butter in a small skillet. Place potato mixture in center of each tortilla. Top with eggs. Spread with salsa, fold over edges, and roll up. Place in greased 9 x 12-inch pan. Top with green chile and cheese. Bake in preheated 350° oven for 20 minutes.

✦ 9 servings.

Hint: Egg beaters may be used for eggs. Leftover potatoes also work well.

✦ Nutritional information per serving

Calories: 291.9	Cholesterol: 84mg	Calories from Fat: 27.4%
Protein: 15.1g	Saturated Fat: 3.7g	Calories from Carbohydrate: ... 52.2%
Carbohydrate: 38.5g	Dietary Fiber: 3.8g	Calories from Protein: 20.5%
Total Fat: 9.0g	Sodium: 532mg	

WILD WEST ENCHILADAS

Dairy

1½ cups shredded Monterey Jack
  cheese, divided
1½ cups shredded cheddar cheese,
  divided
4 ounces cream cheese, softened
1 cup salsa, divided
1 medium red bell pepper, seeded
  and chopped
½ cup sliced green onions
1 teaspoon cumin
8 medium flour tortillas
2 cups shredded lettuce
1 medium tomato, chopped

✦ Combine 1 cup each Monterey Jack and cheddar cheese with cream cheese, ¼ cup salsa, red bell pepper, onion, and cumin. Mix well. Spread ¼ cup cheese mixture down center of each tortilla and roll up. Place seam side down in a greased 9 x 13-inch glass baking dish. Spoon remaining salsa evenly over enchiladas. Sprinkle with remaining cheese. Bake in preheated 350° oven for 20 minutes, or until hot and bubbly. Top with lettuce and tomato and serve with additional salsa.

✦ 8 servings.

MAPLE WALNUT FRENCH TOAST

8 eggs
2 cups milk
4 tablespoons brown sugar
1 teaspoon maple flavoring
1 loaf Texas toast
½ cup chopped walnuts
½ cup maple syrup
2 tablespoons cinnamon sugar

✦ Beat eggs, milk, brown sugar and maple flavoring in a large bowl until well blended. Cut each slice of bread into 4 triangles. Dip into egg mixture and place in a well-buttered 9 x 13-inch glass baking dish, overlapping pieces. Pour any remaining egg mixture over bread. Sprinkle with walnuts. Bake in preheated 350° oven 45 minutes to an hour, until edges are golden brown and center is light and puffy. Serve drizzled with syrup and sprinkled with cinnamon sugar.
✦ 10 servings.

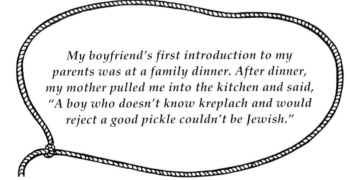

My boyfriend's first introduction to my parents was at a family dinner. After dinner, my mother pulled me into the kitchen and said, "A boy who doesn't know kreplach and would reject a good pickle couldn't be Jewish."

**B
R
U
N
C
H**

BRECKENRIDGE FRENCH TOAST CASSEROLE

1 loaf challah, torn in pieces
12 ounces cream cheese, softened
8 jumbo eggs
¾ cup syrup
2 cups milk
½ cup sugar
cinnamon
maple syrup

✦ Place half of challah pieces in well-buttered 9 x 13-inch glass baking dish. Cube cream cheese and arrange over challah. Top with remaining challah pieces. Beat eggs, syrup, milk and sugar until well blended. Pour over challah, cover and refrigerate overnight. Sprinkle with cinnamon and bake in 350° preheated oven for 45 to 60 minutes, or until firm. Serve with warm syrup.
✦ 12 servings.

Variation: Also great made with raisin challah.

PUFFED BLUEBERRY PANCAKES

4 tablespoons unsalted butter
4 large eggs, beaten
¾ cup milk (not skim)
¾ cup flour
1 cup fresh blueberries
¼ cup firmly packed light brown
    sugar
2 tablespoons lemon juice
blueberry syrup

✦ Place 4 1-cup ramekins on a cookie sheet. Place 1 tablespoon butter in each one. Put into preheated 425° oven long enough to melt butter. Remove from oven. Combine eggs, milk and flour in a medium bowl. Stir until just blended. Divide batter among buttered ramekins. Toss blueberries with brown sugar and lemon juice until coated. Sprinkle over batter. Bake until puffed and golden, about 15 minutes. Serve with blueberry syrup.
✦ 4 servings.

✦ Replace liquid in pancakes and waffles with
club soda for the lightest ones ever.

GERMAN PANCAKE

½ cup unsifted flour
½ cup canned evaporated milk
¼ teaspoon salt
4 extra large eggs
2 tablespoons butter
powdered sugar
syrup

Hint: Great served with fruit in the center.

✦ Preheat oven to 425°. Combine flour, evaporated milk and salt. Mix well. Add eggs, one at a time, whipping with a wire whisk after each addition. Melt butter in a 10-inch ovenproof skillet. Pour in batter. Cook over moderate heat until edges are firm enough to loosen around skillet with spatula. Make a crisscross slash with spatula through the pancake. Bake 15 minutes or until puffed and golden brown. Pancake should puff up into billowy, irregular mounds. Remove from oven and sprinkle with powdered sugar. Cut into wedges and serve immediately, topped with syrup.
✦ 8 servings

CHEESE BLINTZES

4 large eggs
1 cup potato starch
1 cup water
pinch of salt
butter (about 1 stick, total)
14 ounces farmers cheese or dry
    cottage cheese
1 (8 ounce) package cream cheese,
    softened
1 egg
1 tablespoon sour cream
cinnamon
sugar

Hint: Blintzes may be prepared ahead. After rolling, place on cookie sheet and freeze until hard, then store in plastic bags until ready to use. Perfect for Passover.

✦ Beat 4 eggs lightly and add potato starch, water and salt. Beat until smooth. Heat 1-2 teaspoons butter in a 7-inch skillet over high heat until butter begins to sizzle. Pour about ⅓ cup batter into skillet, or enough to cover bottom of pan. Cook until center is dry but not crispy. Remove to waxed paper, cooked side up, and cover with a damp cloth. Repeat with remaining batter. Combine cheeses, remaining egg, sour cream and cinnamon and sugar to taste. Beat until smooth. Place a dollop of cheese filling at bottom of blintz one inch from edge. Fold bottom edge over filling, fold sides in, and roll completely. Lightly brown both sides in butter and serve immediately.

✦ 12 servings

B R U N C H

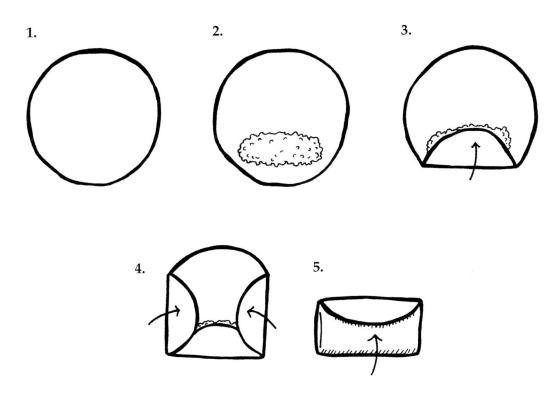

1. 2. 3.

4. 5.

59

NANA'S SALMON BLINTZES Dairy

11 large eggs
¼ pound unsalted butter, softened
¾ cup flour
¾ cup water
1 pound, 8 ounces farmers cheese
4 ounces smoked salmon, cut in
  ½-inch pieces
butter (1 stick, total)

*Variation: 8 ounces cream cheese plus 1
  pound ricotta may be substituted for farmers cheese.*
*Hint: Blintzes may be prepared ahead.
  After rolling, place on cookie sheet
  and freeze until hard, then store in
  plastic bags until ready to use. See
  illustration, page 59.*

✦ Blend 10 eggs, butter and flour in mixer. Slowly add water until consistency of an easily poured batter. Refrigerate for ½ to 1 hour. Combine cheese, salmon and remaining egg and beat until creamy. Heat 1-2 teaspoons butter in a 7-inch skillet over high heat until it begins to sizzle. Pour about ⅓ cup batter into skillet, or enough to cover bottom of pan. Cook until center is dry but not crispy. Remove to waxed paper and cover with a damp cloth. Repeat with remaining batter. Place a dollop of cheese filling at top of blintz one inch from edge. Roll top edge over filling, fold sides in, and roll completely. Lightly brown both sides in butter and serve immediately.
✦ 18 servings

ANASAZI GREEN CHILE CORN BREAD Dairy

1 cup yellow cornmeal
1 tablespoon baking powder
½ teaspoon salt
3 eggs
1 cup buttermilk
½ cup butter, melted
1 cup corn, fresh, frozen or canned
  (drained)
1 (4 ounce) can chopped green chiles,
  drained
2 cups shredded cheddar cheese

✦ Combine cornmeal, baking powder and salt in a large bowl. Beat eggs in another bowl until well mixed. Add buttermilk, butter and corn. Blend egg mixture into cornmeal mixture. Pour one-third of batter into greased 9-inch square baking dish. Top with half of chiles and sprinkle with half of cheese. Pour remaining batter into pan. Top with remaining chiles and cheese. Bake in preheated 350° oven for 45 minutes. Serve warm, cut in 2-inch squares.
✦ 8 servings.

CHILE RELLENO PUFFS

Dairy

3 (4 ounce) cans diced green chiles, drained
2 pounds marble cheese (Monterey Jack and colby), shredded
4 eggs, separated
⅔ cup canned evaporated milk
½ teaspoon salt
½ teaspoon pepper
1 tablespoon flour

✦ Combine chiles and cheese in a large bowl. Divide into well-buttered muffin tins. Beat egg whites until stiff. In another bowl, blend egg yolks, milk, salt, pepper and flour. Fold egg whites into mixture. Pour over cheese mixture in muffin tins. Bake in preheated 325° oven for 45 minutes. Remove from tins while still hot.
✦ Yields 30 puffs.

MOUNTAIN PEAK GRAPEFRUIT ALASKA

Dairy

3 grapefruit
2 tablespoons powdered sugar
3 egg whites
⅛ teaspoon salt
6 tablespoons sugar
1 teaspoon vanilla
1 pint vanilla ice cream or frozen yogurt

✦ Preheat oven to 450°. Cut each grapefruit in half, remove center and cut around each section. Sprinkle each half with 1 teaspoon powdered sugar and chill. Beat egg whites until foamy, add salt, and continue beating until beginning to stiffen. Gradually add sugar and beat until very stiff. Add vanilla. Place a heaping spoonful of ice cream in center of each grapefruit and cover fruit edge to edge with meringue. Place on baking sheet and brown in oven for 3 to 4 minutes. Serve immediately.
✦ 6 servings.

✦ **Nutritional information per serving**

Calories: 193.5	Saturated Fat: 3.0g	Calories from Fat: 22.2%
Protein: 4.0g	Cholesterol: 19mg	Calories from Carbohydrate: ... 69.8%
Carbohydrate: 35.2g	Dietary Fiber: 1.3g	Calories from Protein: 8.0%
Total Fat: 5.0g	Sodium: 107mg	

**B
R
U
N
C
H**

AVOCADO DELIGHT

3 large avocados, thinly sliced
juice of 1 lime
10 ounces light sour cream
2 teaspoons garlic powder
1½ teaspoons seasoned salt
1 (12 ounce) bottle mild taco sauce
1 cup grated New York sharp white
    cheddar cheese
½ cup chopped green onions
tortilla chips

*Hint: Can be made several hours before
    serving.*

✦ Layer the avocado slices in a 9 x 13-inch serving dish. Sprinkle with lime juice. Combine sour cream, garlic powder and seasoned salt. Spread over avocado. Spread taco sauce over sour cream mixture. Sprinkle with cheese and green onion. Serve with tortilla chips.
✦ 10 servings.

CHERRY CHOCOLATE STREUSEL CAKE

½ cup semisweet chocolate mini chips
1 tablespoon cocoa
2 teaspoons cinnamon
1⅔ cups sugar, divided
1½ sticks butter, softened
3 cups flour
1½ teaspoons baking soda
1½ teaspoons baking powder
2 teaspoons vanilla extract
½ teaspoon salt
2 cups light sour cream
3 eggs
⅔ cup maraschino cherries, drained
powdered sugar

Note: Freezes well.

✦ Preheat oven to 350°. Combine chocolate chips, cocoa, cinnamon and ⅓ cup sugar in a small bowl. Set aside. Cream butter and remaining sugar in mixer on low speed until blended. Increase speed to medium and beat 2 minutes, occasionally scraping bowl. Reduce speed to low and add flour, baking soda, baking powder, vanilla, salt, sour cream, and eggs. Beat until well mixed. Increase speed to medium and beat an additional 2 minutes, scraping bowl occasionally. Add cherries. Spread one-third of batter in greased and floured bundt pan. Sprinkle with half of chocolate mixture. Top with half of remaining batter and sprinkle with remaining chocolate. Spread rest of batter on top. Bake for 1 hour and 10 minutes, or until toothpick inserted in center comes out clean. Cool cake in pan for 30-45 minutes, then remove to a serving plate. Sprinkle with powdered sugar before serving.

CRANBERRY SWIRL COFFEE CAKE

Dairy

¼ pound margarine, softened
1 cup sugar
1 teaspoon almond extract
2 eggs
2 cups flour
1 teaspoon baking soda
1 teaspoon baking powder
½ teaspoon salt
1 cup sour cream
1 (16 ounce) can whole cranberry
  sauce
½ cup crushed nuts

Topping:
¾ cup powdered sugar
2 teaspoons warm water
½ teaspoon almond extract
¼ cup crushed nuts

✦ Preheat oven to 350°. Cream margarine in mixer and add sugar gradually. Add extract. Add eggs one at a time, beating well after each addition. Combine flour, baking soda, baking powder and salt. Add to creamed mixture alternately with sour cream, ending with dry ingredients. Pour half of batter into greased bundt pan. Top with half of cranberry sauce and half of nuts. Gently swirl with a knife to marbleize. Repeat layers. Bake for 55 minutes. Cool for 15 minutes before removing from pan.
✦ For topping, combine powdered sugar, water and extract. Drizzle over cooled cake. Sprinkle with nuts.

ALL-OCCASION COFFEE CAKE

Dairy

3 cups flour
2 cups sugar
3 teaspoons baking powder
dash salt
½ cup butter, softened
½ cup margarine, softened
1 (12 ounce) can evaporated milk
2 eggs
1 teaspoon vanilla

Topping:
½ cup firmly packed brown sugar
2 teaspoons cinnamon
½ cup chopped pecans or walnuts

✦ Preheat oven to 350°. Sift together flour, sugar, baking powder and salt. Mix with butter and margarine to form crumbs. Reserve ½ cup crumbs for topping. Add evaporated milk, eggs and vanilla to remaining butter mixture and beat until smooth. Combine reserved crumbs with topping ingredients and mix well. Sprinkle one-third of topping in bottom of greased bundt pan. Top with half of batter. Sprinkle most of remaining topping over batter. Add remaining batter and sprinkle with rest of topping. Bake for one hour.
✦ 14 servings.

Note: This moist coffee cake stays fresh for several days and freezes well also.

COFFEE CAKES

SOUR CREAM COFFEE CAKE

1 stick butter, softened
1 cup sugar
2 eggs
¼ teaspoon salt
1 teaspoon vanilla
1 teaspoon baking powder
1 teaspoon baking soda
2 cups flour
1 cup sour cream

Filling:
½ cup firmly packed brown sugar
½ cup chopped nuts
2 teaspoons cinnamon

✦ Preheat oven to 350°. Cream butter in mixer. Add sugar and beat until light and fluffy. Add eggs one at a time, beating well after each addition. Add salt and vanilla. Blend well. Add baking powder and baking soda and mix well. Add flour alternately with sour cream and continue beating until well blended. Place half of batter in a greased tube pan. Combine filling ingredients and sprinkle half over batter. Spoon in remaining batter and sprinkle with rest of filling. Bake for 40 to 50 minutes, or until a toothpick inserted in center comes out clean. Cool in pan for one hour, remove onto serving plate.

CHOCOLATE CHIP COFFEE RING

1 stick butter, softened
1 cup sugar
2 cups flour
1 cup sour cream
¼ teaspoon lemon juice
1½ teaspoons water
2 eggs
1 teaspoon baking soda
¾ teaspoon baking powder
¼ teaspoon salt
1 teaspoon vanilla
½ cup semisweet chocolate chips

Topping:
½ cup flour
½ cup firmly packed light brown
    sugar
1½ teaspoons cocoa
4 tablespoons butter, softened
¾ cup walnut pieces
½ cup semisweet chocolate chips

✦ Preheat oven to 350°. Cream butter and sugar in mixer until light and fluffy. Add flour, sour cream, lemon juice, water, eggs, baking soda, baking powder, salt and vanilla. Beat at low speed until combined, then increase speed to medium, scraping sides often, for three minutes. Batter will be thick. Stir in chocolate chips. Spread batter in well-greased, but not floured 9-inch tube pan.
✦ For topping, mix flour, sugar and cocoa. Blend in butter with fingers. Stir in nuts and chocolate chips and crumble evenly over batter. Bake for 55 to 60 minutes, or until toothpick inserted in center comes out clean. Cool in pan for one hour, then invert onto serving plate.

ORANGE KISS-ME CAKE

Dairy

1 (6 ounce) can frozen orange juice
   concentrate, thawed and divided
2 cups flour
½ cup milk
1 cup sugar
2 eggs
1 teaspoon salt
1 cup raisins
2 sticks margarine, softened
⅓ cup chopped walnuts
1 teaspoon baking soda

Topping:
⅓ cup sugar
¼ cup chopped walnuts
1 teaspoon cinnamon

✦ Preheat oven to 350°. Combine ½ cup orange juice concentrate with remaining ingredients. Beat for 3 minutes with an electric mixer. Pour into greased and floured 9 x 13-inch pan. Bake for 40 to 45 minutes. Remove from oven and drizzle with remaining orange juice concentrate. Combine topping ingredients and sprinkle over warm cake.

Note: This also makes great muffins and freezes well.

LEMON BLUEBERRY BREAD

Pareve

1 cup oil
4 eggs
1¼ pounds fresh or frozen
   blueberries
zest of 1 lemon
3 cups flour
1 teaspoon baking soda
1 teaspoon salt
1½ teaspoons cinnamon
2 cups sugar
1½ cups chopped pecans

✦ Preheat oven to 350°. Beat oil and eggs until fluffy. Add blueberries and lemon zest. Combine flour, baking soda, salt, cinnamon and sugar in another bowl. Add to blueberry mixture and beat until well blended. Add nuts. Pour into 2 greased 9 x 5-inch loaf pans. Bake for 1 hour, until a toothpick inserted in center comes out clean. Cool in pan for 20 minutes, then turn onto rack and cool completely.
✦ Yields 2 loaves.

COFFEE CAKES

65

WILDERNESS RASPBERRY SQUARES

1 stick butter or margarine, softened
1 cup sugar
1¾ cups flour
2 teaspoons baking powder
1 egg
½ cup milk
1 teaspoon vanilla
1½ cups fresh raspberries

Hint: Unthawed frozen raspberries may be substituted for fresh. Also good with blueberries.

✦ Preheat oven to 350°. Cream butter and sugar together in mixer until light and fluffy. Add flour, baking powder, egg, milk and vanilla and mix well. Fold in raspberries. Pour into greased 8-inch square pan and bake for 40 to 45 minutes.
✦ 12 servings.

OVERNIGHT STICKY ROLLS

¼ cup chopped nuts
½ cup raisins
1 (24 count) package frozen white dinner rolls
1 teaspoon cinnamon
½ (3 ounce) package butterscotch pudding mix (not instant)
¼ pound butter or margarine
½ cup firmly packed brown sugar

✦ Sprinkle nuts and raisins in bottom of greased bundt pan. Layer rolls on top. Sprinkle with cinnamon and dry pudding mix. Melt butter and stir in brown sugar. Pour over rolls. Cover lightly with plastic wrap and towel. Let rise overnight on counter. Do not refrigerate. Uncover and bake in preheated 350° oven for 30 minutes. Cool for 5 minutes and invert onto serving dish. Serve immediately.
✦ 16 servings.

CINNAMON RAISIN CREAM CHEESE

1 (8 ounce) package cream cheese, softened
1½ teaspoons cinnamon
½ cup raisins

✦ Combine cream cheese and cinnamon in a small bowl. Stir in raisins and refrigerate until ready to serve. Spread on bagels or sweet fruit bread.
✦ Yields 1¼ cups.

STRAWBERRY DELIGHT

 Dairy

1 cup whipping cream
⅓ cup powdered sugar
½ cup sour cream
½ teaspoon grated fresh orange rind
2 pints strawberries, hulled
grated dark, sweet or milk chocolate

✦ Beat cream in mixer until stiff. Fold in sugar, sour cream and orange rind. Place strawberries in a glass bowl and top with cream and grated chocolate.
✦ 8 servings.

Variation: This also works well with raspberries and blueberries.

LOX SPREAD

 Dairy

1 (8 ounce) package cream cheese, softened
3 tablespoons sour cream
1 tablespoon chopped chives
2 teaspoons lemon juice
¼ pound lox pieces

✦ Combine cream cheese, sour cream, chives and lemon juice. Blend well, then fold in lox. Refrigerate until ready to serve. Spread on dill, rye, pita bread or bagels.
✦ Yields 1½ cups.

MICROWAVE PLUM JAM

 Pareve

2 cups unpeeled, chopped, pitted Italian plums
1 tablespoon lemon juice
1½ tablespoons powdered pectin
1½ cups sugar

✦ Combine plums, lemon juice and pectin in a 3-quart casserole. Cover tightly. Microwave on high 5 to 8 minutes or until mixture comes to a rolling boil. Stir in sugar. Microwave, covered, 3½ to 5 minutes, or until boiling. Skim off foam. Remove from microwave and stir for 2 to 3 minutes. Pour into freezer carton. Keeps in refrigerator for up to 2 weeks or can be frozen up to 6 months.
✦ Yields 1½ cups.

S
P
R
E
A
D
S

QUICK PEACH PRESERVES

7 ounces dried peaches, chopped fine 2 cups water 1 cup sugar 1 tablespoon fresh lemon juice	✦ Combine all ingredients in a 3-quart saucepan. Cook over high heat until mixture boils. Reduce heat and simmer 5 minutes. Remove from heat and cool 30 minutes. Refrigerate until ready to serve. ✦ Yields 2 cups.

BERRYNANA SMOOTHIE

1 pint strawberries, hulled 1 large ripe banana, sliced 2 cups vanilla nonfat yogurt 10 ice cubes	✦ Blend all ingredients for 1 minute on high in blender. Serve in chilled glasses. ✦ 6 servings.

Hint: Add vodka or rum for a picker-upper!

ORANGECRAN BUBBLY

1 quart cranberry-raspberry juice, chilled 2 cups orange juice 2 cups ginger ale, chilled 2 cups lemon-lime seltzer, chilled orange and lime slices cranberries	✦ Mix juices and ginger ale in a 3-quart pitcher. Refrigerate until ready to serve. Just before serving, stir in seltzer and garnish with fruit slices and cranberries. ✦ 10 servings.

B
R
E
A
D
S

BREAD INDEX

THE SCIENCE OF BREAD-MAKING

Many factors influence the success or failure of making bread — the humidity, the age, type and amount of flour, the freshness of the yeast, the warmth of the kitchen, the amount of sugar, salt, and fat, and the altitude (ever notice how much faster bread dough rises in Colorado?). Furthermore, it often doesn't matter if one kind of liquid is used for another, if honey is substituted for sugar, if spices or dried fruits are added to a recipe, if the dough is shaped into a long French loaf or into dinner rolls, or if the shaped dough is glazed with butter or misted with water. Making bread is truly a creative endeavor.

A bread recipe is an approximation. Our recipes are based on approximately 3 cups of flour to 1⅛ cups liquid, so that the dough may be made in a standard 1 to 1½ pound-capacity bread machine or by any conventional method. Adjustments may need to be made, so that dough is neither too sticky, nor so dry that it won't work into a smooth ball when kneaded. One must recognize through practice what workable dough feels like.

PREPARING THE DOUGH

The doughs for the yeast bread recipes have been made either in a bread machine (using the "dough cycle" only) or by the conventional method (using a mixer with a dough hook, a food processor, or by hand).

Using your bread machine: Follow manufacturer's instructions for placing the ingredients into the bread pan. Select the "dough" cycle. To prevent items such as raisins, nuts, seeds, chopped onions or sun-dried tomatoes from becoming too finely chopped, add to the machine toward the end of the cycle. This process takes about 2 hours (depending on the machine), after which time the dough will have risen once. Remove dough promptly when cycle is complete.

Using a conventional method:

a. Combine half of total amount of flour and all other dry ingredients, including the yeast, in a large mixing bowl. Set aside.
b. Heat the liquids (water, milk, honey, butter, etc.) in a small saucepan until very warm (120° to 130°).
c. Pour liquid mixture over mixed dry ingredients. Blend at low speed of electric mixer or mix by hand until moistened. Add eggs, if any. Beat on medium speed or vigorously by hand for about 3 minutes. Add items such as raisins, nuts, seeds, chopped onion or sun-dried tomatoes. Stir in enough remaining flour to make dough easy to handle.
d. Knead dough on a floured surface until smooth and elastic, about 8 to 10 minutes.
e. Place in greased bowl. Turn greased side up. Cover with plastic wrap and let rise in warm place until light and doubled in size.

Once the dough has doubled in size, knead lightly to extract air, then let rise, covered with plastic wrap, for 5 to 10 minutes. It is now ready for shaping and baking according to the suggestions given in the recipe or as desired.

HINTS

1. Use active dry yeast or yeast made specifically for the bread machine. Yeast must be fresh. In Colorado the amount of yeast called for in a recipe may need to be reduced. Two teaspoons active dry yeast or 1½ teaspoons bread machine or rapid rise yeast is usually sufficient for a recipe calling for 3 cups white bread flour. Slightly more might be required for recipes using whole grains or with added fruits and nuts. Our recipes have already been adjusted for Colorado use.
2. Bread flour helps develop gluten, which gives structure to bread.

3. Start with slightly less than the amount of flour called for. It is easier to add flour than it is to restore dough once too much flour has been incorporated. Once dough no longer sticks to hands, no additional flour should be added. In fact, oil (rather than flour) should then be used on the kneading surface and on hands as dough is kneaded further and shaped. Remember if dough is to be shaped into a free standing loaf, such as a French loaf baked on a cookie sheet, the dough will need to be stiffer in order to hold its shape while baking.

4. The air is dry in Colorado. Dough should be exposed to the air as little as possible. Always keep dough oiled and covered with plastic wrap.

5. If the dough is ready before you are, don't worry. Dough can be punched down and allowed to rise several times. It also can be punched down, refrigerated overnight, then kneaded slightly and allowed to rise again in the morning before baking. In fact, up to a certain point (beyond 4 or 5 risings the yeast begins to lose energy), the more risings, the better the flavor.

6. Dough rises best in warm locations away from drafts. For instance, dough could be allowed to rise in an oven, turned on to 200° for 1 minute, then turned off *before* placing the bowl of dough on the oven rack. Placing a bowl of hot water on the oven rack below the dough helps maintain the heat and adds necessary moisture; replenish the water as it cools. No one can tell precisely how many minutes might be required for the dough to double. Many factors affect the timing - the density of the dough, the altitude, the number of times the dough has risen previously (it takes less time with each successive rising), the amount of yeast, *and* the temperature of the dough and its environment. In general, if the dough is not chilled, has not risen previously, and is made with mostly white flour, the dough will double in size in about 30 to 40 minutes (in Colorado).

7. Dough is doubled in size when an impression remains if the dough is pressed about ½ inch into top with a finger. If dent fills in, let dough rise for another 15 minutes and test again.

8. Grease all baking containers. Spray products work well.

9. Baking time depends on oven temperature and the shape of the bread. In general, bread should be baked at 375° (always preheat), unless the dough is sweet or some sort of sweet topping has been used, in which case the oven should be set at 350°. Bread baked in 9 x 5-inch or 8 x 4-inch bread pans take approximately 30 to 40 minutes. Rolls take 15 to 20 minutes and rolls baked in 9-inch square or 9 x 13-inch pans about 20 to 25 minutes. French loaves take about 30 minutes, depending on the diameter of the loaf. They can bake in a slightly hotter oven - 400°. Bread is done when the top is nicely browned, the bottom sounds hollow when tapped and the bread shrinks slightly from the sides of the pan.

10. Once baked, bread should be removed from baking pans or sheets immediately and allowed to cool on a wire rack. Do not wrap bread for storage until it has cooled completely.

11. Cut fresh bread with a serrated bread knife.

BE CREATIVE AND HAVE FUN: Try cranberry juice instead of water, cutting down slightly on the amount of sugar in recipe. Use Mexican spices in a loaf of French bread. Add sun-dried tomato bits and chopped onion to foccacia. Work in currants, chopped apple and cinnamon, or sunflower seeds while kneading dough. Try different glazes on the top - cornstarch and water for a hard crust; egg white for a crispy crust; egg yolk for a beautiful golden glaze; butter, margarine or oil for a soft crust; or just water from a mister. Sprinkle with poppy, caraway, or other seeds. Substitute whole wheat flour for half of the white flour. Shape the dough as a long French loaf, bread sticks, pan rolls, different-sized round balls to form a teddy bear, or whatever. Bake bread in a well-greased, clean flower pot or use a cake pan instead of a loaf pan. The rules are few.

RED ROCKS RYE BREAD

Dough:
2¼ cups bread flour
1 cup rye flour
1½ teaspoons salt
2 tablespoons sugar
1 tablespoon cocoa powder, optional,
  for a darker bread
½ cup sour cream
1 cup minus 1 tablespoon water
2 teaspoons active dry yeast

✦ Prepare dough according to directions on page 71. Shape into a large French bread loaf on greased baking sheet. Make 4 one-inch slits in top of loaf. Cover with plastic wrap and let rise until almost double. Mist with water before baking. Bake in preheated 375° oven for 20 to 25 minutes. Remove from baking sheet and let cool on rack.
✦ Yields 1 loaf.

CRUSTY FRENCH BREAD

Dough:
3 cups bread flour
1 teaspoon salt
1 teaspoon sugar
1⅛ cups water
2 teaspoons active dry yeast
cornmeal for baking sheet

Glaze:
1 egg beaten with ½ teaspoon salt

✦ Prepare dough according to directions on page 71. Cut dough in half. Roll each half into a small French loaf and place on a greased cookie sheet sprinkled with cornmeal. Make 4 one-inch slits in top of each loaf. Cover with plastic wrap and let rise until almost double. Brush with glaze, being careful not to drip on baking sheet. Bake in preheated 425° oven for 20 to 25 minutes. Remove from sheet and let cool on rack.
✦ Yields 2 loaves.

**Y
E
A
S
T**

My grandfather used to make bread and rolls for his Denver grocery store. His challahs were perfectly braided, using six strands of dough. When my brother was ten, he asked grandfather to teach him how to make the braid. Grandfather took six strands of string, tied them together at one end, and taught him. My brother put the string away in a drawer. Years later, long after grandfather died, we decided to make our own challah. My brother found the string and studied it. My mother made the dough, my father rolled the six strands and joined them at one end. After many false starts, my brother suddenly felt grandfather guiding his hands, and he made a perfectly braided challah.

HONEY TWIST CHALLAH

Dough:
3 cups bread flour
1½ teaspoons salt
¼ cup honey
¼ cup corn oil
¾ cup water
1 egg yolk
1 egg
2 teaspoons active dry yeast

Glaze:
1 egg, beaten
pinch of salt
sesame or poppy seeds

Hint: This dough can also be used to make pletzel. See recipe on page 80.

✦ Prepare dough according to directions on page 71. Divide dough in half. Divide each half into 3 equal pieces. Roll to form strands of equal length, about 10 to 12 inches long and tapered slightly at the ends. Braid the three strands together and place on greased baking sheet. Repeat with remaining strands. Cover with plastic wrap and let rise until almost double. For glaze, combine egg and salt. Brush on loaves. Sprinkle with sesame or poppy seeds. Bake loaves in preheated 350° oven for 30 minutes. Remove from baking sheets immediately and cool on wire rack.
✦ Makes 2 loaves.

✦ **Nutritional information per serving**

Calories: 102.3	Saturated Fat: 0.5g	Calories from Fat: 28.2%
Protein: 2.8g	Cholesterol: 27mg	Calories from Carbohydrate: ... 60.8%
Carbohydrate: 15.5g	Dietary Fiber: 0.5g	Calories from Protein: 11.1%
Total Fat: 3.2g	Sodium: 140mg	

1.

2.

3.

4.

5.

ITALIAN PARMESAN BREAD

Dough:
3 cups bread flour
3 tablespoons sugar
1 tablespoon dried oregano
1 teaspoon salt
3 ounces fresh Parmesan or Romano
   cheese, grated
1 cup water
1½ tablespoons olive oil
2 teaspoons active dry yeast

Hint: This recipe also makes nice rolls.

✦ Prepare dough according to directions on page 71. Cut dough in half. Roll each half into a small French loaf and place in greased French loaf pans or on cookie sheets. Make 4 one-inch slits in top of each loaf. Cover with plastic wrap and let rise until almost double. Bake in preheated 375° oven for 30 minutes. Remove from pans immediately and let cool on rack.
✦ Yields 2 loaves.

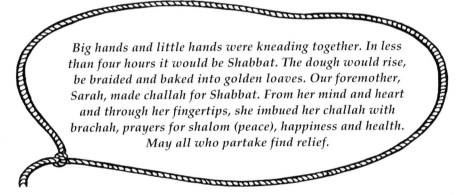

Big hands and little hands were kneading together. In less than four hours it would be Shabbat. The dough would rise, be braided and baked into golden loaves. Our foremother, Sarah, made challah for Shabbat. From her mind and heart and through her fingertips, she imbued her challah with brachah, prayers for shalom (peace), happiness and health. May all who partake find relief.

YEAST

DRIED TOMATO-BASIL BREAD

Dough:
2½ cups white bread flour
1 cup whole wheat flour
1½ teaspoons salt
1 tablespoon dried basil
2 tablespoons olive oil
1¼ cups water
⅓ cup dried tomatoes
   (not oil-packed), chopped or
   snipped (to be added toward end
   of dough-making process)
2 teaspoons active dry yeast

✦ Prepare dough according to directions on page 71. Cut dough in half. Roll each half into a small French loaf and place in greased French loaf pans or on baking sheets. Make 1 long slit in top of each loaf. Cover with plastic wrap and let rise until almost double. Bake in preheated 375° oven for 30 minutes. Remove from pans immediately and let cool on rack.
✦ Yields 2 loaves.

CONEJOS DILL BREAD

Dough:
3 cups bread flour
2 tablespoons dry milk
1 tablespoon sugar
1 teaspoon salt
1 tablespoon dill seed
¼ teaspoon garlic powder
1½ teaspoons instant minced onion
1 tablespoon shortening
1⅛ cups water
2 teaspoons active dry yeast

Glaze:
water or egg white
1 teaspoon coarse salt, optional

Hint: This also makes excellent dinner rolls or sandwich buns.

✦ Prepare dough according to directions on page 71. Cut dough in half. Roll each half into a small French loaf and place in greased French loaf pans or on baking sheets. Make 4 one-inch slits in top of each loaf. Cover with plastic wrap and let rise until almost double. Mist tops with water or brush with slightly beaten egg white. Sprinkle with coarse salt, if desired. Bake in preheated 375° oven for 30 minutes. Remove from pans immediately and let cool on rack.
✦ Yields 2 small French loaves.

BEST BRIOCHE

Dough:
3 cups bread flour
1½ teaspoons salt
3 tablespoons sugar
1 cup milk
4 tablespoons butter
2 eggs
2 teaspoons active dry yeast

Glaze:
1 egg, beaten
1 tablespoon sugar

Hint: This dough also makes an excellent challah.

✦ Prepare dough according to directions on page 71. Divide dough into 12 large balls and 12 small balls. Place large balls into greased muffin tins. Press down in center of each one to form an indentation. Place small ball of dough in each indentation. Cover with plastic wrap and let rise until almost double. Combine glaze ingredients and brush over tops. Bake in preheated 375° oven for 15 to 20 minutes. Remove from muffin tins immediately and let cool on rack.
✦ Yields 12 brioche.

✦ **Nutritional information per serving**

Calories: 206.3	Saturated Fat: 3.3g	Calories from Fat: 27.8%
Protein: 6.6g	Cholesterol: 66mg	Calories from Carbohydrate: ... 59.3%
Carbohydrate: 30.4g	Dietary Fiber: 1.0g	Calories from Protein: 12.9%
Total Fat: 6.3g	Sodium: 332mg	

ONION FOCACCIA

Dough:
2 cups bread flour
1 tablespoon sugar
1 teaspoon salt
2 tablespoons olive oil
¾ cup water
2 teaspoons active dry yeast

Topping:
3 tablespoons margarine or butter
2 medium onions, sliced
2 cloves garlic, finely chopped
¾ cup shredded mozzarella cheese
2 tablespoons grated Parmesan cheese

✦ Prepare dough according to directions on page 71. Pat dough into 12-inch circle on a greased baking sheet. Cover with plastic wrap. Let rise until almost double. Melt margarine in a medium skillet over medium-low heat. Add onions and garlic and sauté 15 to 20 minutes, stirring occasionally, until onions are brown and caramelized. Remove from heat. Make deep depression in dough at 1-inch intervals with finger or handle of wooden spoon. Spread onion topping over dough. Sprinkle with cheese. Bake in preheated 400° oven until edges are golden brown, 15 to 18 minutes. Remove from baking sheet and cool slightly. Cut into wedges and serve warm.

✦ 8 servings.

✦ **Nutritional information per serving**

Calories: 244.1	Saturated Fat: 2.7g	Calories from Fat: 38.8%
Protein: 8.3g	Cholesterol: 7mg	Calories from Carbohydrate: ... 47.5%
Carbohydrate: 28.9g	Dietary Fiber: 1.6g	Calories from Protein: 13.7%
Total Fat: 10.5g	Sodium: 535mg	

SOURDOUGH-LIKE BEER BREAD

Dough:
3 cups bread flour
2 tablespoons sugar
¾ teaspoon salt
1⅛ cups warm beer
1½ tablespoons oil
2 teaspoons active dry yeast
cornmeal for baking sheet

✦ Prepare dough following directions on page 71. Divide into 2 parts. Roll each half into a 7 x 11-inch rectangle. Starting with longer side, roll up tightly, pressing dough into roll with each turn. Pinch edges and ends to seal. Place seam-side down on greased cookie sheet sprinkled with cornmeal. Make 5 diagonal slashes across top with a sharp knife. Cover with plastic wrap. Let rise until almost double. Bake in preheated 375° oven for 30 to 35 minutes. Remove from baking sheet and let cool on rack.

✦ Yields 2 loaves.

BUBBIE'S BABKA

Dough:
3¾ cups bread or all-purpose flour
⅓ cup sugar
1 teaspoon salt
¼ cup vegetable oil
1 cup milk
2 eggs
2 teaspoons active dry yeast

Cinnamon Filling:
½ stick butter, melted
¾ cup firmly packed brown sugar
1 tablespoon cinnamon

or

Chocolate Filling:
2 ounces bittersweet chocolate
¼ cup sugar
½ stick butter
¼ cup milk
1 teaspoon vanilla

Meringue:
2 egg whites
¼ cup sugar

Note: This is a family tradition for Yom Kippur fast-breaking.

✦ Prepare dough according to directions on page 71. Divide in half. Roll out each half on floured board.
✦ For Cinnamon Filling, spread each dough section with half the melted butter. Combine brown sugar and cinnamon and sprinkle over each dough section.
✦ For Chocolate Filling, melt chocolate over double boiler. Stir in sugar, butter and milk. Cook, stirring constantly, until thickened, about 15 minutes. Add vanilla. Chill in refrigerator. Beat egg whites with sugar to make a stiff, but not dry, meringue. Spread each dough section with half of chilled chocolate filling and top with half of meringue.
✦ Roll up jelly-roll fashion starting at the long side. Braid rolls together to form a twist and place in greased bundt pan. Seal edges and cover with plastic wrap. Let rise until almost double. Bake in preheated 350° oven for 50 minutes. Remove from pan immediately and let cool slightly on a rack.
✦ 16 servings.

"Bubbie, make a babka," is the common cry from my daughters when my mother visits. She and my aunt developed the recipe when they tried to reproduce my Bubbie's babka. When my aunt couldn't grasp the twisting of the two dough rolls, my mother rolled up two tea towels and demonstrated. The number of twists, or rolls, in a babka became the signatures of the sisters. My mother does four twists, but my aunt only three. My children swear there is a difference in the taste because of the twists.

MOM'S OATMEAL BREAD

Dairy

Dough:
¾ cup boiling water
½ cup quick-cooking oats
¼ cup firmly packed brown sugar
3 tablespoons margarine, melted
1 teaspoon salt
3 cups bread flour
¼ cup water
1 egg
2 teaspoons active dry yeast

✦ Combine water, oats, brown sugar, margarine and salt in a bowl; stir well. Let cool slightly, then prepare dough according to directions on page 71, using oat mixture as liquid. Shape dough into a 9 x 5-inch loaf and place in a greased loaf pan. Cover with plastic wrap and let rise until almost double. Bake in preheated 375° oven for 40 minutes. Remove from pan immediately and let cool on rack.
✦ Yields 1 loaf.

TASTY RAISIN BREAD

Dairy

Dough:
3 cups bread flour
1½ teaspoons salt
¼ cup sugar
1½ tablespoons dry milk
1½ teaspoons cinnamon
2 tablespoons butter
1⅛ cups water
2 teaspoons active dry yeast
⅔ cup raisins (to be added at end of
   dough-making process)

Topping:
2 tablespoons sugar
¼ teaspoon cinnamon

Variation: Dried cranberries or chopped dried apricots can be used in place of raisins.

✦ Prepare dough according to directions on page 71. Cut dough in half and roll each half into two small French bread loaves. Place in greased French loaf pans or on baking sheets. Make four 1-inch slits in top of each loaf. Cover with plastic wrap and let rise until almost double. Mist loaves lightly with a spray bottle of water. Combine topping ingredients and sprinkle over loaves. Bake in preheated 375° oven for 20 to 25 minutes. Remove from pans and let cool on rack.
✦ Yields 2 small loaves.

Y E A S T

PLETZEL

Dough:
3½ cups bread flour
1½ teaspoons salt
1 egg yolk
1 egg
¾ cup water
¼ cup honey
¼ cup vegetable oil
2 teaspoons active dry yeast
1 tablespoon poppy seeds (to be added at end of dough-making process)
1 small onion, minced (to be added at end of dough-making process)
cornmeal for baking sheet

Topping:
1 egg, beaten
1 small onion, coarsely chopped
2 tablespoons poppy seeds
pinch of salt

✦ Prepare dough according to directions on page 71. Divide dough into 12 balls. Place on 2 greased baking sheets which have been lightly sprinkled with cornmeal. Cover with plastic wrap and let rise until almost double. Flatten each ball by hand. Brush with egg and sprinkle with remaining topping ingredients. Bake in preheated 375° oven for 15 to 20 minutes, or until golden brown. Remove from baking sheet immediately and cool on rack.
✦ Yields 12 rolls.

✦ Nutritional information per serving

Calories: 246.9	Saturated Fat: 1.2g	Calories from Fat: 27.4%
Protein: 7.1g	Cholesterol: 53mg	Calories from Carbohydrate: ... 61.1%
Carbohydrate: 37.8g	Dietary Fiber: 2.2g	Calories from Protein: 11.5%
Total Fat: 7.5g	Sodium: 371mg	

My fond memories of cooking started when my mother asked me to fix breakfast for a cousin shortly before my wedding. I cut a grapefruit for him, the wrong way, and I am still intimidated by that fruit! When my new husband asked me to fix him scrambled eggs the day after we returned from our honeymoon, I had to call my mother to find out what to do with eggs! But I think my greatest coup was to bake a marble cake that really came out as hard as marble. I am happy to say that was then, when I was a young bride, but since then I have learned a great deal about cooking, and my children and husband have not only survived, but have enjoyed!

TIMBER CREEK ROLLS

Dairy

Dough:
**3 cups bread flour
2 tablespoons sugar
1 teaspoon salt
1⅛ cups milk
2 tablespoons shortening, butter,
    margarine or vegetable oil
2 teaspoons active dry yeast**

For Cinnamon Rolls:
cinnamon sugar

Glaze: Your choice of
**milk,
melted butter,
egg white, or
egg yolk,
    mixed with 2 teaspoons water**

✦ Prepare dough according to directions on page 71.

on page 71.

✦ For bowknots, divide dough into 12 equal pieces. Roll each piece into ½-inch diameter ropes about 6 inches long. Tie each loosely into a knot and place on greased baking sheet.

✦ For cloverleaf rolls, divide dough into 36 balls. Dip in melted butter and place 3 balls into each section of a greased muffin tin.

✦ For cinnamon rolls, roll dough out ¼-inch thick, brush with melted butter and sprinkle generously with cinnamon sugar. Roll up jelly-roll style and cut into 1-inch slices. Place on a greased baking sheet.

✦ Cover shaped rolls with plastic wrap and let rise until almost double. Brush with your choice of glaze. Bake in preheated 375° oven for 15 to 20 minutes. Remove from baking sheet immediately and cool on rack.

✦ Yields 1 dozen rolls.

**Y
E
A
S
T**

✦ **Flash Freezing Instructions:**
While still warm, place freshly baked or
cooked food on a cookie sheet in a single layer.
Freeze until very firm. Remove from cookie sheet,
seal in containers, and refreeze.

CINNAMON SWIRL BREAD

Dairy | Lighter

Dough:
3 cups bread flour
¼ cup firmly packed brown sugar
1 teaspoon salt
2 tablespoons dry milk
1 egg yolk
1 egg
1½ teaspoons vanilla
1 stick butter or margarine
⅞ cup water
2 teaspoons active dry yeast

Filling:
melted butter or margarine
¼ cup cinnamon
¾ cup sugar

Icing:
½ cup powdered sugar
1½ teaspoons butter or margarine,
  softened
½ teaspoon corn syrup
1½ teaspoons hot water

✦ Prepare dough according to directions on page 71. Roll out dough with a rolling pin into a 4 x 12-inch strip. Brush with butter or water. Combine cinnamon and sugar and sprinkle over dough. Roll up tightly and seal. Place in a greased 9 x 5-inch loaf pan, seam-side down. Cover with plastic wrap and let rise until almost double. Bake in preheated 375° oven for 30 to 40 minutes. Remove from pan immediately and let cool on rack. Combine icing ingredients and spread on completely cooled bread or sprinkle with powdered sugar.
✦ Yields 1 loaf.

✦ Nutritional information per serving

Calories: 148.4	Saturated Fat: 2.7g	Calories from Fat: 28.7%
Protein: 2.8g	Cholesterol: 29mg	Calories from Carbohydrate: ... 64.0%
Carbohydrate: 24.0g	Dietary Fiber: 1.1g	Calories from Protein: 7.3%
Total Fat: 4.8g	Sodium: 314mg	

My grandmother used to come to visit us once or twice a year. She would spend a lot of her time in our kitchen, baking yeast rolls — plain or with onion. They were delicious, but best of all, the entire house smelled like freshly rising dough and warm baked bread. It was an incredible smell! Now I'm the one in the family who bakes yeast rolls, and as my home fills with these wonderful aromas, memories of my grandmother and of my mother's kitchen return to me once again.

CHEESE SCONES

1½ cups all-purpose flour
1½ teaspoons baking powder
1 teaspoon dry mustard
½ teaspoon salt
4 tablespoons cold unsalted butter,
  cut up
1 cup shredded sharp cheddar cheese
2 tablespoons grated Parmesan cheese
1 egg
½ cup milk

*Note: Scones can be frozen before baking,
then thawed and baked when ready
to serve.*

✦ Preheat oven to 400°. Combine flour, baking powder, dry mustard and salt in a large bowl. Add cold butter and cut it in with a pastry blender until mixture looks like fine granules. Add cheese and toss to mix. Break egg into milk and beat with a fork to blend well. Pour over flour mixture and stir with a fork until a dough forms. Turn onto a lightly floured board and knead 10 to 12 times. Cut in half. Knead each half briefly into a ball, turn smooth side up, and pat into a 6-inch circle. Cut each circle into 6 wedges. Place on an ungreased baking sheet. Bake for 12 to 15 minutes, or until medium brown. Cool, loosely wrapped in a dish towel, on a wire rack.

✦ Yields 12 scones.

HERB-OLIVE OIL SCONES

2 cups all-purpose flour
1 tablespoon baking powder
¼ cup coarsely grated Parmesan
  cheese
½ teaspoon salt
¼ teaspoon freshly ground black
  pepper
½ cup buttermilk or plain yogurt
⅓ cup olive oil
1 egg
2 teaspoons lemon juice
½ teaspoon minced fresh garlic
2 tablespoons snipped chives
1 tablespoon chopped fresh basil
1 teaspoon coarsely chopped fresh
  marjoram, thyme or oregano

✦ Preheat oven to 350°. Combine flour, baking powder, Parmesan, salt and pepper in a large bowl. Stir to mix well. In another bowl, whisk buttermilk, oil, egg, lemon juice, garlic, chives and herbs until well blended. Pour into flour mixture and stir until a soft dough forms. Turn dough onto a lightly floured board and knead 10 to 15 times. Gather dough into a ball and cut in half. Place both halves on an ungreased baking sheet and pat into an 8-inch round. Cut each round into 8 wedges, but do not separate the wedges. Bake for 15 to 20 minutes or until lightly browned. Cool on a wire rack for 5 minutes, then wrap in a dish towel and continue cooling at least 15 minutes more before serving.

✦ Yields 16 scones.

ASPEN APRICOT SCONES

Dairy

4 ounces dried apricots, finely
   chopped
2 tablespoons honey
2 (2-inch) strips lemon peel
1 tablespoon lemon juice
3 cups flour
1 tablespoon baking powder
¼ teaspoon salt
2 sticks unsalted butter, softened
¼ cup sugar
3 eggs
1 teaspoon vanilla
⅓ cup buttermilk or plain yogurt

*Note: Scones may be frozen before baking
   and stored in freezer in plastic bags
   up to 6 weeks. Thaw before baking.*
*Variation: Any other dried fruit may be
   used in place of apricots.*

✦ Place apricots, honey, lemon peel, lemon juice and ¼ cup water in a small saucepan. Bring to a boil, reduce heat and cover. Simmer 10 minutes, or until apricots are very soft. Discard lemon peel. Mash apricots until a coarse, thick puree. While apricots are cooking, mix flour, baking powder and salt in a medium bowl. Beat butter in large bowl with mixer on medium speed until smooth. Add sugar and beat 2 to 3 minutes, until light and fluffy. Add eggs one at a time, beating well after each addition. Add vanilla. Scrape sides of bowl and reduce speed to low. Add flour mixture. Beat only until blended. Scrape sides again, add buttermilk and mix only until blended. Fold in apricot puree with a rubber spatula just until puree is swirled through. Scoop ⅓ cupful of dough onto an ungreased baking sheet, placing mounds 2 inches apart. Loosely cover with plastic wrap and refrigerate 45 minutes. Uncover and bake in preheated 350° oven for 15 minutes. Reduce heat to 325° and bake until pale golden brown, 10 to 13 minutes longer. Cool, uncovered, on a wire rack.

✦ Yields 2 dozen scones.

EASY CHEESY
STUFFED BREAD

Dairy

2 medium loaves French bread
¾ cup shredded Swiss cheese
½ cup butter, softened
¼ cup mayonnaise
⅛ cup shredded Parmesan cheese
salt and pepper

✦ Preheat oven to 400°. Diagonally slice bread almost, but not completely through. Place on large piece of heavy foil. Combine remaining ingredients. Spread between bread slices and over top. Bring sides of foil up, loosely covering sides of bread but not the top. Bake for 20 minutes.

✦ 12 servings.

CHEESE AND
ONION PINWHEELS

Dairy

1 tablespoon butter or margarine
1 large onion, finely chopped
1 (1 pound) loaf frozen white bread
    dough, thawed
8 ounces shredded sharp cheddar
    cheese
paprika, optional

✦ Melt butter in a medium skillet over medium heat. Sauté onion, stirring occasionally, until tender, about 5 minutes . Remove
from heat. Roll out dough on a lightly
floured surface, using a lightly floured rolling pin, into a 12 x 14-inch rectangle. Arrange onions over dough. Sprinkle with
cheese, leaving a ¾-inch border along one
12-inch side. Roll up jelly-roll style. Cut
dough into 12 rolls with a sharp knife. Place
rolls on greased baking sheets, leaving 1
inch between each roll. Pat into rounded
shapes, cover with a damp kitchen towel
and set aside to rise 20 minutes or until
doubled. Sprinkle with paprika, if desired,
and bake in preheated 350° oven for 15 minutes or until golden.
✦ Yields 1 dozen rolls.

PUMPKIN HARVEST LOAF

Dairy

1¾ cups flour
1 cup sugar
1 teaspoon baking soda
½ teaspoon salt
1 teaspoon cinnamon
½ teaspoon nutmeg
¼ teaspoon ginger
¼ teaspoon ground cloves
2 eggs
1 cup butter, softened
1 cup canned pumpkin
½ cup applesauce
1 cup chopped walnuts
½ cup chocolate chips
orange sauce, optional (page 227)

✦ Preheat oven to 350°. Combine flour,
soda, salt and spices in a small bowl. Cream
butter in a large bowl. Add sugar and beat
until light and fluffy. Add eggs one at a
time, beating well after each addition. Add
flour mixture alternately with pumpkin and
applesauce, beginning and ending with dry
ingredients. Stir in nuts and chocolate chips.
Pour into buttered bundt pan. Bake for 60 to
65 minutes, or until toothpick inserted in
center comes out clean. Cool before removing from pan. Serve with lemon or orange
sauce, if desired.
✦ 12 servings.

ANNA BANANA BREAD

3 medium very ripe bananas, 1½ cups
3 eggs
2¼ cups sugar
2 sticks plus 2 tablespoons margarine
   or unsalted butter, softened
6 tablespoons plain yogurt
1 tablespoon vanilla
1 tablespoon dark rum
2 cups plus 2 tablespoons flour
1½ teaspoons baking soda
¼ teaspoon salt

Brown Sugar Glaze:
½ cup unsalted butter
½ cup firmly packed light brown
   sugar
½ cup powdered sugar
1 teaspoon vanilla

◆ Preheat oven to 350°. Place bananas in work bowl of food processor fitted with steel blade. Pulse until almost smooth, but still retaining some texture. Remove from bowl. Add eggs, sugar and butter to processor and blend until fluffy, stopping once to scrape down sides. Add yogurt, vanilla and rum and process for 5 seconds. Combine flour, baking soda and salt in a large bowl. Fold in egg mixture and 1½ cups banana puree gently but thoroughly. Save any extra banana for another use. Spoon batter into 2 greased 9 x 5-inch loaf pans or bundt pan. Bake for 45-50 minutes, or until toothpick inserted in center comes out clean. Cool in pan 5 minutes. Remove from pan.
◆ For glaze, melt butter in a small saucepan. Stir in brown sugar and cook over low heat until bubbly, stirring occasionally. Increase heat to medium-high and cook 2 more minutes, stirring constantly. Add milk and cook 1 minute. Remove from heat and add powdered sugar and vanilla. Stir until smooth. Spread over warm bread.
◆ Yields 2 loaves.

BANANA CHOCOLATE CHIP BREAD

1 stick butter, softened
1⅔ cups sugar
2 eggs, slightly beaten
¼ teaspoon salt
1½ teaspoons baking powder
½ teaspoon baking soda
¼ cup sour cream
1 cup mashed bananas
1 cup chopped nuts
2 cups sifted cake flour
1 teaspoon vanilla
½ cup mini chocolate chips

◆ Preheat oven to 350°. Cream butter and sugar in a large mixing bowl on medium speed until light and fluffy. Add eggs and salt. Mix well. Dissolve baking powder and baking soda in sour cream. Add to creamed mixture. Stir in bananas and nuts. Add flour gradually and mix until blended. Stir in vanilla and chocolate chips. Pour into greased 9 x 5-inch loaf pan and bake for 65 to 75 minutes, or until toothpick inserted in center comes out clean.
◆ Yields 1 loaf.

LEMONY LEMON BREAD

Dairy

1½ cups flour
¼ teaspoon baking powder
⅛ teaspoon baking soda
1 cup sugar
1 stick butter, softened
3 eggs
½ cup sour cream
grated peel of 1 lemon

Glaze:
⅓ cup lemon juice
⅓ cup sugar

Note: Great for muffins, too!

✦ Preheat oven to 325°. Combine flour, baking powder and baking soda in a bowl. Beat sugar and butter in a large bowl at high speed, until light and fluffy, about 5 minutes. Add eggs one at a time, beating well after each addition. Add flour mixture alternately with sour cream, beating until well blended. Stir in lemon peel. Pour batter into greased and floured 9 x 5-inch loaf pan. Bake for 1 to 1¼ hours, or until toothpick inserted in center comes out clean. Prepare glaze by combining lemon juice and sugar. Spoon evenly over hot bread in pan. Cool bread in pan on wire rack.
✦ Yields 1 loaf.

GRANDMA'S CHOCOLATE ZUCCHINI BREAD

2 cups sugar
1 cup vegetable oil
1 teaspoon vanilla
2 eggs
2¾ cups flour
¼ cup cocoa
1 teaspoon baking soda
¼ teaspoon baking powder
1 teaspoon salt
3 cups grated zucchini
1 cup shredded coconut
1 cup chopped nuts
1 cup pareve mini chocolate chips

Note: Makes a great bundt cake!

✦ Preheat oven to 350°. Combine sugar, oil, vanilla and eggs. Stir in flour, cocoa, baking soda, baking powder and salt. Fold in remaining ingredients. Pour into 2 greased 9 x 5-inch loaf pans. Bake for 1 hour, or until toothpick inserted in center comes out clean. Can also bake in bundt pan for 1 hour and 10 minutes.
✦ Yields 2 loaves.

AWESOME BLUEBERRY MUFFINS

¾ cup sugar
¼ cup butter, softened
1 egg
2 cups flour
2 teaspoons baking powder
½ teaspoon salt
½ cup milk
2 cups blueberries

Topping:
½ cup sugar
¼ cup butter, softened
½ teaspoon cinnamon

✦ Preheat oven to 400°. Cream butter, sugar and egg until light and fluffy. Combine flour, baking powder and salt in another bowl. Add to creamed mixture alternately with milk. Blend well. Fold in berries. Fill greased muffin tins two-thirds full. Mix topping ingredients and sprinkle over top. Bake for 20 to 25 minutes.
✦ Yields 1 dozen muffins.

✦ **Nutritional information per serving**

Calories: 250.0	Saturated Fat: 5.1g	Calories from Fat: 30.6%
Protein: 3.2g	Cholesterol: 40mg	Calories from Carbohydrate: ... 64.3%
Carbohydrate: 40.9g	Dietary Fiber: 0.7g	Calories from Protein: 5.1%
Total Fat: 8.6g	Sodium: 239mg	

✦ **When a muffin recipe calls for butter or a solid
shortening, replace the fat with a substitute:
use half as much fruit juice, applesauce or fruit purée.
If oil is an ingredient, replace all or three-fourths
with one of the substitutes.**

SUN-KISSED
DATE NUT MUFFINS

2 cups flour
½ cup sugar
½ teaspoon salt
2 teaspoons baking powder
¼ teaspoon baking soda
1 tablespoon grated orange rind
2 eggs, well beaten
½ cup buttermilk
½ cup vegetable oil
¼ cup chopped walnuts
½ cup chopped dates
melted butter

Topping:
2 teaspoons grated orange rind
¼ teaspoon cinnamon
1 teaspoon orange juice
⅓ cup sugar

✦ Preheat oven to 400°. Sift flour, sugar, salt, baking powder and baking soda into mixing bowl. Combine rind with eggs, buttermilk and oil. Pour into dry ingredients and stir to blend. Stir in walnuts and dates. Fill well-greased muffin pans two-thirds full. Coat tops with melted butter. Combine topping ingredients and sprinkle over muffins. Bake for 20 minutes.

✦ Yields 1 dozen muffins.

MOCHA MUFFINS

1 tablespoon instant espresso powder
¼ cup hot water
½ cup buttermilk
½ cup vegetable oil
2 large eggs
1 teaspoon vanilla
1¾ cups flour
½ cup sugar
½ cup firmly packed light brown
   sugar
3 tablespoons cocoa
1 teaspoon baking powder
1 teaspoon baking soda
1 teaspoon salt
1½ cups milk chocolate chips
1 cup coarsely chopped pecans,
   toasted •
12 chocolate coffee beans, optional

✦ Preheat oven to 375°. Dissolve espresso powder in hot water in a medium bowl. Add buttermilk, oil, eggs and vanilla and whisk until well blended. Mix flour, sugar, brown sugar, cocoa, baking powder, baking soda and salt in a large bowl. Add buttermilk mixture and stir just until combined. Stir in chocolate chips and pecans. Divide batter into 12 muffin cups lined with paper liners. Bake for 25 minutes, or until toothpick inserted in center of muffin comes out clean. Top each muffin with a chocolate coffee bean, if desired. Transfer to wire rack and cool.

✦ Yields 1 dozen muffins.

SPICED COCONUT-
CARROT MUFFINS

2 cups flour
1 tablespoon baking powder
1 tablespoon cinnamon
¼ teaspoon ground cloves
¼ teaspoon ground ginger
¼ teaspoon ground nutmeg
¼ teaspoon salt
1 cup firmly packed dark brown
   sugar
¾ cup sugar
1 cup sweetened shredded coconut
1 cup shredded peeled carrot
1 cup yellow raisins
1 small tart green apple, peeled and
   coarsely chopped
½ cup chopped walnuts
1 cup vegetable oil
3 eggs
1 tablespoon vanilla

✦ Preheat oven to 375°. Sift flour, baking powder, spices and salt into a large bowl. Mix in both sugars. Add coconut, carrot, raisins, apple and nuts. Whisk oil, eggs and vanilla together in a medium bowl to blend. Gradually pour oil mixture into dry ingredients, occasionally scraping down sides of bowl. Mix until well blended. Divide batter among 18 muffin cups lined with foil liners. Bake until toothpick inserted in center comes out clean and tops are deep golden brown, about 25 minutes. Transfer to rack and cool.

✦ Yields 1½ dozen muffins.

SOUPS AND SALADS

SOUP AND SALAD INDEX

BASIC CHICKEN SOUP

Meat | Traditional

1 (4 pound) chicken or 4 pounds chicken parts, well trimmed of excess fat
3 quarts water
4 carrots, peeled and cut in 1-inch diagonal slices
4 celery stalks, including leaves, cut into thirds
1 large onion, cut in half
2 large sprigs parsley
salt and pepper to taste
1 tablespoon chicken bouillon granules, or 2 cubes
few dashes garlic powder

✦ Wash chicken thoroughly, inside and out. Add 3 quarts of water, or enough to cover chicken in a stock pot. Bring to a boil. Place chicken in pot and return to a boil. Skim foam off as it forms on top. After all foam is removed, add remaining ingredients. Cover, reduce heat, and simmer 1½ hours. If using a stewing chicken, simmer for 2 hours. Remove chicken and reserve for other uses. Strain soup, reserving carrots for garnish. Refrigerate for several hours or overnight and remove congealed fat from top of soup.

✦ 10 servings.

Hint: Leftover chicken from the soup is handy to have. Debone it and use for sandwiches and salads. It also freezes well.

Shabbat was special when I was growing up. Coming home from school on Friday afternoon, I was overwhelmed by the fragrant smells emanating from the kitchen. Smells of chicken soup mixed with potato kugel and frying chicken drifted through the house. The table glowed with fresh linen and the good china. The silver candlesticks were polished and ready to be lit. Daddy came home, showered and put on a freshly starched white shirt. We all stood and watched Mother light the candles. Then Daddy would recite the kiddush, and we all sipped sweet wine. The kids dipped the challah in the wine and loved every bite! The meal was joyous, with talk about our week at work and at school and the fun things we would do over the weekend. Shabbat dinner gave us the time to be together and be thankful for our loving family. It was a night to stay at home and observe our Jewish heritage, feel nourished in body and spirit, and strengthen the bond of our family. As the years go by, I always think of these beautiful memories, especially on Friday night when I light the candles and my husband recites the kiddush for our family.

SOUPS

GRANDMA'S SECRET CHICKEN SOUP

1 (4 pound) roasting chicken
8 ounces flanken of beef, or meat
  from short ribs
3 large carrots, peeled, cut in half
3 large celery stalks, cut in half
2 large onions
1 large parsnip, peeled, cut in half
10 cups water
2 teaspoons salt
pepper

✦ Clean chicken, but do not remove fat, unless planning to serve soup on the same day. If this is necessary, remove all visible fat. Remove fat from beef. Place chicken, including neck and gizzard, meat and remaining ingredients in a large stock pot. Bring to a boil, then reduce heat to simmer. Skim foam as it forms on top. When foam no longer appears, about 30 minutes, cover pot. Simmer 1½ to 2 hours, until chicken leg meat pulls away from the bone. Cool. Remove chicken, meat and vegetables. Save chicken and vegetables for another use. Strain soup and refrigerate. Remove congealed fat from top of soup before serving. To serve, reheat and adjust seasonings. Slice reserved carrots into soup for garnish, if desired.

✦ 10 servings.

My grandmother was a caterer in Russia. She lived with us and prepared wonderful foods. She made lockshen (noodles) every Sabbath. She would spread a special tablecloth out on the dining room table with a bowl under it in the center to give it a little rise. Then she would roll out the dough until it was moderately thin and begin to work it on the back of her hands over her curved knuckles, crossing her arms as she would lift and stretch one section at a time until the dough was as large as the table. Then she would lift up the cloth and gently roll the dough into a long log. Then she would slice it thinly, lift the dough off the table and drop it. As the noodles fell back to the table, they would dry.

KREPLACH

1 large yellow onion, sliced
1 teaspoon vegetable oil
  or chicken fat
1 pound trimmed cooked beef
  (brisket, steak, pot roast
  or ground beef)
5 eggs, divided
salt and pepper
1⅓ cups flour

Note: *To prepare ahead, freeze cooked kreplach on cookie sheets and store in plastic bags until ready to use.*
Hint: *Wonton skins may be substituted for the dough. Reduce cooking time to 3 minutes.*
Variation: *To serve as a first course, place kreplach on a greased baking sheet, brush with oil and cook in preheated 375° oven until brown.*

✦ Sauté onion in oil until tender. Grind meat and onion in a grinder or food processor. Add 2 eggs and salt and pepper to taste. Mix well. Beat remaining eggs in a medium bowl. Add flour and ¼ teaspoon salt and mix well. Place on floured board and knead until smooth and no longer sticky. Cover with a cloth and let rest for 30 minutes. Roll dough to a 17 x 22-inch rectangle. Cut into 3-inch squares. Place 1 heaping teaspoon of meat mixture in center of square. Moisten edges of dough with water and pinch together tightly to form a triangle. Repeat with remaining squares. Drop in boiling salt water or chicken soup. Reduce heat and simmer 30 minutes, or until done. Remove with slotted spoon and place in soup.
✦ Yields 3 dozen.

1.
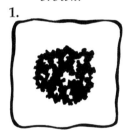
2.
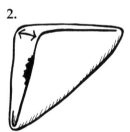
3.
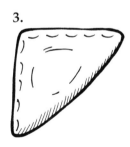

MAMA'S MATZO BALLS

4 tablespoons chicken fat or
  vegetable oil
4 eggs
1 cup matzo meal
1½ teaspoons salt, divided
4 tablespoons seltzer water

Note: *These are very light and fluffy. Great for Passover and all through the year.*

✦ Combine oil or chicken fat (schmaltz) and eggs. Stir in matzo meal and ½ teaspoon salt, then seltzer. Blend well. Cover with plastic wrap and refrigerate 1 to 2 hours, or until mixture is firm enough to roll into balls. Roll into 16 balls. Bring a large pot of water to a rapid boil. Add remaining salt. Drop balls into water, cover pot and boil for 1¼ hours. Remove from water with a slotted spoon. Add to soup or freeze for later use.
✦ Yields 16 matzo balls.

✡ See Pareve Food Preparation, page 30

S
O
U
P
S

95

BEET BORSCHT

2 bunches red beets (10 to 12)
2 quarts water
8 tablespoons sugar
juice of 3 lemons
1 tablespoon salt
1 tablespoon sour salt (citric acid)
sour cream, optional

*Note: Delicious, refreshing and great for
Passover!*

✦ Clean and trim beets. Place in pot with water to cover. Cook over medium heat until tender, about 20 to 30 minutes. Drain and cool beets. When cool enough to handle, grate beets. Place in a pot with 2 quarts water. Add remaining ingredients except sour cream. Bring to a boil. Add additional lemon and sugar to taste. Remove from heat and refrigerate. Serve chilled, with a dollop of sour cream in each bowl if desired.
✦ 10 servings.

✡ See Pareve Food Preparation, page 30

✦ Nutritional information per serving

Calories: 61.6	Saturated Fat: 0g	Calories from Fat: 0.5%
Protein: 0.4g	Cholesterol: 0mg	Calories from Carbohydrate: ... 97.0%
Carbohydrate: 16.0g	Dietary Fiber: 0.6g	Calories from Protein: 2.4%
Total Fat: 0g	Sodium: 823mg	

CABBAGE BORSCHT

3 pounds beef chuck roast or short ribs
2 tablespoons vegetable oil
1 large onion, chopped
1 (3 pound) green cabbage, thickly
  sliced
3 to 4 quarts water
1 (28 ounce) can diced tomatoes,
  undrained
1 (10¾ ounce) can tomato puree
2 teaspoons salt
1 teaspoon pepper
½ cup sugar
½ cup firmly packed brown sugar
¾ cup lemon juice
½ cup white raisins
20 prunes, with pits

Note: This is best when made a day ahead.

✦ Cook meat in preheated 425° oven until brown. While meat is browning, heat oil in large stock pot. Add onion and sauté until soft. Add cabbage and sauté 3 to 5 minutes more. Add browned meat. Add water to cover, about 3 to 4 quarts. Bring to a boil, reduce to a simmer and skim foam from soup. When no more foam appears, add tomatoes, tomato puree, salt, pepper, sugars and lemon juice. Simmer 1 hour. Taste and adjust seasonings, adding more sugar and lemon juice as needed. Cook 1 more hour. Add raisins and prunes and cook 1 more hour. Adjust seasonings. Cool, remove fat and cut meat into pieces. Reheat before serving. Serve with rye bread.
✦ 8 servings.

SPINACH BORSCHT

1½ quarts water
2 (10 ounce) packages frozen
    chopped spinach
1 cup chopped onion
½ teaspoon garlic salt
½ teaspoon pepper
⅓ cup lemon juice
¼ cup firmly packed brown sugar
1 cup sour cream
1 cucumber, diced
1 hard boiled egg, sliced, optional

✦ Combine water, spinach, onion, garlic salt and pepper in a saucepan. Bring to a boil. Reduce heat and simmer 10 minutes. Add lemon juice and sugar. Simmer 5 minutes more. Taste and correct seasonings. Refrigerate. Serve chilled with spoonfuls of sour cream and cucumber mixed into each bowl. Garnish with egg slices, if desired. Serve with pumpernickel or rye bread.

✦ 10 servings.

✦ **Nutritional information per serving**

Calories: 43.5	Saturated Fat: 0g	Calories from Fat: 4.2%
Protein: 2.1g	Cholesterol: 0mg	Calories from Carbohydrate: ... 79.3%
Carbohydrate: 9.9g	Dietary Fiber: 2.2g	Calories from Protein: 16.5%
Total Fat: 0.2g	Sodium: 109mg	

CREAMY CUCUMBER SOUP

¾ cup coarsely chopped walnuts
2 large cloves garlic, halved
3 tablespoons olive oil
4 cups plain yogurt
3 medium cucumbers, pared and
    seeded
1 teaspoon salt
⅛ teaspoon freshly ground pepper
2 tablespoons lemon juice
2 tablespoons chopped fresh mint,
    divided
chopped walnuts for garnish

Note: Refreshing and delicious - great as an appetizer or a light summer supper.

✦ Place walnuts and garlic in blender and blend until coarsely ground. Add oil and blend until smooth. Gradually blend in yogurt, scraping down sides of container frequently with spatula. Pour into a glass bowl. Shred cucumbers and drain in a colander. Press out excess liquid. Stir cucumbers, salt, pepper, lemon juice and 1 tablespoon mint into yogurt mixture. Cover and refrigerate until thoroughly chilled, at least 2 hours. Garnish with remaining mint and chopped walnuts.

✦ 8 servings.

S O U P S

LIME TORTILLA SOUP

2 tablespoons vegetable oil
1 large red bell pepper, seeded and
  chopped
1 onion, minced
1 clove garlic, minced
2 tomatoes, peeled, seeded and
  chopped
3 fresh jalapeño or serrano chiles,
  seeded and minced
6 cups chicken broth
1 lime
1½ cups cooked, shredded chicken
  breast
salt and pepper
tortilla chips
6 lime slices

✦ Heat oil in a saucepan. Add red bell pepper, onion and garlic and cook over low heat, stirring, until pepper is softened. Add tomatoes and cook, stirring, for 2 minutes. Add chiles, and broth. Rinse lime, halve it crosswise and squeeze juice into saucepan. Add lime skins to pan and bring to a boil. Reduce heat and simmer 5 minutes. Remove and discard lime skins. Add chicken and simmer until chicken is heated thoroughly. Season with salt and pepper to taste. Ladle into bowl and top with a handful of tortilla chips. Float a lime slice in the center of each bowl.
✦ 6 servings.

BORDER BROCCOLI CHEESE SOUP

¼ cup butter or margarine
½ onion, chopped
2 stalks celery, cut into ¼-inch slices
1 teaspoon minced garlic
42 ounces chicken-style pareve
  bouillon or vegetable broth
4 cups chopped fresh broccoli
1 potato, cut in 1-inch dice
1 teaspoon dried thyme
1 teaspoon salt
¼ teaspoon freshly ground pepper
1 cup half and half or
  whipping cream
4 cups grated cheddar cheese
2 cups cooked broccoli florets

Variation: Cauliflower, asparagus, or zucchini all work well in this recipe.
Note: This soup should not be frozen.

✦ Melt butter in a large stock pot. Sauté onion and celery until onion is translucent. Add garlic and sauté another minute. Add bouillon, chopped broccoli, potato, thyme, salt and pepper. Bring to a boil, reduce heat, and simmer 10 to 15 minutes, until potatoes and broccoli are tender. Remove from heat, strain liquid from vegetables and return liquid to pot. Process vegetables in food processor, in batches, until fairly smooth. Add a little reserved liquid if necessary. After each batch of vegetables is processed, return them to pot. Reheat over medium-low heat. Gradually add half and half, stirring constantly. Do not allow to boil. When half and half is completely mixed, add cheese, stirring constantly, until cheese is melted. Add broccoli florets. Heat, stirring, for a few more minutes and serve.
✦ 6 servings.

KETTLE POTATO AND LEEK SOUP

2 large leeks
2 tablespoons olive oil
1 cup chopped onion
8 cups chicken stock or pareve
  chicken-flavored broth
1½ pounds potatoes, peeled and
  diced into 2-inch pieces
1 cup nondairy creamer
½ teaspoon salt
1 teaspoon pepper
fresh chopped chives for garnish

✦ Trim root end of leeks. Cut off top, leaving leek 6 to 7 inches long. Cut in half lengthwise. Cut each half into ¼-inch slices. Soak in cold water to clean, then drain. Heat oil in a large heavy pot. Add leek and onion and cook over medium-low heat for 5 to 10 minutes until soft and slightly brown. Add stock, potatoes, salt and pepper. Bring to boil, reduce heat and simmer until potatoes are tender, 25 to 30 minutes. Strain liquid from soup into a bowl and reserve. Puree vegetables, in batches, in food processor. Add some of reserved liquid if needed. Return reserved liquid and pureed vegetables to pot. Stir to blend. Gradually add non-dairy creamer, stirring constantly over medium-low heat. Salt and pepper to taste. Heat until steamy. Garnish with chives.

✦ 8 servings.

✡ See Pareve Food Preparation, page 30

✦ **Nutritional information per serving**

Calories: 237.7	Saturated Fat: 2.0g	Calories from Fat: 30.0%
Protein: 11.2g	Cholesterol: 6mg	Calories from Carbohydrate: ... 51.4%
Carbohydrate: 30.7g	Dietary Fiber: 3.0g	Calories from Protein: 18.7%
Total Fat: 8.0g	Sodium: 1,346mg	

S
O
U
P
S

99

SKIERS' VEGETABLE SOUP

Meat

6 pounds crosscut beef shanks
4 teaspoons salt, divided
10 cups water
3 stalks celery, diced
3 large carrots, diced
2 medium onions, diced
1 (28 ounce) can tomatoes, chopped
½ cup chopped fresh parsley
½ teaspoon dried basil
½ teaspoon dried thyme leaves
½ teaspoon pepper
1 (10 ounce) package frozen lima
    beans
1 (10 ounce) package frozen corn
1 (10 ounce) package frozen peas
2 cups sliced mushrooms

✦ Place beef, 2 teaspoons salt and water in a large stock pot. Bring to a boil over high heat and skim off all foam. Reduce heat to a simmer and add celery, carrots, onions, tomatoes, herbs and pepper. Cover and simmer 3 hours. Stir in frozen vegetables, mushrooms and remaining salt. Continue cooking for 1 hour, until meat and vegetables are done. Remove meat from soup and cut into cubes. Return to soup. Skim off fat and adjust seasonings. Flavor is best if made a day ahead.
✦ 14 servings.

Note: This hearty one dish meal freezes well.

FRENCH VEGETABLE SOUP

Meat or Pareve ✡

2 tablespoons pareve margarine or
    vegetable oil
1 cup diced leeks, white part only
1 cup diced carrots
1 cup diced red potatoes
½ cup chopped celery
½ cup sliced green beans
½ cup diced green bell pepper
8 cups chicken or vegetable stock
½ cup frozen peas
⅓ cup small shell pasta
½ cup diced zucchini
1 cup sliced mushrooms
1 large clove garlic
1 tablespoon fresh basil
3 tablespoons tomato paste
3 tablespoons olive oil
salt, pepper and cayenne pepper

✦ Heat oil in a stock pot. Add leeks, carrots, potatoes and celery, and sauté 10 minutes. Add green beans and green pepper. Pour in stock. Add peas, pasta, zucchini and mushrooms. Place garlic, basil, tomato paste and olive oil in blender and puree. Add to soup with salt, pepper and cayenne to taste. Bring to a boil, cover, reduce heat and simmer for one hour.
✦ 6 servings.

✡ See Pareve Food Preparation, page 30

Note: Can be frozen.

LENTIL SOUP DURANGO

Dairy | Lighter

1 tablespoon olive oil
1 cup sliced carrots
1 cup chopped onion
2 cups water
1 cup uncooked dried lentils, rinsed
   well
⅓ cup uncooked long grain rice
1 teaspoon salt
½ teaspoon ground cumin
¾ teaspoon pepper
2 (13¾ ounce) cans vegetable broth
1 (8 ounce) can tomato sauce
2 cups milk

✦ Heat oil in a large Dutch oven over medium-high heat. Add carrots and onions and sauté until tender, about 5 minutes. Add remaining ingredients except milk. Mix well. Bring to a boil, cover and reduce heat. Simmer until lentils are tender, about 1 hour. Puree half of lentil mixture in food processor until smooth. For a smooth soup, repeat with remaining lentils. For chunky soup, leave remaining lentils unprocessed. Return lentils to pan and stir in milk. Cook over low heat until thoroughly heated.
✦ 8 servings.

Note: Great accompanied by a salad and crusty bread for a football party or after a long day on the slopes.

✦ Nutritional information per serving

Calories: 286.7	Saturated Fat: 2.4g	Calories from Fat: 21.5%
Protein: 14.6g	Cholesterol: 12mg	Calories from Carbohydrate: ... 58.5%
Carbohydrate: 42.8g	Dietary Fiber: 12.1g	Calories from Protein: 20.0%
Total Fat: 7.0g	Sodium: 1,179mg	

BUTTERNUT SQUASH SOUP

Dairy or Pareve ✡

2 tablespoons pareve margarine or
   butter
1 cup chopped onion
2½ cups peeled, cubed butternut
   squash
½ teaspoon ground sage
½ teaspoon dried thyme
3-4 cups low salt chicken broth or
   vegetable broth
cayenne pepper
salt
Parmesan cheese, optional
½ cup coarsely chopped walnuts

✦ Melt butter in a large saucepan. Sauté onion until tender, about 10 minutes. Add squash and sauté 10 more minutes. Add sage and thyme and stir for a minute. Add broth and bring to a boil. Reduce heat and simmer until squash is tender, about 30 minutes. Process in small batches in blender or food processor until smooth. Season with cayenne pepper and salt to taste. Serve hot, garnished with walnuts and Parmesan cheese, if desired.
✦ 4 servings.

✡ See Pareve Food Preparation, page 30

Note: Delicious and healthy!

S O U P S

MUSHROOM BARLEY SOUP   `Meat`

3 pounds beef short ribs
2 large onions, chopped
3 stalks celery, chopped or sliced
3 carrots, chopped or sliced
1 pound fresh mushrooms, sliced
1½ teaspoons pepper
2 teaspoons salt
1 teaspoon minced garlic
1 cup medium barley
3 medium tomatoes, diced
1½ quarts water
1½ quarts beef broth

✦ Place meat, onions, celery and carrots in a roasting pan. Bake in preheated 400° oven for 30 to 40 minutes, until browned. Drain off fat. Transfer to a stock pot, add remaining ingredients and bring to a boil. Reduce heat and simmer for several hours, until meat is tender. Let cool or refrigerate overnight. Skim fat off top, remove ribs and debone. Shred meat and return to soup. Reheat soup, adding water if too thick. Adjust seasonings. Serve with crusty bread.
✦ 8 servings.

✦ If soups and other foods are too salty, add a teaspoon each of vinegar and sugar and reheat.

OVEN BEEF BARLEY SOUP   `Meat`

1 cup barley
2 medium onions, chopped
3 (14½ ounce) cans beef broth
2 (28 ounce) cans chopped tomatoes, undrained
5 stalks celery, sliced
5 carrots, sliced
1 parsnip, sliced
3 pounds stew beef
3 pounds soup bones
2 teaspoons salt
1 teaspoon pepper
½ teaspoon garlic powder

✦ Combine all ingredients in a large roaster or 8-quart stock pot. Add water if needed to reach top of pot. Cover and bake in preheated 250° oven for 5 to 6 hours. Remove from oven and cool. Remove meat from soup and debone. Return to the soup. Skim off fat and adjust seasonings. Tastes even better if prepared a day ahead. Serve with crusty French bread.
✦ 12 servings

Variation: To make in crock pot, cut all ingredients in half.

SOUTH FORK SHIITAKE MUSHROOM SOUP

Meat

3 tablespoons vegetable oil, divided
4½ pounds beef short ribs, cut crosswise into 2-inch pieces
1 tablespoon salt, divided
½ teaspoon freshly ground pepper, divided
1 cup minced shallots
1 pound fresh white mushrooms, chopped
½ pound fresh shiitake mushrooms, stemmed, caps thinly sliced
1 cup dry red wine
¾ cup barley, rinsed and drained
2 teaspoons ground cumin
1½ teaspoons chili powder
4 sprigs fresh thyme or ¾ teaspoon dried
1 bay leaf
1 (28 ounce) can Italian peeled tomatoes, chopped, and juice reserved
3 tablespoons chopped Italian parsley

Variation: Portobello mushrooms may be used in place of shiitake mushrooms.

✦ Heat 2 tablespoons oil in a stock pot over high heat. Add half of meat and sauté, turning until browned, about 4 minutes. Remove meat to a bowl and season with half of salt and pepper. Repeat with remaining meat. Drain fat from pot. Add remaining oil and heat over moderately high heat. Add shallots and mushrooms and cook until softened and lightly browned, about 8 minutes. Add wine and bring to a boil. Boil until reduced by half, about 5 minutes. Stir in 8 cups water, barley, cumin, chili powder, thyme and bay leaf. Return meat to pot. Bring to a boil. Reduce heat to low and simmer, partially covered, until meat is tender, about 1½ hours. Remove ribs to cutting board. Discard bones and cut meat into ½-inch pieces, trimming any excess fat. Skim fat from soup and return meat to pot. Return to boil and add tomatoes and juice. Simmer, uncovered, about 10 minutes. Adjust seasonings, garnish with parsley and serve.
✦ 8 servings

✦ How to remove foam and fat from soup:
When soup comes to a boil, skim off the dark or frothy foam that forms on top before adding the remaining ingredients. If possible, chill soup before serving and remove all fat from surface.

S
O
U
P
S

DIVINE SALAD

Dressing:
1 cup cider vinegar
½ cup sugar
2 tablespoons minced red onion
2 tablespoons canola oil
½ teaspoon poppy seeds

Salad:
**4 cups tightly packed torn romaine
  lettuce**
**4 cups tightly packed torn Boston or
  leaf lettuce**
½ cup thinly sliced red onion
**2 (11-ounce) cans mandarin oranges,
  drained**

✦ Combine all dressing ingredients in blender and process until smooth. May be made a day ahead. For salad, place all ingredients in a large bowl. Pour ½ cup dressing over and toss well. Save remaining dressing.

✦ 5 servings.

✦ **Nutritional information per serving**

Calories: 169.4	Saturated Fat: 0.4g	Calories from Fat: 29.0%
Protein: 1.8g	Cholesterol: 0mg	Calories from Carbohydrate: ... 67.0%
Carbohydrate: 30.5g	Dietary Fiber: 2.8g	Calories from Protein: 4.0%
Total Fat: 5.9g	Sodium: 8mg	

SALAD MEXICANA

Pareve

1 large head romaine lettuce, torn
   into pieces
2 Roma tomatoes, thinly sliced
1 green bell pepper, seeded,
   quartered and sliced
1 small red onion, thinly sliced and
   separated into rings
1 medium jícama, cut in eighths and
   thinly sliced
1 avocado, diced
1 bunch radishes, thinly sliced
2 cucumbers, cut in half lengthwise
   and sliced

Dressing:
1 large clove garlic
juice of 1 lemon
½ cup olive oil
salt and freshly ground pepper

✦ Toss all salad ingredients together. For dressing, place garlic in food processor and pulse until finely chopped. Add lemon juice and olive oil and blend until creamy. Add seasonings to taste. Toss salad with dressing and serve immediately. Use only enough of the dressing to coat salad. Reserve leftover dressing for another time. It will keep up to a week in refrigerator.
✦ 8 servings.

ORIENTAL SPINACH SALAD

1 (10 ounce) package fresh spinach
8 ounces fresh bean sprouts
1 (8 ounce) can water chestnuts,
   drained and sliced
½ pound fresh mushrooms, sliced
3 hard boiled eggs, sliced, optional
1 cup croutons or to taste

Dressing:
1 cup vegetable oil
½ cup white vinegar
¼ cup sugar
¼ cup firmly packed brown sugar
⅓ cup ketchup
1 tablespoon Worcestershire sauce
1 medium onion, chopped
dash of salt

✦ Wash, dry and remove stems from spinach. Tear into pieces and place in salad bowl. Add bean sprouts, water chestnuts, mushrooms, and eggs, if desired. Toss lightly. Combine dressing ingredients in a blender and run on high speed for a few seconds, until well blended. Pour enough dressing over salad to coat and toss gently. Sprinkle with croutons before serving. Extra dressing keeps well in the refrigerator.
✦ 8 servings.

STRAWBERRY SPINACH SALAD

 Pareve

1 pound fresh spinach, washed, stems removed and torn into bite-sized pieces
1 head bibb lettuce, washed and torn into bite-sized pieces
1 pint fresh strawberries, hulled and sliced
½ cup thinly sliced red onion
¼ cup finely chopped toasted pecans

Dressing:
⅓ cup raspberry vinegar
¼ teaspoon salt
¼ cup sugar
1 tablespoon poppy seeds
2 teaspoons dried instant minced onion
¼ cup canola oil

✦ Place spinach, lettuce, strawberries, onions and pecans in a large salad bowl. Combine all dressing ingredients in a small bowl. Mix with a wire whisk until salt and sugar are dissolved. Pour over salad and toss.
✦ 8 servings.

BASIC VINAIGRETTE

 Dairy or Pareve ✿

1 teaspoon Dijon mustard
¼ teaspoon salt
freshly ground pepper to taste
2 tablespoons red wine vinegar
1 teaspoon lemon juice
2 tablespoons vegetable oil
¼ cup olive oil

✦ Whisk ingredients together thoroughly and add to 10 to 12 cups salad greens.

✿ See Pareve Food Preparation, page 30

Variation: Stir in minced garlic.
Note: Add garlic, crushed anchovies, croutons and grated Parmesan for Caesar Salad.
Add chopped shallots for marinated mushrooms or green beans.
Add chopped capers and minced red onion. Pour over warm boiled potatoes.

DIPSY DOODLE DRESSING

Pareve

¼ cup chopped, drained oil-packed
   sun-dried tomatoes
2 teaspoons Dijon mustard
2 teaspoons honey
3 tablespoons balsamic vinegar
¼ cup olive oil
salt and pepper to taste

✦ Combine sun-dried tomatoes, mustard and honey in a small bowl. Whisk in vinegar, then oil. Season with salt and pepper to taste.

AUTHENTIC ROQUEFORT DRESSING

Dairy

1 cup mayonnaise
4 ounces Roquefort cheese, crumbled
½ cup buttermilk
1 teaspoon finely minced garlic
1 tablespoon finely minced onion
1 tablespoon freshly grated pepper
1 teaspoon lemon juice
2 tablespoons white wine

✦ Combine mayonnaise and cheese and blend thoroughly. Add remaining ingredients and mix well.

YOGURT DRESSING AND DIP

Dairy

6 walnut halves
1 clove garlic
1 tablespoon olive oil
1 cup plain yogurt
¼ cup peeled, seeded and finely
   diced cucumber
½ teaspoon lemon juice

✦ Place walnuts, garlic and oil in blender and blend well. Stir in remaining ingredients. Chill well.

Note: *Makes a great salad dressing or may be served as an appetizer with crackers and raw vegetables.*

107

TANGY REDSTONE COLE SLAW

1 head cabbage, chopped
1 medium onion, chopped
1 (4 ounce) jar pimentos, drained and chopped
1 teaspoon chopped parsley
1 cup chopped carrots
6 tablespoons vinegar
1 teaspoon pepper
5 tablespoons sugar
1½ teaspoons salt
dash of garlic powder
4 tablespoons salad oil
½ teaspoon celery seed

✦ Combine cabbage, onion, pimento, parsley and carrots in a bowl. Combine remaining ingredients and blend well. Pour over cabbage mixture and toss well. Refrigerate overnight or chill several hours before serving.
✦ 8 servings.

Variation: For a quick and easy version, substitute the packaged slaw mix for the cabbage mixture.

✦ Keep cookbooks and recipe cards clean while cooking by placing them under an inverted glass pie plate — which also magnifies them!

SUMMER CORN SALAD

⅓ cup balsamic vinegar
⅓ cup red wine vinegar
½ cup chopped fresh basil
1 tablespoon minced garlic
1 tablespoon chopped fresh tarragon
2 teaspoons Asian red chile paste, or more to taste
½ cup olive oil
3 cups corn kernels, cut from cooked corn on cob
⅓ cup diced green bell pepper
⅓ cup diced red bell pepper
¼ cup diced red onion

✦ Place vinegars, basil, garlic, tarragon and chile paste in food processor. Pulse until blended. With motor running, slowly add olive oil. Combine corn, peppers and onion in a serving bowl. Top with ⅓ cup of dressing and toss. Reserve remaining dressing for other uses. Chill salad until ready to serve.
✦ 4 servings

Note: A great summer salad served with grilled salmon.

JOSEPH'S COAT VEGETABLE SALAD

1 cup sliced carrots
1 head cauliflower, cut into florets
½ cup chopped onion
1 green bell pepper, seeded and diced
1 cup diced celery
1 (4 ounce) jar pimentos, drained
1 (6 ounce) can water chestnuts,
   drained and sliced
¼ pound mushrooms, sliced

Dressing:
⅓ cup salad oil
½ cup white vinegar
1 teaspoon salt
dash of pepper
2 tablespoons flour
2 tablespoons prepared mustard
¼ cup fresh lemon juice

✦ Combine all salad ingredients in a bowl. Combine all dressing ingredients in a small saucepan. Bring to a boil, stirring. Reduce heat and continue cooking, stirring constantly, until thickened, about 5 minutes. Remove from heat and cool. Pour over salad and refrigerate. Will keep several days.

MEDITERRANEAN CHICK PEA PASTA SALAD

Dressing:
¼ cup olive oil
¼ cup balsamic vinegar
½ teaspoon minced garlic
½ teaspoon salt
¼ teaspoon pepper

Salad
1 (16 ounce) can chick peas, rinsed
   and drained
1 (9 ounce) package frozen French cut
   green beans, thawed and drained
½ cup pitted black olives
12 cherry tomatoes, quartered, or
   1½ cups diced plum tomatoes
1 cup crumbled feta cheese
¼ cup loosely packed fresh basil
   leaves
8 ounces bowtie pasta, cooked
   al dente and drained

✦ Whisk dressing ingredients in large bowl until blended. Add salad ingredients and mix well.
✦ 8 servings.

EGGPLANT ORIENTAL

2 (1 pound) eggplants
2 teaspoons finely chopped fresh
  ginger
3 tablespoons chopped fresh cilantro
  or parsley
2 tablespoons soy sauce
2 teaspoons finely chopped garlic
1 tablespoon rice wine vinegar
1 tablespoon dark sesame oil
½ teaspoon sugar
¼ teaspoon hot chili oil or hot pepper
  sauce
2 medium tomatoes, sliced

*Variation: The eggplant makes a good
appetizer served on toast
rounds or crackers.*

✦ Place whole eggplants on a baking sheet and bake in preheated 400° oven for 30 minutes. Remove from oven and cool. When cool enough to handle, peel and cut into ½-inch pieces. Combine remaining ingredients except tomatoes in a large bowl. Add eggplant and mix well. Arrange tomato slices on a plate. Spoon eggplant mixture evenly over tomatoes and serve. The eggplant mixture is even better if made 2 or 3 days in advance, as the flavors develop in the refrigerator. Place on tomatoes just before serving.

✦ 6 servings.

✦ Nutritional information per serving

Calories: 90.3	Saturated Fat: 0.4g	Calories from Fat: 25.7%
Protein: 2.8g	Cholesterol: 0mg	Calories from Carbohydrate: 63.1%
Carbohydrate: 15.9g	Dietary Fiber: 4.8g	Calories from Protein: 11.2%
Total Fat: 2.9g	Sodium: 289mg	

ROASTED EGGPLANT WITH TOMATO SALAD

Pareve   Lighter

1 (1¼ pound) eggplant, unpeeled
½ teaspoon salt
½ cup finely chopped scallions
¼ cup red wine vinegar
3 tablespoons olive oil
2 tablespoons finely chopped shallots
2 tablespoons chopped fresh basil or oregano
1 teaspoon minced garlic
½ teaspoon salt
½ teaspoon freshly ground pepper
4 medium tomatoes, peeled, seeded and diced

Note: This low fat salad makes a lovely presentation.

✦ Trim eggplant and cut lengthwise into ½-inch slices. Place on baking sheet coated with nonstick vegetable spray. Lightly coat top of eggplant with cooking spray and sprinkle with salt. Bake in preheated 400° oven for 25 minutes. Turn slices over and continue baking for 10 minutes longer. Combine remaining ingredients except tomatoes in a large bowl. Add tomatoes and toss well. Arrange eggplant on a platter and mound tomato mixture on top.
✦ 6 servings

GRILLED VEGETABLE PASTA SALAD

1 medium yellow bell pepper, halved and seeded
1 medium green bell pepper, halved and seeded
3 (8 ounce) Japanese eggplants, halved lengthwise
1 medium red onion, sliced
¼ cup olive oil
½ pound macaroni or rotini pasta, cooked and drained according to package directions
12 cherry tomatoes, halved
1 ounce sun-dried tomatoes, rehydrated and diced
½ cup Kalamata olives, pitted
¼ cup snipped fresh basil leaves
¾ cup Caesar salad dressing
¼ cup finely shredded Parmesan cheese

✦ Brush cut surfaces of peppers, eggplant and onion with olive oil. Grill directly over hot coals until tender and slightly charred, about 5 minutes per side for the peppers, and 3 minutes per side for the eggplant and onions, turning once. Remove from grill. Place peppers in a plastic bag and seal. Let cool for 15 minutes, then peel skin, but do not rinse. Coarsely chop, cover and refrigerate until needed, or up to 24 hours.
✦ Combine the grilled vegetables, pasta, tomatoes, sun-dried tomatoes, olives and basil in a large bowl. Add salad dressing and toss gently to coat. Cover and chill at least 2 hours or overnight. Before serving, add additional dressing if needed and sprinkle with Parmesan cheese.
✦ 10 servings.

SUNSHINE SALAD

Sun-Dried Tomato Vinaigrette:
2 ounces dehydrated sun-dried
  tomatoes
2 cups boiling water
¾ cup tomato juice
2 tablespoons olive oil
2 tablespoons balsamic vinegar
1 tablespoon tomato paste
1 garlic clove
½ teaspoon pepper
¼ teaspoon salt

Salad:
4 cups torn spinach, washed and
  well-drained
8 ounces small seashell macaroni,
  cooked and drained according to
  package directions
1 cup chopped tomato
½ cup thinly sliced red onion
1 (6 ounce) jar marinated artichoke
  hearts, drained and chopped
12 oil-cured ripe olives
3 ounces feta cheese, crumbled

*Hint: The vinaigrette is fabulous over hot
  pasta also.*

✦ For vinaigrette, cover sun-dried tomatoes with boiling water in a bowl. Let stand 20 minutes. Drain, reserving ¾ cup water. Put tomatoes, reserved water and remaining ingredients in a food processor or blender. Process until smooth. The dressing may be made in advance.
✦ For salad, combine spinach, macaroni, tomato, onion, artichoke hearts and olives in a large bowl. Pour 1 cup vinaigrette over spinach mixture and toss well. Sprinkle with feta cheese.
✦ 4 servings.

✦ Nutritional information per serving

Calories: 601.6	Saturated Fat: 4.6g	Calories from Fat: 22.3%
Protein: 21.8g	Cholesterol: 19mg	Calories from Carbohydrate: ... 63.6%
Carbohydrate: 97.6g	Dietary Fiber: 7.8g	Calories from Protein: 14.2%
Total Fat: 15.2g	Sodium: 1,016mg	

CHUTNEY RICE SALAD

1 cup long grain rice
6 ounces marinated artichokes,
    drained and chopped, marinade
    reserved
3 green onions, thinly sliced
½ cup pimento-stuffed olives, sliced
½ large green bell pepper, chopped
½ large red bell pepper, chopped
½ cup chopped celery
½ cup raisins
¼ cup minced fresh parsley
1 grilled chicken breast, cubed,
    optional

Dressing:
½ cup light mayonnaise
1 teaspoon curry powder
¼ cup mango chutney
salt and pepper to taste
½ cup chopped Granny Smith apple

✦ Cook rice according to package directions. Place in salad bowl. Add artichokes, onions, olives, green and red bell pepper, celery, raisins, parsley and chicken, if desired. Combine mayonnaise, reserved marinade, curry and chutney in another bowl. Stir into rice mixture and mix thoroughly. Add salt and pepper to taste. Refrigerate overnight. Add apple just before serving.
✦ 6 servings.

✡ See Pareve Food Preparation, page 30

Note: Keeps well for several days. Great for picnics and barbecues.
Variation: Substitute 3 cups cooked orzo for the rice.

My Sephardic grandmother was called "Steta."
She taught my mother early on to cook Sephardic dishes.
My father's cousin lived with us for a very long time. She would
make the most delectable Syrian specialties, always cooking up
whatever I loved especially for me. Syrian salad, rice and bedda
belumune were standard accompaniments to every meat meal,
especially on Friday night with roast chicken and potatoes,
zucchini stuffed with meat and rice, or keftes (meat balls).
Sachuhenna! (bon appétit).

ORZO SALAD

2⅓ cups cooked orzo (about 1 cup
   uncooked)
2 cups diced tomatoes
½ cup diced cucumber
½ cup diced green bell pepper
½ cup crumbled feta cheese
½ cup chopped red onion
½ cup chopped celery
3 tablespoons sliced ripe olives
1 (6 ounce) can chunk light tuna in
   water, drained or fresh grilled tuna,
   optional

Dressing:
½ cup red wine vinegar
2 tablespoons water
1 tablespoon olive oil
½ teaspoon dried basil
½ teaspoon dried oregano
1 garlic clove, minced

✦ Combine salad ingredients in a large bowl and toss well. Combine salad dressing ingredients in a blender and process until well mixed. Pour over salad and toss well. Cover and chill. Serve with carrot and celery sticks, pita triangles and green grape clusters.

✦ 8 servings

Variation: Substitute cooked rice for orzo.

✦ Nutritional information per serving

Calories: 228.6	Saturated Fat: 1.9g	Calories from Fat: 22.3%
Protein: 13.4g	Cholesterol: 17mg	Calories from Carbohydrate: ... 54.5%
Carbohydrate: 31.5g	Dietary Fiber: 2.1g	Calories from Protein: 23.2%
Total Fat: 5.7g	Sodium: 251mg	

I remember that my mother and mother-in-law were very competitive about holiday cooking and baking. Every year each would try to get up earlier than the other to start her preparation, in order to have perfection. This went on for years, until the time my mother stayed up all night and got no sleep in order to get a head start. For the record, they were both great cooks!

SHOGUN SALAD

Meat

1 head cabbage, shredded
½ cup shredded carrots
½ cup sliced green onions
½ pound cooked chicken or turkey,
  cut in bite-sized pieces
4 ounces chow mein noodles
½ cup chopped peanuts or cashews

Dressing:
½ teaspoon dry mustard
2 tablespoons sugar
2 teaspoons soy sauce
1 tablespoon sesame oil
¼ cup salad oil
3 tablespoons rice vinegar

✦ Place cabbage, carrots, onion and chicken in serving bowl. Combine all dressing ingredients in blender or food processor. Pour over cabbage mixture and toss. Top with noodles and nuts and mix gently.
✦ 6 servings.

Hint: The dressing can be doubled or tripled and keeps well in refrigerator.
Variation: For a vegetarian salad, omit chicken. Optional ingredients are mandarin oranges, water chestnuts, pineapple chunks, raisins or flaked tuna.

CHINESE CHICKEN AND KIWI SALAD

Meat

2 cups cubed cooked chicken
1 red bell pepper, seeded and diced
1 cup shredded carrots
½ cup dry roasted, unsalted cashews
¼ cup thinly sliced green onions
4 cups shredded green cabbage
3 kiwis, peeled and sliced ¼-inch
  thick

Dressing:
⅓ cup vegetable oil
3 tablespoons light soy sauce
2 tablespoons wine vinegar
1 tablespoon honey
½ teaspoon ground ginger

✦ Combine all salad ingredients except kiwi. Combine dressing ingredients, whisk thoroughly and pour over salad. Toss to combine and garnish with kiwi.
✦ 4 servings.

ORIENTAL CHICKEN SALAD   Meat

Chicken:
2 tablespoons hoisin sauce
2 tablespoons soy sauce
1 teaspoon crushed garlic
1 tablespoon sesame oil
1½ pounds boneless, skinless chicken
   breasts

Salad:
4 large leaves romaine lettuce
1 cup bean sprouts
1 cucumber, thinly sliced
4 tablespoons fresh cilantro
fresh mint leaves to taste
½ cup unsalted roasted peanuts

Dressing:
½ cup lemon juice
¼ cup hoisin sauce
2 tablespoons soy sauce
2 tablespoons sesame oil
1 tablespoon sugar
1½ teaspoons Vietnamese chili garlic
   sauce, or to taste
1 teaspoon crushed garlic

✦ For chicken, combine hoisin sauce, soy sauce, garlic and sesame oil. Pour over chicken and cover. Refrigerate at least 2 hours or overnight. Grill or broil chicken on high heat for 7 minutes per side, or until done. Slice thinly.
✦ For salad, tear lettuce into bite-sized pieces and mound on platter with bean sprouts, cucumber, cilantro and mint. Top with chicken and peanuts.
✦ For dressing, combine all ingredients in blender and blend well. Serve dressing on the side. Use cautiously; it's spicy.
✦ 4 servings.

Note: Rave reviews on this one!

A favorite recipe was given to me by my maternal grandmother. Actually, I caught the recipe by putting a measuring cup out to capture each ingredient before it was added to the mixture. Nana never measured anything; it was just her natural instinct to know what would taste good. I was very close to her and fortunate to have her in my life until I was 43 years old. She was my best friend and mentor, just what a grandmother should be. Her spirit is always with me, especially when I make one of her recipes.

STREAMLINE CURRY CHICKEN SALAD

Meat | Lighter

1 green apple, seeded, cored and
chopped
lemon juice
1 cup fat-free mayonnaise
1½ teaspoons curry powder,
or to taste
¼ teaspoon each salt, pepper,
cayenne pepper, cinnamon,
allspice, nutmeg, cumin, dried
parsley flakes, garlic powder
and dried lemon peel
4 skinless chicken breasts cooked
and cut into bite-sized pieces
1 cup halved green seedless grapes
¼ cup shredded carrots
¼ cup currants
¼ cup chopped celery

✦ Sprinkle apple with lemon juice to prevent browning. Combine mayonnaise and seasonings. Place remaining ingredients, except apples, in a bowl. Top with mayonnaise mixture. Just before serving, add apple slices and toss. Serve on lettuce leaves or as a sandwich or pita pocket filling.
✦ Serves 4.

✦ Nutritional information per serving

Calories: 284.9	Saturated Fat: 0.8g	Calories from Fat: 9.8%
Protein: 39.1g	Cholesterol: 96mg	Calories from Carbohydrate: 34.6%
Carbohydrate: 24.3g	Dietary Fiber: 1.7g	Calories from Protein: 55.6%
Total Fat: 3.1g	Sodium: 990mg	

SOUTH OF THE BORDER SALAD

1 small head lettuce, torn into bite-sized pieces
2 tomatoes, seeded and sliced
1 can ranch style beans, rinsed and drained
1 can pitted black olives, drained
3 green onions, chopped
8 ounces grated cheddar cheese
1 avocado, diced
1 small bag corn chips
1 small bottle Catalina or French dressing

Variation: Add cooked hamburger or chicken for a main course salad.

✦ Mix together lettuce, tomatoes, beans, olives, onions and cheese. Just before serving, add avocado and chips. Top with dressing and toss to combine.
✦ 6 servings.

Jonathan remembers giving a recipe to a college roommate that required the use of a "zippel," which Jonathan assumed was an English term. When no one knew what he was talking about, he asked his family and found that "zippel" is Yiddish for "strainer."

SILVER PEAK
SALAD NIÇOISE

Pareve

3 (7 ounce) cans tuna, drained and
 flaked, or 1½ pounds fresh tuna,
 grilled
1 pound green beans, parboiled until
 tender
3 stalks celery, sliced
5 cooked medium red potatoes,
 unpeeled and diced
1 small red onion, sliced
6 hard boiled eggs, sliced
2 tablespoons chopped fresh basil
1 green bell pepper, seeded and sliced
½ red bell pepper, seeded and sliced
1 pint cherry tomatoes
1 (2¼ ounce) can pitted black olives,
 drained
½ cup sliced scallions
½ cup chopped parsley
1 (2 ounce) can anchovies, drained,
 optional

Dressing:
5 tablespoons lemon juice
4 teaspoons spicy mustard
5 tablespoons wine vinegar
2 cloves garlic, minced
2 tablespoons vegetable oil
5 tablespoons olive oil
2 teaspoons dried thyme
freshly ground pepper to taste

✦ Combine all salad ingredients in a large bowl. Refrigerate until ready to serve. Combine all salad dressing ingredients and mix well. Pour over salad just before serving. Serve on a bed of fresh lettuce.
✦ 10 servings.

TUNA CAESAR SALAD

Dairy

Dressing:
1 large clove garlic
½ cup olive oil
¼ cup fresh lemon juice
3 tablespoons sour cream
1 tablespoon Worcestershire sauce
1 teaspoon Dijon mustard
1 teaspoon anchovy paste
½ teaspoon salt
¼ teaspoon coarsely ground pepper

Salad:
2 (¾-inch) thick tuna steaks
   (about ½ pound each)
salt and freshly ground pepper
   to taste
3 small heads romaine lettuce, torn
   into bite-sized pieces
1½ cups freshly grated Parmesan
   cheese, divided
1 pint cherry tomatoes, optional
1 cup croutons, or to taste

✦ For dressing, mince garlic in blender or processor. Add remaining ingredients and blend well. This can be done a day ahead, covered and refrigerated.

✦ For salad, heat barbecue grill or broiler. Brush 1 tablespoon dressing on one side of tuna. Season with salt and pepper. Grill seasoned side down 3 minutes. Brush top with 1 tablespoon dressing. Season with salt and pepper, turn and cook until just cooked through, about 3 minutes. Transfer to a plate and tent with foil to keep warm. Place lettuce in a large bowl. Add remaining dressing, 1 cup cheese and pepper. Taste and adjust seasonings. Divide salad among plates. Cut each fish steak into 4 pieces. Arrange 2 pieces in center of each salad. Sprinkle with 2 tablespoons Parmesan and pepper. Add tomatoes, if desired, and croutons.

✦ 4 servings.

FRUITA HOT FRUIT COMPOTE

Pareve

1 box dried pitted prunes
1 (16 ounce) can peeled apricots,
   drained
1 (16 ounce) can pear slices, drained
1 (24 ounce) can peach halves
   or slices, drained
1 (16 ounce) can pineapple chunks,
   juice reserved
1 (21 ounce) can cherry pie filling
¼ cup apricot brandy

✦ Layer prunes, apricots, pears, peaches and pineapple in a large glass casserole dish. Spread cherry pie filling on top. Add brandy, slowly and evenly. Add ½ cup reserved pineapple juice, slowly and evenly. Bake in preheated 350° oven until liquid begins to boil.

✦ 10 servings.

PALISADE FALL FRUIT SALAD

6 cups mixed chopped fruit (apples, pears, grapes, tangerines, oranges, bananas and berries)

Dressing:
½ cup orange marmalade
2 tablespoons orange liqueur
2 tablespoons orange juice
2 tablespoons dry vermouth

Hint: Make the same day as serving for best results.
Variation: Great on French toast or pancakes!

✦ Place fruit in serving bowl. Combine all dressing ingredients and mix well. Pour over fruit and stir gently. Chill 1 to 3 hours before serving.
✦ 10 servings.

✦ **Nutritional information per serving**

Calories: 143.7	Saturated Fat: 0g	Calories from Fat: 3.2%
Protein: 0.6g	Cholesterol: 0mg	Calories from Carbohydrate: ... 95.2%
Carbohydrate: 34.1g	Dietary Fiber: 3.0g	Calories from Protein: 1.6%
Total Fat: 0.5g	Sodium: 12mg	

STEAMBOAT GOURMET CRANBERRIES

1 (1 pound) bag fresh cranberries, rinsed and picked over
1½ cups sugar
1 cup sliced, toasted almonds
1 cup orange marmalade
3 tablespoons orange liqueur
juice of ½ lemon
1 teaspoon grated lemon rind, optional

Note: Delicious with turkey.

✦ Combine cranberries and sugar in a casserole dish. Cover and bake in preheated 350° oven for 1 hour. Add remaining ingredients, stir and refrigerate.
✦ 10 servings.

POTPOURRI

121

COLUMBINE CRANBERRY CHUTNEY

1 (1 pound) bag fresh cranberries,
  rinsed and picked over
1 cup sugar
½ cup firmly packed brown sugar
1 cup peeled, chopped apples
½ cup raisins
2 teaspoons cinnamon
1½ teaspoons ground ginger
¼ teaspoon ground cloves
¼ teaspoon allspice
1 cup water
1 tablespoon unsalted butter or pareve
  margarine
½ cup chopped onion
½ cup chopped celery

✦ Combine cranberries, sugar, brown sugar, apples, raisins, spices and water in a large saucepan or Dutch oven. Cook over medium heat until juices are released from cranberries, about 15 minutes. Meanwhile, melt butter in a sauté pan and sauté onions and celery until soft, about 10 minutes. Fold onion mixture into cranberries and simmer, uncovered, until thick, about 40 minutes, stirring frequently. Cool before serving.
✦ 8 servings.

Note: Chutney can be kept tightly covered in the refrigerator for up to 4 weeks.

SUNLIGHT STRAWBERRY RHUBARB SAUCE

4 cups rhubarb, washed and cut into
  1-inch pieces
1 cup sugar
3 tablespoons water
1 (10 ounce) package frozen
  strawberries, thawed and drained

✦ Place rhubarb, sugar and water in a heavy saucepan. Cook over low heat, stirring often, until rhubarb is very soft, about 30 minutes. Add strawberries and stir. Remove from heat and cool. Transfer to a serving dish and chill before serving.
✦ 6 servings.

✦ Non-fat evaporated milk adds a
creamy texture to soups, sauces and desserts.

CRANBERRY-RASPBERRY MOLD

3 small packages raspberry gelatin
3 cups boiling water
2 cans jellied raspberry-cranberry
   sauce
2 (8 ounce) containers raspberry
   yogurt
fresh raspberries, optional

Hint: This can be made a day ahead.

✦ Dissolve gelatin in boiling water. Let cool until slightly thickened. Beat in remaining ingredients until very well blended. Pour into a mold which has been coated with nonstick vegetable spray and chill. Unmold just before serving. Garnish with fresh raspberries or other fresh fruits, if desired.
✦ 12 servings.

✦ Nutritional information per serving

Calories: 111.5	Saturated Fat: 1.0g	Calories from Fat: 12.1%
Protein: 1.7g	Cholesterol: 6mg	Calories from Carbohydrate: ... 82.1%
Carbohydrate: 23.7g	Dietary Fiber: 0.6g	Calories from Protein: 5.8%
Total Fat: 1.6g	Sodium: 39mg	

✦ **Grease gelatin molds to make unmolding easy.**

POTPOURRI

123

WEST SIDE DILL PICKLES

Pareve

1 rounded tablespoon kosher salt
¾ teaspoon pickling spice
2 cloves garlic, sliced
1 sprig and flower fresh dill
1 dried red pepper
1 pound firm pickling cucumbers

✦ Wash quart jar and lid well. Place salt, spice, garlic slices, dill and red pepper in jar. Pack cucumbers into jar, starting with larger cucumbers. Fill jar with cold water, seal with lid and tighten well. Turn jar upside down overnight. Retighten lids the next day and store in a cool place. Do not refrigerate for 2 weeks, at which time the pickles will be ready to eat.

✦ 1 quart.

My grandfather retired as a fish monger to become a salad chef at a Catskills resort. He was renowned as a wonderful dill pickle expert who always had a small batch brewing on his kitchen counter. To this day, when I walk past the fresh dill in my garden or in the produce section of the store, that wonderful fragrance reminds me of my grandfather and the summers I spent visiting his home in upstate New York.

COCONUT-CRANBERRY SAUCE

Pareve

1 pound cranberries, washed and
   picked over
1 (12 ounce) jar orange marmalade
1 cup chopped pecans
½ cup flaked coconut
½ cup sugar
½ cup water

Note: Can be made 1-2 days ahead. Perfect for your Thanksgiving dinner.

✦ Combine all ingredients and spread in a 9 x 13-inch pan. Bake 45 minutes at 350°.

✦ 8 servings.

ENTREES

ENTRÉE INDEX

DENVER BUFFALO COMPANY ®

GARLIC AND CHILI-RUBBED BUFFALO STEAKS

| Meat | Lighter |

2 large cloves garlic, chopped
1 teaspoon salt
2 tablespoons chili powder
1 teaspoon ground cumin
¾ teaspoon sugar
3½ tablespoons Worcestershire sauce
4 (1-inch thick) buffalo rib eye steaks

Note: Also great on beef steaks and chicken.

✦ Combine garlic and salt in a small bowl and mash to a paste. Add chili powder, cumin and sugar and mix well. Stir in Worcestershire sauce. Arrange steaks on a plate large enough to hold them in one layer. Rub both sides of steaks with chili paste. Transfer to a zip-lock plastic bag and refrigerate for at least 4 hours and up to 2 days.

✦ Grill steaks on an oiled rack 5 inches over glowing coals, 5 minutes per side for medium rare. Transfer to serving plates and let rest 5 minutes.

✦ 4 servings.

M E A T

✦ **Nutritional information per serving**

Calories: 253.4	Saturated Fat: 1.0g	Calories from Fat: 14.1%
Protein: 46.9g	Cholesterol: 104mg	Calories from Carbohydrate: 9.8%
Carbohydrate: 6.0g	Dietary Fiber: 1.4g	Calories from Protein: 76.1%
Total Fat: 3.9g	Sodium: 838mg	

DENVER BUFFALO COMPANY®

BUFFALOAF

2 tablespoons pareve margarine
1 cup minced onion
1 cup minced celery
2 cloves garlic, minced
1 cup ketchup, divided
2 pounds ground buffalo
⅓ cup bread crumbs
2 eggs
1 tablespoon Worcestershire sauce
2 tablespoons lemon juice
½ teaspoon cumin powder
½ teaspoon black pepper
½ teaspoon salt
dash hot pepper sauce
1 tablespoon chopped fresh parsley

✦ Melt margarine in a skillet over medium heat. Sauté onion, celery and garlic until soft. Remove to a large mixing bowl. Add ½ cup ketchup and remaining ingredients. Mix well and shape into a loaf. Place in a greased 9 x 13-inch pan and bake in preheated 350° oven for 35 minutes. Remove from oven and top with remaining ketchup. Bake 15 to 20 minutes longer. Let stand 15 minutes before slicing.

✦ 8 servings.

✦ **Nutritional information per serving**

Calories: 289.1	Saturated Fat: 2.0g	Calories from Fat: 25.5%
Protein: 34.9g	Cholesterol: 140mg	Calories from Carbohydrate: ... 26.2%
Carbohydrate: 18.9g	Dietary Fiber: 1.7g	Calories from Protein: 48.3%
Total Fat: 8.2g	Sodium: 985mg	

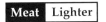

BRONCO BUFFALO CHILI

Meat | Lighter

1 pound ground buffalo
2 tablespoons canola oil
¾ cup chopped onion
1½ tablespoons chili powder
1½ teaspoons chopped garlic
1½ cups diced tomatoes
1 tablespoon vinegar
1 teaspoon ground coriander
½ jalapeño pepper, chopped
pinch of ground cloves
1 teaspoon ground cumin
1 tablespoon dried oregano, crumbled
2 teaspoons brown sugar
2 cups beef broth
1 (12 ounce) can red kidney beans, drained
1 (12 ounce) can pinto beans, drained
cayenne pepper, optional

✦ Brown meat in oil in a deep pot. Add onions and cook until tender. Add remaining ingredients and stir to combine. Bring to a boil, then reduce heat, cover and simmer 2 hours.

✦ 6 servings.

M E A T

✦ **Nutritional information per serving**

Calories: 580.1	Saturated Fat: 1.7g	Calories from Fat: 18.5%
Protein: 50.8g	Cholesterol: 53mg	Calories from Carbohydrate: ... 47.1%
Carbohydrate: 69.7g	Dietary Fiber: 21.5g	Calories from Protein: 34.4%
Total Fat: 12.1g	Sodium: 1,011mg	

HAIMISHEH BRISKET

1 (5 to 6 pound) first cut beef brisket,
   well-trimmed
1 teaspoon salt, divided
1 teaspoon pepper, divided
3 tablespoons vegetable oil, divided
3 large yellow onions, cut in ½-inch
   dice
4 large cloves garlic, minced
1 teaspoon Hungarian paprika

*Variation: Add a can of stewed tomatoes
   when blending gravy and
   onions.*

✦ Pat brisket dry and season with ½ teaspoon salt and ½ teaspoon pepper. Place 1 tablespoon oil in Dutch oven and heat in preheated 375° oven for 10 minutes. Place brisket in oil, fat side up, and bake, uncovered, for 30 minutes. Sauté onions in remaining oil in a large skillet over moderately high heat, stirring until softened and beginning to turn golden. Reduce heat to medium and continue cooking until deep golden, about 20 minutes, stirring occasionally. Add garlic, paprika and remaining salt and pepper and cook 1 minute. Stir in 3 cups water and bring to a boil. Spoon over brisket. Reduce oven to 350 degrees. Place lid on Dutch oven ½ inch ajar and bake 3½ hours or until brisket is tender. Add more water if liquid gets too low. Remove from oven and let cool 1 hour. Remove brisket from sauce, scraping any clinging onions back into sauce. Wrap brisket in foil and refrigerate overnight. Strain gravy, pressing onions to produce as much gravy as possible. Store gravy and onions in separate containers and refrigerate overnight.
✦ The following day, remove congealed fat from gravy and add enough water to make 2¾ cups liquid. Place in blender or food processor and add reserved onions. Blend until smooth. Slice brisket against the grain. Place brisket and gravy in a roasting pan and cover with foil. Bake in preheated 350° oven for 30 minutes.
✦ Serves 8 to 10.

TANTE'S BRISKET

1 (5 pound) brisket, well-trimmed
2 large cloves garlic, cut into slivers
pepper and paprika to taste
¾ cup honey
2 cups ketchup
1 envelope onion soup mix
1 tablespoon soy sauce
1 tablespoon Worcestershire sauce

✦ Make slits in top of brisket and insert slivers of garlic. Season with pepper and paprika. Place in a Dutch oven. Combine remaining ingredients and stir until well blended. Pour over brisket and cover. Bake in preheated 325° oven for 4 hours. Remove from oven and refrigerate overnight.
✦ The following day, remove congealed fat from sauce. Slice brisket and reheat in sauce.
✦ 8 servings.

COLORADO BARBECUED BRISKET

1 (4-5 pound) brisket, well-trimmed
2 tablespoons liquid smoke
2 tablespoons Worcestershire sauce
garlic powder, onion powder, salt,
  pepper
½ cup firmly packed brown sugar
1 (8 ounce) can tomato sauce
1 cup barbeque sauce
¼ cup lemon juice

✦ Sprinkle meat with liquid smoke, Worcestershire sauce, garlic powder, onion powder, salt and pepper. Seal in heavy duty foil and place on a cookie sheet with sides. Bake in a 350° oven for 3½ to 4 hours. Remove from oven and cool. Remove meat from foil saving juices. Refrigerate meat. Mix remaining ingredients with pan juices and refrigerate.
✦ The following day, remove congealed fat from sauce. Slice brisket and reheat in sauce for one hour at 350°. Serve with sauce on the side.
✦ Serves 6 to 8.

KIBBITZER'S KISHKA

2 yards kishka casings
2 pounds flour
1 tablespoon kosher salt, or to taste
1 teaspoon pepper
2 tablespoons paprika
2 pounds meat suet, ground on coarse
    blade
3 large yellow onions, ground
    or diced
vegetable oil

Kishka Gravy:
2 medium onions, diced
1 teaspoon minced garlic
3 medium carrots, sliced
2 stalks celery, sliced
1 cup canned tomatoes, broken into
    pieces
beef bones or top rib
salt, pepper and paprika to taste

✦ Cut kishka casings into 6 pieces. Run cold water through each piece. Tie one end with string and turn fat side out. Combine flour and seasonings. Add suet and mix well. Sauté onions in oil until soft. Add to suet mixture and mix well. To stuff, turn one end of casing inside about one inch and stuff suet mixture through the casing. Continue, turning casing inside out with the fat side on the inside. Stuff until casing is full but not tightly packed. Tie open end closed with string and drop in boiling water for 15 minutes. Remove and clean in cold water.
✦ For gravy, add all ingredients to a roasting pan. Add kishka, cover and roast in preheated 350° oven for 2 hours. Uncover and continue roasting until brown.
✦ Yields 2 dozen pieces.

*Hint: A sausage attachment makes kishka
        easier to stuff.*

Dinner at my parents' house wasn't just food at a table big enough for all of us to sit around. Dinner was, still is, and I hope always will be, an EVENT! The food goes fast, as do the double entendres tossed about by everyone, and the chairs stay warm because no one is eager to be the first to move away. No topic is taboo and everyone joins in. As the plastic plate our daughter made when she was small says, "Dinner is fun at our house"!

SABBATH CHOLENT

2 tablespoons vegetable oil
3 pounds short ribs, well-trimmed
2 onions, chopped
1 envelope onion soup mix
1½ cups dry baby lima beans
¾ cup barley
6 large potatoes, peeled and cubed
1½ tablespoons honey
1½ tablespoons ketchup
½ teaspoon nutmeg
salt and pepper to taste

✦ Heat oil in a Dutch oven over medium-high heat. Add ribs and onion and cook until browned. Add remaining ingredients and enough water to barely cover meat and vegetables. Cover and bake in a preheated 250° oven for 14 hours.
✦ 8 servings.

Note: *Place this in the oven and see what develops - your Shabbat will be special.*

✦ **Oil the cup or spoon before measuring honey or molasses.**

MOM'S GEDEMPTE POT ROAST WITH FRUIT

1 cup dried apricots
2 medium onions, minced
1 (3 pound) chuck roast, well-trimmed
1 tablespoon vegetable oil
1 cup dried prunes
2 tablespoons brown sugar
2 tablespoons honey
1 tablespoon lemon juice
1 bay leaf
1 teaspoon cinnamon
½ teaspoon salt or to taste
2 medium red or white potatoes, peeled and quartered
2 medium sweet potatoes, peeled and quartered
3 large carrots, cut in 2-inch pieces, optional

✦ Soak apricots with just enough water to cover for one hour. Brown onions and beef in oil in a large stock pot. Add apricots, apricot water, prunes, brown sugar, honey, lemon juice, bay leaf, cinnamon and salt. Cover and cook over low heat for 1½ hours. Remove bay leaf. Add potatoes and carrots, if desired. Cook an additional hour.
✦ 6 servings.

**M
E
A
T**

133

BEEF BLINTZES

Blintzes:
4 eggs, lightly beaten
½ teaspoon salt
⅔ cup flour
1⅓ cups water
4 tablespoons pareve margarine or
vegetable oil, divided

Filling:
2 pounds cooked roast beef, brisket
or steak, cut into chunks
salt and pepper to taste
garlic powder, lemon pepper,
seasoned salt, optional
2 large onions, sliced
1 tablespoon pareve margarine
2 eggs

Note: See illustration for folding cheese blintzes, page 59.

✦ For blintzes, combine eggs, salt, flour and water. Blend well and strain out any lumps. Spray a 6-inch skillet with nonstick vegetable spray and place over medium to medium-high heat. Lightly cover bottom with blintz batter, about ⅓ cup. Tilt pan from side to side until batter is set. Invert onto a clean dish towel, browned side up. Repeat until all batter is used, spraying pan with additional nonstick spray as needed.
✦ For filling, season beef with desired seasonings. Sauté onion in margarine until soft. Place beef, onion and eggs in a food processor or meat grinder. Chop well.
✦ To assemble, place ⅓ cup beef mixture on each blintz. Spread, leaving a 1 inch border. Fold top over filling, then fold in sides. Roll from top to bottom. Heat 1 tablespoon margarine or vegetable oil in a large skillet. Fry blintzes until browned on each side. Add more margarine as needed.
✦ Yields 1 dozen blintzes.

BUBBIE'S FRICASSEE

1 pound ground beef
½ cup bread crumbs
1 egg, lightly beaten
1 large onion, chopped
1 tablespoon vegetable oil
1 (16 ounce) can tomatoes
1 (28 ounce) can tomato sauce
1½ pounds chicken feet, wings,
gizzards and necks
salt and pepper
1 teaspoon garlic powder, or to taste
½ cup honey
½ to 1 cup firmly packed brown sugar
2 tablespoons lemon juice or
sour salt (citric acid) to taste

Note: The aroma will carry you back in time.
Can use chicken pieces.

✦ Combine ground beef, bread crumbs and egg and shape into small balls. Sauté onion in oil in a roasting pan until soft. Add tomatoes and tomato sauce and stir to combine. Add chicken and season with salt, pepper and garlic powder. Add meatballs and cover. Bake in preheated 350° oven for 2 hours. Combine remaining ingredients, add to roaster, cover and bake an additional 2 hours, basting occasionally.
✦ 6 servings.

STUFFED CABBAGE

1 large cabbage, washed and cored
1½ pounds ground beef
1 large onion, grated
2 eggs, lightly beaten
2 tablespoons uncooked white rice
¼ cup bread crumbs
¼ cup water
1 pound beef short ribs, well-trimmed
salt, pepper and paprika to taste
1 (6 ounce) can tomato paste
1 (8 ounce) can tomato sauce
1 large onion, chopped
¼ cup sugar
½ cup firmly packed brown sugar
1½ teaspoons sour salt (citric acid)
1 cup water

✦ Place cabbage in a plastic bag and freeze for at least 2 days. Place in very hot water and remove leaves one at a time. Drain and pat leaves dry. Combine ground beef, grated onion, eggs, rice, bread crumbs and water. Place ¼ cup filling in center of a cabbage leaf, about 1 inch from core end. Fold end over filling, roll once, then turn in sides. Carefully finish rolling. Repeat with remaining leaves until all filling is used. Chop any leftover leaves and place in bottom of roaster. Season short ribs with salt, pepper and paprika. Place on chopped leaves. Place cabbage rolls, seam-side down, on ribs. Combine remaining ingredients and pour over all. Add 1 cup water. Cover and bake in preheated 350° oven for 3 hours, basting occasionally. Remove lid last 30 minutes of cooking to brown top.
✦ 8 servings.

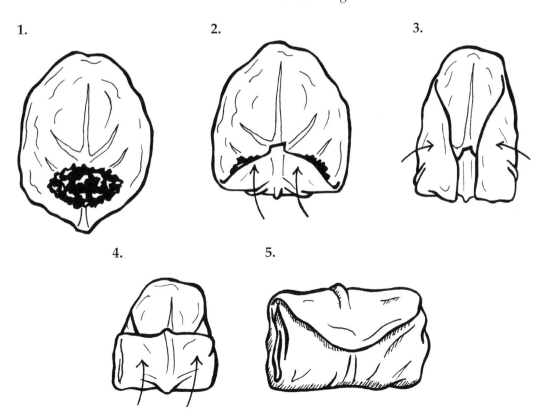

1.

2.

3.

4.

5.

M
E
A
T

135

SWEET AND SOUR STUFFED CABBAGE

2 large cabbage heads, washed and
   cored
2 pounds ground beef
1 medium potato, peeled and grated
1 medium onion, grated
¼ cup uncooked rice
2 eggs, lightly beaten
¼ cup water
1 teaspoon salt
¼ teaspoon pepper
garlic powder to taste
1 onion, sliced
1 (1 pound) can sauerkraut, with juice
1 (20 ounce) bottle ketchup
1 (16 ounce) can jellied cranberry
   sauce
½ cup firmly packed brown sugar

*Variation: Increase rice and water to ½
cup each and eliminate potato.*

✦ Place cabbages in a plastic bag and freeze for at least 2 days. Place in very hot water and remove leaves one at a time. Drain and pat leaves dry. Combine ground beef, grated potato, grated onion, rice, eggs, water, salt, pepper and garlic powder to taste. Place ¼ cup beef mixture on cabbage leaf, about 1 inch from core end. Fold end over filling, roll once, then turn in sides. Carefully finish rolling. Repeat with remaining leaves until all filling is used. Slice any leftover leaves and place in bottom of a roasting pan. Place sliced onion and sauerkraut over sliced leaves. Top with cabbage rolls, seam side down. Combine remaining ingredients and pour over all. Cover and bake in preheated 325° oven for 3 hours, basting occasionally. Add more water if needed.
✦ Yields 1½ dozen rolls.

One of our family's favorite entrées for Sukkot is stuffed cabbage rolls, which have as many names as there are shtetls from which the recipes originate. Our family's recipe calls for three or four hours in the oven. My daughter prepared the recipe, and it had been in the oven for about an hour and a half when my granddaughter, age four, came into the kitchen from her playroom and said, "Mommy! Could you please turn down the smell?"

UNSTUFFED CABBAGE

Soup:
1 large onion, diced
2 pounds cabbage, diced
1 (8 ounce) can tomato sauce
1 (28 ounce) can tomatoes, with juice
1 cup water
¼ cup honey
¼ cup lemon juice
⅓ cup firmly packed brown sugar
¼ cup raisins, optional

Meatballs:
1 pound ground beef
2 teaspoons Worcestershire sauce
½ teaspoon salt, or to taste
pepper
1 egg
½ onion, grated
½ cup uncooked rice

✦ Combine all soup ingredients, except raisins, in a stock pot. Bring to a boil. Combine all meatball ingredients and mix well. Shape into small balls and add to boiling soup. Reduce heat, cover and simmer for 2 hours. Remove cover, add raisins, if desired, and continue cooking for 30 more minutes.
✦ 8 servings.

Note: For best flavor, prepare a day ahead and reheat. Can be frozen.

**M
E
A
T**

Grandma always cooked the roast the day before we were coming to dinner so she could remove the fat, reheat the meat and be ready to sit down to eat with us. Of course, the fact that my father and two of his kids preferred their beef medium-rare didn't matter. Roast beef dinner at Grandma's was always well done!

REDSTONE RIB ROAST WITH WATERCRESS SAUCE

¾ teaspoon seasoned salt
2 teaspoons minced garlic
1¼ teaspoons freshly ground pepper, divided
1 (3½ to 4 pound) small end, boneless rib roast
2 pounds baby carrots
2 teaspoons olive or vegetable oil
½ teaspoon salt

Watercress Sauce:
1 tablespoon water
1 tablespoon vegetable oil
½ teaspoon salt
1 cup chopped watercress
1 cup chopped fresh parsley
3 tablespoons mayonnaise

✦ Combine seasoned salt, garlic and 1 teaspoon pepper in a small bowl. Press over surface of roast. Place roast in 11 x 17-inch roasting pan. Combine carrots, oil, salt and remaining pepper in a large bowl. Toss to coat. Arrange carrots around beef. Place on upper rack of preheated 375° oven. Cook 16 minutes per pound for rare or 20 minutes per pound for medium, or until internal temperature of beef reaches 125° to 135° on a meat thermometer. Transfer roast and carrots to a serving platter and cover loosely with foil. Let stand 20 minutes before carving.

✦ For Watercress Sauce, combine water, oil and salt in blender. Add watercress and parsley. Pulse to puree. Add mayonnaise and pulse once to blend. Serve over meat.

✦ 6 servings.

AIOLI SAUCE

6 cloves garlic
1 teaspoon olive oil
¼ cup low-fat or nonfat mayonnaise
1 tablespoon chopped fresh chives
1 tablespoon fresh lemon juice
salt and pepper to taste

Note: This sauce is an alternative to the Watercress Sauce. It also goes well with fish and vegetables.

✦ Place garlic on a piece of foil and top with olive oil. Seal tightly and bake in preheated 375° oven for 30 minutes, or until tender. Remove cloves from oven and squeeze from skins into a small bowl. Mash with a fork. Add remaining ingredients and mix well. Chill in refrigerator.

FLANK STEAK WITH CITRUS SALSA

1½ pounds flank steak, well-trimmed
¾ cup frozen orange juice concentrate, thawed
1 jalapeño pepper, seeded and chopped
1 teaspoon paprika
1 teaspoon pepper
½ cup water

Citrus Salsa:
2 oranges, peeled, seeded and chopped
¼ cup sliced green onions
2 tablespoons chopped fresh parsley
1 tablespoon lime juice
dash salt

Note: If you like it hot, garnish with chopped jalapeño pepper and sliced oranges to cut the bite.

✦ Place steak in a zip-lock bag. Combine orange juice, jalapeño, paprika and pepper. Reserve 2 tablespoons of this mixture for the salsa. Add water to remaining marinade and pour over steak. Refrigerate at least 24 hours, turning occasionally.

For salsa, combine reserved marinade and remaining ingredients. Stir and chill at least 30 minutes.

✦ Remove meat from marinade, reserving marinade, and grill over hot coals 3 to 4 minutes per side for medium rare, 4 to 5 minutes for medium. Baste with remaining marinade. Slice thinly and serve with salsa and warm tortillas.

✦ 6 servings.

FABULOUS FLANK STEAK

1½ pounds flank steak, well-trimmed
½ cup soy sauce
4 tablespoons white wine vinegar
2 large cloves garlic, minced
1 tablespoon minced fresh ginger
1 tablespoon sugar
2 tablespoons dried onion flakes

Note: May be served hot or cold.

✦ Place steak in a zip-lock plastic bag. Combine remaining ingredients and pour over steak. Refrigerate at least 24 hours, turning bag occasionally. Remove meat from marinade, reserving marinade, and grill over hot coals 3 to 4 minutes per side for medium rare, 4 to 5 minutes for medium. Baste with remaining marinade.

✦ 6 servings.

RIB EYE SHIITAKE

1 tablespoon pareve margarine, divided
1 large clove garlic, finely minced
⅓ cup finely chopped shallots
½ pound shiitake mushrooms, sliced if large
1½ cups dry red wine, divided
1 (10¼ ounce) can beef broth, divided
4 (1-inch thick) rib eye steaks, well-trimmed
freshly ground pepper
1 tablespoon soy sauce
2 teaspoons cornstarch
1 teaspoon dried thyme

✦ Melt 1½ teaspoons margarine in a large skillet. Sauté garlic, shallots and mushrooms on medium-high heat for 4 minutes. Add ¾ cup wine and ½ can beef broth. Cook over medium heat for 5 more minutes, stirring occasionally. Remove mushrooms and continue cooking wine mixture until reduced to about ⅔ cup. Pour over mushrooms. Rinse skillet and dry it. Add remaining margarine and melt over medium heat. Season steak with pepper and add to skillet. Cook 3 minutes on each side, or until desired degree of doneness is achieved. Remove to a warm platter. Combine soy sauce and cornstarch and mix well. Add remaining beef broth and wine to skillet. Add mushroom mixture, cornstarch mixture and thyme. Bring to a boil and boil 2 minutes, stirring constantly. Correct seasonings and pour over steaks. Serve immediately.

✦ 4 servings.

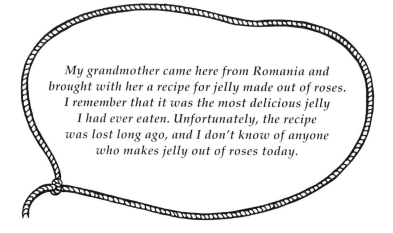

My grandmother came here from Romania and brought with her a recipe for jelly made out of roses. I remember that it was the most delicious jelly I had ever eaten. Unfortunately, the recipe was lost long ago, and I don't know of anyone who makes jelly out of roses today.

BULGOGGI

Korean Beef Barbecue

2 tablespoons sesame seeds
2 cloves garlic, minced
1 teaspoon minced fresh ginger
1 cup Japanese-style soy sauce
¼ cup water
¼ cup dry red wine
2 tablespoons sesame oil
2 pounds flank steak, well-trimmed
   and sliced paper thin
½ red apple, sliced ½-inch thick
½ cup sugar
1 tablespoon cornstarch

✦ Toast sesame seeds in a nonstick skillet over medium-high heat until golden brown, stirring constantly. Combine garlic, ginger, soy sauce, water, wine and sesame oil in a medium bowl. Layer beef and apples in a deep bowl. Cover with wine mixture and sprinkle with sesame seeds and sugar. Mix well. Cover tightly and refrigerate overnight.

✦ The following day, discard apples and remove meat from marinade, reserving marinade. Coat a large skillet or wok with nonstick vegetable spray. Stir-fry meat on medium high to high heat in 3 separate batches, stirring constantly. Remove from pan when desired doneness is reached. Pour marinade in pan, add cornstarch, and cook until sauce thickens. Serve with short grain rice.

✦ 6 servings.

MEXICAN SALSA BURGER WITH GUACAMOLE

Burgers:
1 pound lean ground beef or turkey
¼ cup finely crushed tortilla chips
¼ cup thick and chunky salsa
1 teaspoon minced garlic
⅛ teaspoon cumin powder
½ teaspoon chili powder
4 sandwich buns

Guacamole:
1 small jalapeño pepper, seeded
1 large clove garlic
2 ripe avocados, peeled and pitted
1 tablespoon lemon juice
½ medium tomato, quartered
1½ tablespoons salsa, optional
salt and pepper

✦ Combine meat with remaining burger ingredients. Form into four patties. Grill or broil 9 to 13 minutes, turning once, until desired degree of doneness is achieved. Serve on sandwich buns with extra salsa and guacamole.

✦ For guacamole, drop jalapeño and garlic into running food processor and process until finely minced. Add remaining ingredients and pulse only to chop well. Do not puree.

✦ 4 servings.

BLACK CANYON CHILI

Meat

1 tablespoon vegetable oil
1½ cups finely chopped onion
1 cup chopped green bell pepper
1¼ pounds ground beef or turkey
1½ tablespoons minced garlic
2½ tablespoons chili powder, or to
   taste
1 teaspoon ground cumin
1 teaspoon dried oregano, crumbled
1 bay leaf
½ teaspoon pepper
1 (28 ounce) can crushed tomatoes
1 (15 ounce) can tomato sauce
1 tablespoon red wine vinegar
¼ teaspoon crushed red pepper
1 (15 ounce) can kidney beans,
   drained
1 tablespoon sugar
½ teaspoon salt, optional

✦ Heat oil in a large saucepan. Add onion and green pepper and sauté until onion is wilted. Add meat and brown, stirring to break up lumps. Sprinkle with garlic, chili powder, cumin and oregano. Stir to blend. Add remaining ingredients. Bring to a boil, reduce heat to low, cover and simmer one hour, stirring occasionally.
✦ 4 servings.

Note: Freezes well.

SAVORY LAMB
SHISH KEBAB

Meat

2 pounds boneless lamb, cut into
   1½-inch cubes
½ medium onion, cut into wedges
½ cup chopped fresh parsley
¼ cup fresh lemon juice
2 cloves garlic, minced
1 teaspoon salt
½ teaspoon freshly ground pepper
¼ teaspoon thyme
¼ teaspoon oregano
¼ cup olive oil
cherry tomatoes
whole mushrooms

✦ Place lamb and onion in a large bowl. Add parsley, lemon juice, garlic and seasonings. Let stand 10 minutes. Add olive oil and toss lightly. Cover and marinate in refrigerator 24 hours, turning occasionally. Thread meat on skewers alternately with onion wedges. Thread separate skewers with cherry tomatoes and mushrooms that have been dipped in the marinade. Grill over hot coals or under broiler about 5 minutes per side for medium. Baste with remaining marinade.
✦ 6 servings.

ROSEMARY MARINATED LAMB CHOPS

Meat

4 (1-inch thick) lamb chops, trimmed
1 small onion, sliced
2 tablespoons wine vinegar
2 tablespoons lemon juice
2 teaspoons dry mustard
3 tablespoons olive oil
1 clove garlic, minced
1 teaspoon dried rosemary
¼ teaspoon ground ginger
¼ teaspoon salt

✦ Place lamb chops in a deep ceramic or glass bowl. Top with onion slices. Combine remaining ingredients and pour over chops. Marinate in refrigerator overnight. Broil over a hot charcoal fire or under an oven broiler for 4 to 6 minutes per side for medium rare.

✦ 4 servings.

✦ Trim excess fat from meat before cooking.
✦ How to remove fat from pan juices:
Chill pan juices; remove congealed fat from top;
or pour juices into a gravy strainer.

HERB CRUSTED RACK OF LAMB

Meat

2 racks of lamb, well-trimmed
2 tablespoons olive oil
½ cup minced onion
2 cloves garlic, minced
1 teaspoon chopped fresh sage
1 teaspoon chopped fresh rosemary
½ cup chopped fresh parsley
4 teaspoons Dijon mustard
½ teaspoon minced fresh ginger
1 teaspoon sugar
salt and pepper to taste

✦ Brown lamb in olive oil in roasting pan. Combine remaining ingredients and rub on meat. Bake in preheated 425° oven 30 minutes. Remove from oven and let rest 10 minutes before carving.

✦ 6 servings.

**M
E
A
T**

VICTOR VEAL PICCATA

1½ pounds veal, sliced ¼ to ½-inch
   thick, trimmed
salt and pepper to taste
¼ cup flour
4 tablespoons olive oil, divided
2 cloves garlic, minced
½ pound fresh mushrooms, sliced
2 tablespoons fresh lemon juice
¾ cup dry white wine
1 tablespoon capers
2 teaspoons juice from capers
½ cup chicken broth
fresh chopped parsley
thinly sliced lemon

✦ Sprinkle veal with salt and pepper, then dip in flour. Shake off any excess flour. Heat 2 tablespoons oil in a large skillet over high heat. Add veal and brown quickly on both sides. Remove veal and reduce heat to medium. Add remaining oil and sauté garlic and mushrooms 3 minutes, scraping up any browned bits in bottom of pan. Add lemon juice, wine, capers, caper juice and chicken broth. Stir well. Return veal to pan and simmer about 10 minutes, or until veal is tender, basting occasionally. Add additional chicken broth if sauce becomes too thick. Garnish with parsley and lemon slices.
✦ 4 servings.

VEAL CHOPS WITH CARAMELIZED ONIONS

4 (1-inch thick) veal chops, trimmed
2 tablespoons minced garlic
¼ cup fresh lemon juice
¾ cup water
½ teaspoon cumin powder
½ teaspoon paprika
salt and pepper to taste

Caramelized Onions:
3 cups sliced red onions
¼ cup water
¼ cup firmly packed brown sugar
½ cup dry white wine
¼ cup white vinegar
1 teaspoon olive oil
¼ teaspoon salt
¼ teaspoon pepper
⅛ teaspoon cayenne pepper

✦ Place veal in a marinating dish or zip-lock plastic bag. Combine garlic, lemon juice, water, cumin, paprika and salt and pepper. Mix well and pour over veal. Cover or seal bag and refrigerate overnight.
✦ The following day, prepare onions: place onions and water in a saucepan, cover and cook over medium heat for 5 minutes. Add remaining ingredients and reduce heat to medium low. Cover and cook 50 minutes, stirring occasionally.
✦ Remove chops from the marinade. Coat a large skillet with nonstick vegetable spray. Brown chops on medium for 3 to 4 minutes per side for medium doneness. Remove from pan, top with onions and serve immediately.
✦ 4 servings.

STUFFED BREAST OF VEAL WITH WILD RICE

Meat

1 whole veal breast
¾ pound mushrooms
3 shallots
½ cup toasted cashews or almonds, optional
6 ounces cooked white rice
4 ounces cooked wild rice
garlic powder
salt and pepper
paprika
1 to 2 cups chicken stock, divided
1 cup dry white wine, divided

✦ Have butcher make a pocket in the veal and trim all visible fat. Place mushrooms, shallots and nuts in food processor. Chop fine. Turn into a medium bowl and add rices, seasonings to taste and 6 tablespoons chicken stock. Rub veal inside and out with seasonings. Stuff as much dressing into pocket as possible. Bake any additional dressing, moistened with more stock, in a separate casserole. Pour ½ cup stock and ½ cup wine into a large roasting pan. Add veal and cover loosely with foil. Bake in preheated 375° oven until meat is white and a meat thermometer reaches 170°, about 3½ to 4 hours. Baste occasionally. Add more stock and wine during roasting, if necessary. Remove foil and roast for an additional 15 minutes to brown.

✦ 10 servings.

GLAZED CORNED BEEF

Meat

1 (3 to 4 pound) corned beef
⅔ cup firmly packed brown sugar
10 tablespoons ketchup
6 tablespoons white vinegar
2 tablespoons pareve margarine, melted
2 tablespoons yellow, spicy or honey mustard

✦ Cook corned beef according to package directions until tender. Combine remaining ingredients in a saucepan and simmer until well-blended. Place corned beef in a roasting pan which has been coated with non-stick vegetable spray. Pour sauce over beef and bake in preheated 350° oven, uncovered, for 45 minutes or until glazed. Baste occasionally. Cool slightly and slice against the grain.

✦ 6 servings.

M
E
A
T

✦ Partially freeze meat to make slicing thin easier.

TANTALIZING TONGUE

1 large beef tongue
1 tablespoon pickling spice
2 tablespoons garlic powder
2 tablespoons paprika
salt and pepper
1 can tomato soup
1 cup dry red wine
1 large onion, diced

Note: Also wonderful cold and in sandwiches.

✦ Place tongue and pickling spice in a large pot. Add water to cover. Bring to a boil, reduce heat, cover and simmer one hour. Remove tongue and cool. Remove skin and season tongue with garlic powder, paprika, salt and pepper. Cover and refrigerate overnight.

✦ The following day, place tongue in roasting pan. Add soup, wine and onion. Cover and roast in preheated 325° oven for 2 to 3 hours, basting occasionally. Uncover and bake an additional hour to brown. Remove tongue from juices and chill juices so that excess fat can be removed. Slice tongue thinly and serve with reheated juice.

Cleaning and preparing poultry:

✦ If using a whole chicken or turkey, first remove everything inside.

✦ Rinse well to clean thoroughly.

✦ Pat dry.

✦ Remove all excess fat.

✦ Keep raw poultry separate from cooked poultry. Never return cooked poultry to the same dish or pan used when it was raw. Always clean countertops and cutting board where raw poultry was placed with a bleach solution to remove bacteria.

✦ To test poultry for doneness, cut between the thigh and drumstick. Poultry is done when the juices run clear.

SHABBAT ROAST CHICKEN

½ teaspoon garlic powder
2 teaspoons paprika, or more
¾ teaspoon kosher salt, to taste
¼ teaspoon seasoning salt, or to taste
½ teaspoon pepper
4 pounds chicken pieces
2 teaspoons minced garlic
1 medium onion, diced
1 (8 ounce) can diced tomatoes
¼ cup water

Hint: Chill juices to harden fat; remove.

✦ Combine garlic powder, paprika, kosher salt, seasoning salt and pepper. Sprinkle some over chicken, coating both sides. Place minced garlic and onion in bottom of an 11 x 15-inch roasting pan. Sprinkle with remaining seasoning. Add tomatoes and water. Top with chicken, skin side down. Cover and bake in a preheated 350° oven for 45 minutes. Uncover and increase temperature to 375°. Turn skin side up. Sprinkle with additional paprika and add water if needed. Continue baking 45 minutes, basting occasionally. Strain gravy.

GARLIC LOVERS' CHICKEN

1 (3½ to 4 pound) chicken
1 tablespoon olive oil
1 tablespoon chopped fresh rosemary
   or 1 teaspoon dried
1 tablespoon chopped fresh thyme
   or 1 teaspoon dried
1 tablespoon chopped fresh basil
   or 1 teaspoon dried
salt and pepper
2 whole heads garlic, unpeeled
1 bay leaf
¾ cup dry white wine, divided
paprika

✦ Place chicken in a roasting pan and rub with olive oil. Combine herbs with salt and pepper to taste. Rub some of the herb mixture inside chicken cavity and remainder on skin. Separate unpeeled garlic into cloves; scatter some in pan, place some in cavity and tuck remainder under skin. Place bay leaf in pan and add ½ cup wine. Sprinkle chicken with paprika. Bake, uncovered, in preheated 400° oven for 1½ hours, basting often. Add a little water and remaining wine if needed. To test for doneness, cut between thigh and drumstick. Juices should run clear. Remove liquid from pan and chill until fat hardens. Remove fat and return liquid to pan and reheat. Serve chicken with garlic cloves, which will pop out of skins when squeezed and make a delicious spread for bread.

POULTRY

MOUNTAIN MUSHROOM CHICKEN

Meat

1 (2 package box) dry onion soup mix
1 chicken, cut up
¾ pound fresh mushrooms, sliced
3 tablespoons pareve margarine
paprika
½ cup water

✦ Place soup mix in a shallow bowl and stir to blend. Dip chicken pieces into soup mix and place in roasting pan, skin side down. Add water to the bottom of the pan. Cover and bake in preheated 350° oven for 45 minutes. While chicken is baking, sauté mushrooms in margarine until browned and tender. Turn chicken over and bake an additional 15 minutes. Uncover, sprinkle with paprika and top with mushrooms. Bake an additional 30 minutes, basting often. Add additional water as needed for pan juices.
✦ 6 servings.

✦ Use garlic or onion *powder* instead of garlic or onion *salt* to reduce the sodium.

COMPANY CRANBERRY CHICKEN

Meat

10 chicken pieces
pepper
garlic powder
2 boxes long grain and wild rice mix
    with seasoning
1 (16 ounce) can whole cranberry
    sauce
1 cup water
3 tablespoons pareve margarine
4 tablespoons soy sauce
2 tablespoons lemon juice
½ cup sliced, toasted almonds,
    optional

✦ Season chicken with pepper and garlic powder. Place rice and its seasonings in bottom of a 9 x13-inch glass baking dish. Top with chicken. Place cranberry sauce, water, margarine, soy sauce and lemon juice in a saucepan. Cook over low heat until cranberry sauce has melted. Pour over chicken and cover with foil. Bake in preheated 325° oven for 1 hour and 15 minutes. Remove foil and bake an additional 15 minutes, or until chicken is browned. Garnish with almonds, if desired.
✦ 6 servings.

MI AMORÉ CACCIATORE

2 to 3 pounds chicken pieces
1 cup flour
1 teaspoon salt
½ teaspoon pepper
vegetable oil
1 pound mushrooms, sliced
1 large onion, diced
1 green bell pepper, seeded and diced
3 cloves garlic, minced
2 (15 ounce) cans Italian stewed
   tomatoes
2 teaspoons chicken bouillon
   granules
½ teaspoon garlic powder
1 tablespoon dried basil
1 teaspoon oregano
1 tablespoon chopped fresh parsley
½ cup dry red wine
¼ teaspoon red pepper flakes

✦ Coat chicken pieces with a mixture of flour, salt and pepper. Film bottom of a large skillet with oil. Heat over medium high and brown chicken. Remove to a large baking pan. Sauté mushrooms, onions, green pepper and minced garlic in skillet. Add stewed tomatoes, bouillon granules, garlic powder, basil, oregano, parsley, red wine, and red pepper flakes. Bring to a boil, reduce heat and simmer until bouillon granules are dissolved. Add additional salt and pepper to taste. Pour over chicken, cover and bake in preheated 350° oven for 30 minutes. Uncover and bake an additional 30 minutes.

Variation: Omit flour. Broil well seasoned chicken, place in baking pan, pour on sauce.

✦ How to flatten chicken breasts:
Place chicken breast between two pieces of waxed paper.
With a rolling pin, roll out to desired thinness,
or use the flat long side of a mallet and
gently pound out to desired thinness.

When an elderly aunt came to Denver from Russia, she brought with her many recipes and kitchen secrets that she was reluctant to share. She learned frugality early in life. When she would invite us over for dinner, there were usually 12 of us. Out of two chickens she could make many courses, including delicious soup, chopped liver, chicken croquettes, chicken blintzes and, of course, roasted chicken. I will never understand how she did all this!

P
O
U
L
T
R
Y

149

ROSEMARY CHICKEN

10 cloves garlic, peeled, divided
½ teaspoon salt
2 tablespoons lemon juice
6 tablespoons olive oil, divided
4 large chicken breast halves with
   bones and skin, about 2 pounds
2 large lemons, thinly sliced
1 pound small red potatoes, quartered
4 plum tomatoes, halved lengthwise
10 stuffed green olives, cut in half
1 tablespoon fresh rosemary leaves,
   or 1 teaspoon dried
salt and pepper to taste

✦ Mince and mash 4 cloves garlic and salt to a paste in a small bowl. Add lemon juice, 4 tablespoons olive oil and salt and pepper to taste. Whisk to combine. Make a bed of lemons in a greased 9 x 13-inch pan and top with chicken. Season chicken with salt and pepper and spread with half of garlic mixture. Toss potatoes, tomatoes, remaining garlic cloves and remaining oil until vegetables are well coated. Arrange around chicken. Sprinkle with olives and rosemary. Roast in middle of preheated 450° oven for 30 minutes. Brush with remaining garlic paste and bake until chicken is cooked through, about 15 minutes. Discard lemon slices. Serve chicken with vegetables and any remaining pan juices.

PEKING DUCK

1 (4 to 5 pound) duckling
½ teaspoon ground ginger
½ teaspoon cinnamon
¼ teaspoon ground nutmeg
¼ teaspoon white pepper
⅛ teaspoon ground cloves
1 tablespoon soy sauce
3 whole green onions, divided
1-inch slice fresh ginger
1 tablespoon honey
chopped Chinese parsley or cilantro
chopped cucumber
½ cup plum sauce

✦ Trim fat from duck. Cut off tail and discard. Combine ginger, cinnamon, nutmeg, pepper and cloves. Sprinkle ½ teaspoon inside of duck. Stir soy sauce into remaining spice mixture and rub evenly over duck. Cut one green onion in half and tuck into cavity of duck. Cover and refrigerate overnight.
✦ The following day, tuck 2 more green onions and ginger slice into duck cavity. Place duck on rack in roasting pan, breast side up. Prick skin all over with fork. Bake in preheated 275° oven for 4 hours, pricking skin several times during baking. Pour off excess fat as it accumulates. Brush duck with honey and bake an additional 15 minutes, until nicely browned. Slice. Garnish with parsley and cucumber. Serve with plum sauce.
✦ 6 servings.

WAGON WHEEL
CHILI CHICKEN

1 tablespoon cinnamon
1 tablespoon chili powder
1 tablespoon cracked black pepper
2 teaspoons salt, or to taste
1 teaspoon cumin powder
1 frying chicken, cut in quarters
1 cup chicken broth
2 tablespoons honey
juice of 2 limes
1 jalapeño pepper, minced

Note: The syrup is worth the wait. Be patient.

✦ Combine cinnamon, chili powder, pepper, salt and cumin. Rub well into skin of chicken. Place chicken skin side up in shallow baking pan. Bake in preheated 450° oven for 45 minutes, or until thigh juices run clear when pierced with fork. While chicken is baking, combine chicken broth, honey, lime juice and jalapeño in a small saucepan. Cook over moderately high heat, uncovered, until mixture is reduced to a syrup, 45 minutes to one hour. When chicken is done, cool slightly and brush glaze on all sides. Serve hot or cold.

BARBECUED
ORANGE CHICKEN

2 chickens, halved
2 tablespoons pareve margarine,
  softened
salt and pepper to taste
1 (12 ounce) can frozen orange juice
  concentrate, thawed
1 cup firmly packed brown sugar
1½ cups bottled barbecue sauce

Variation: Also great with Cornish hens.

✦ Arrange chicken, skin side up, in a large baking dish and rub with margarine. Season with salt and pepper to taste. Bake in preheated 350° oven for 30 minutes. Turn chicken. Combine remaining ingredients. Pour half over chicken. Bake an additional 30 minutes, then turn again and top with remaining sauce. Bake until brown, about 30 more minutes, basting occasionally.
✦ 10 servings.

P
O
U
L
T
R
Y

FIVE-SPICE ORANGE-GLAZED CHICKEN

¾ cup frozen orange juice concentrate, thawed
⅓ cup honey
¼ cup light soy sauce
1½ teaspoons five-spice powder
¾ teaspoon garlic powder
3 pounds skinless chicken pieces
2 oranges, thinly sliced

✦ Combine orange juice concentrate, honey, soy sauce, five-spice powder and garlic powder in a small mixing bowl. Place chicken in a zip-lock bag and pour on marinade. Refrigerate 1 to 2 hours, or overnight. Preheat oven to 350°. Place chicken and marinade in baking pan. Bake, uncovered, basting frequently for one hour, until chicken is nicely glazed. Heat any remaining glaze and serve with chicken. Garnish with orange slices.

✦ 6 servings.

✦ Nutritional information per serving		
Calories: 356.8	Saturated Fat: 2.0g	Calories from Fat: 18.9%
Protein: 37.5g	Cholesterol: 126mg	Calories from Carbohydrate: ... 40.2%
Carbohydrate: 36.9g	Dietary Fiber: 1.6g	Calories from Protein: 40.9%
Total Fat: 7.7g	Sodium: 458mg	

CHICKEN WITH A KICK

½ cup honey
¼ cup Dijon mustard
1 teaspoon curry powder
¾ teaspoon salt
4 tablespoons pareve margarine
6 boneless, skinless chicken breast halves
mandarin oranges, chopped peanuts, coconut, optional

✦ Combine honey, mustard, curry powder and salt in a small bowl. Melt margarine in a 9-inch square baking pan. Dredge chicken in margarine and top with honey mixture. Bake in preheated 375° oven for 30 minutes, basting occasionally. Serve garnished with mandarin oranges, chopped peanuts and coconut, if desired.

✦ 4 servings.

CHEERY CHERRY CHICKEN

Meat

½ cup flour
½ teaspoon salt
½ teaspoon garlic powder
½ teaspoon paprika
½ teaspoon pepper
1 (3 pound) fryer, cut in serving pieces
4½ tablespoons olive oil, divided
½ pound mushrooms, whole or halved
1½ cups chicken broth
½ cup sherry
2 (14 ounce) cans artichoke hearts, drained and halved
1 cup sun-dried cherries

Note: If using boneless chicken breasts, reduce baking time to 20 to 30 minutes.

✦ Combine ½ cup flour, salt, garlic powder, paprika and pepper in a large zip-lock bag. Place chicken in bag, a few pieces at a time. Shake to coat, then remove and shake off any excess flour. Heat 3 tablespoons olive oil in a large skillet. Brown chicken, then remove to a 9 x 13-inch baking pan. Add remaining olive oil to skillet. Sauté mushrooms for 2 minutes. Stir in chicken broth and sherry. Cook and stir one minute, until smooth. Arrange artichoke hearts between chicken pieces. Top with mushroom sauce. Bake in preheated 350° oven for 45 to 50 minutes, basting occasionally. Add cherries last 15 minutes of baking.
✦ 6 servings.

WILD TEQUILA CHICKEN

Meat

½ cup tequila
7 tablespoons lime marmalade, divided
2 tablespoons olive oil
2 tablespoons fresh lime juice
1 teaspoon coarsely ground black pepper
3 medium cloves garlic, peeled and flattened
1 teaspoon hot pepper sauce
½ cup chopped cilantro
8 boneless, skinless chicken breast halves
cilantro sprigs and lime slices, optional

Note: Delicious for cold sandwiches.

✦ Combine tequila, 4 tablespoons marmalade, olive oil, lime juice, pepper, garlic, hot pepper sauce and cilantro in a small mixing bowl. Place chicken and marinade in a large zip-lock bag, seal bag and turn to coat with marinade. Refrigerate 8 hours or overnight, turning bag occasionally.
✦ Remove chicken from marinade. Reserve marinade. Grill chicken on a preheated grill until done. While chicken is cooking, pour marinade into a small saucepan. Bring to a boil, reduce heat and simmer until liquid is reduced by one third. Remove garlic cloves. Add remaining marmalade. Serve over chicken. Garnish with cilantro sprigs and lime slices, if desired.
✦ 8 servings.

POULTRY

153

SUNSET CHICKEN

15 dry-packed sun-dried tomatoes
1½ pounds boneless, skinless chicken
   breast halves
2 tablespoons chopped capers
3 large cloves garlic, minced
12 pitted Kalamata olives, chopped
1 tablespoon olive oil
2 teaspoons fresh lemon juice
1 tablespoon chopped fresh basil
garlic powder
salt and pepper
4 large ripe tomatoes, diced and
   drained
½ cup torn fresh basil leaves
paprika

✦ Place sun-dried tomatoes in boiling water for 2 minutes. Drain and chop fine. Pound chicken breasts thin (¼ inch) between 2 pieces of waxed paper with a mallet. Combine sun-dried tomatoes, capers, garlic, olives, olive oil, lemon juice and basil. Sprinkle chicken with garlic powder and pepper on both sides. Spread 1 tablespoon sun-dried tomato mixture over each breast, reserving ½ tablespoon per breast to top, and roll up. Place diced tomatoes and torn basil in a bowl and sprinkle with garlic powder, salt and pepper. Place half of diced tomato mixture in baking pan. Arrange chicken over tomatoes and sprinkle with paprika. Spread tops with remaining sun-dried tomato mixture. Top with remaining tomato and basil mixture. Cover pan with foil and bake in preheated 350° oven for 30 minutes. Uncover and bake an additional 15 to 20 minutes.

✦ 6 servings.

✦ Nutritional information per serving

Calories: 512.8	Saturated Fat: 1.7g	Calories from Fat: 17.1%
Protein: 47.9g	Cholesterol: 77mg	Calories from Carbohydrate: ... 49.1%
Carbohydrate: 69.4g	Dietary Fiber: 15.0g	Calories from Protein: 33.8%
Total Fat: 10.8g	Sodium: 2,614mg	

CHALLAH STUFFED CHICKEN BREASTS

Meat

Stuffing:
1½ stalks celery, chopped
1 medium carrot, grated
1½ onions, chopped
2 tablespoons pareve margarine
1 loaf challah, cubed and toasted
2 cups chicken broth, divided
2 eggs, lightly beaten
2 tablespoons chopped parsley
thyme, optional
onion powder
salt and pepper

Chicken:
8 boneless, skinless chicken breast
** halves**
vegetable oil
salt and pepper
garlic powder
onion powder
paprika
1 tablespoon vegetable oil
1 large onion, chopped
1 cup chicken broth

✦ For stuffing, sauté celery, carrots and onions in margarine until soft. Place bread cubes in a large bowl and cover with 1 cup broth. Add eggs, sautéed vegetables, parsley and seasonings to taste. Add enough of remaining broth to make moist dressing.

✦ Place chicken breasts between 2 pieces of plastic wrap and flatten with a mallet. Brush both sides with oil and season with salt, pepper, garlic powder, onion powder and paprika. Place ⅓ cup stuffing on each breast and roll up. Heat 1 tablespoon oil in medium skillet and sauté onion until soft. Place onion in bottom of a shallow roasting pan. Season with salt, pepper and paprika. Top with chicken. Add ½ cup chicken broth. Bake in preheated 350° oven, uncovered, for 1 hour, basting often with remaining broth. Any leftover stuffing can be baked in a casserole with additional chicken broth.

✦ 8 servings.

On one of her return trips from Toronto after visiting her parents, my friend brought several frozen chicken feet, gift wrapped, thinking that no one would ask her to open a gift for inspection. But the x-ray machine could not decipher what was in the package, and she had to open the gift after all. After some tears and pleading that she only wanted her chicken soup to taste like her mother's, she was allowed to keep the "gift."

POULTRY

CHICKEN BREASTS WITH MUSTARD PISTACHIO SAUCE

Meat

¼ cup chopped pistachio nuts
4 boneless, skinless chicken breasts
pepper
5 tablespoons pareve margarine,
   divided
1 cup chicken stock or broth
¼ cup dry white wine
1 clove garlic, chopped
2 teaspoons Dijon mustard
6 leaves fresh basil, shredded
¼ teaspoon pepper

✦ Toast pistachio nuts in preheated 325° oven for 5 minutes. Set aside. Sprinkle chicken with pepper. Melt 1 tablespoon margarine in a large skillet over medium-low heat. Add chicken, cover and cook until cooked through, about 4 minutes per side. Remove chicken from pan and keep warm. Add stock and wine to pan. Cook over high heat until reduced to about ¼ cup. Add garlic, mustard, basil and ¼ teaspoon pepper. Reduce heat and whisk in remaining margarine 1 tablespoon at a time until combined with liquid to form a sauce. Slice chicken, top with sauce and sprinkle with pistachio nuts.

✦ 4 servings.

CHICKEN CURRY

Meat

2 tablespoons vegetable oil
1 pound boneless, skinless chicken
   breasts, cut into 1-inch cubes
1 onion, chopped
½ cup sliced mushrooms
½ cup sliced celery
1 tablespoon flour
1 cup chicken broth
2 tablespoons lemon juice
2 tablespoons curry powder
2 teaspoons ground cumin
1 teaspoon ground coriander
½ teaspoon ground cloves
½ teaspoon salt
¼ cup yellow raisins
2 bananas, sliced ¼-inch thick
½ cup light coconut milk
cooked rice
raisins, coconut, chopped peanuts,
   sliced green onions

✦ Heat oil in a large skillet over medium-high heat. Add chicken, onion, mushrooms and celery and sauté until chicken is white and vegetables are soft. Sprinkle with flour and gradually stir in chicken broth. Add lemon juice, curry powder, cumin, coriander, cloves, salt and raisins. Bring to a boil, reduce heat and simmer 15 minutes, stirring occasionally. Add bananas and cook an additional 15 minutes. Stir in coconut milk just before serving. Serve with rice and garnish with raisins, coconut, peanuts and green onions.

✦ 4 servings.

CHICKEN BREASTS IN PHYLLO

Meat

1½ cups mayonnaise
1 cup chopped scallions
⅓ cup lemon juice
3 cloves garlic, minced
2 teaspoons snipped fresh dill
1 tablespoon Dijon mustard
12 boneless, skinless chicken breast
    halves
salt and pepper
24 phyllo sheets
1⅓ cups melted pareve margarine or
    olive oil

Note: Can be made ahead and refrigerated or frozen before baking. Bring to room temperature before baking.

✦ Combine mayonnaise, scallions, lemon juice, garlic, dill and mustard. Lightly sprinkle chicken with salt and pepper. Place one sheet phyllo on work surface. Quickly brush with margarine or olive oil. Repeat with second sheet. Keep remaining phyllo covered with plastic wrap and a damp cloth to prevent its drying out. Dip a chicken breast in mayonnaise mixture. Place on corner of phyllo sheets. Fold corner over breast, fold in sides, then roll up. Place seam side down on ungreased cookie sheet and brush with melted margarine or oil. Repeat with remaining phyllo and chicken. Bake in preheated 375° oven for 20 to 25 minutes, until phyllo is brown and crispy.
✦ 12 servings.

CHICKEN POT PIE

Meat

1 (10 ounce) package frozen peas
    and carrots
½ cup sliced mushrooms
½ cup diced onion
¼ cup pareve margarine
⅓ cup flour
1 cube chicken bouillon dissolved
    in 2 cups boiling water
¾ cup liquid nondairy creamer
½ teaspoon salt
¼ teaspoon ground sage
pepper
3 cups cooked cubed chicken
2 unbaked deep dish pie crusts

Note: An excellent way to use leftover chicken. Can be made in advance and frozen. Defrost before baking.

✦ Cook peas and carrots according to package directions, drain and set aside. Sauté mushrooms and onions in margarine until soft. Add flour and stir well to combine. Gradually add bouillon and creamer, stirring constantly. Add salt, sage and pepper to taste and continue cooking until mixture is bubbling and thick. Stir in chicken and peas and carrots. Pour into pie crust and top with second crust. Crimp edges together and cut 4 slits in top. Bake in preheated 450° oven for 15 minutes, or until lightly browned.
✦ 6 servings.

POULTRY

CHERRY GLAZED CORNISH HENS

6 (1½ pound) Cornish hens
salt and pepper
3 tablespoons diced onion
¼ pound sliced, fresh mushrooms
1 cup uncooked rice
2 tablespoons pareve margarine
2 cups chicken broth
1 teaspoon salt, divided
1 tablespoon lemon juice
½ cup slivered almonds
melted pareve margarine or canola oil

Cherry Sauce:
1 (10 ounce) jar red currant jelly
1 (1 pound) can pitted dark sweet
   cherries, drained and juice reserved
1 tablespoon cornstarch
1 tablespoon orange juice concentrate,
   thawed
½ cup orange liqueur

✦ Sprinkle hens with salt and pepper. Sauté onion, mushrooms and rice in margarine in a medium saucepan until onion is soft. Add broth, ½ teaspoon salt and lemon juice. Bring to a boil, reduce heat, cover and simmer 20 to 25 minutes, until rice is fluffy. Toast almonds in preheated 325° oven for 5 to 10 minutes, until light brown. Add to cooked rice. Stuff hens with rice mixture and close cavity with poultry skewers. Brush hens with a little melted margarine or canola oil. Place breast side down in a roasting pan which has been coated with non-stick vegetable spray. Bake in preheated 350° oven for 30 minutes. While hens are baking, melt currant jelly in saucepan. Add reserved cherry juice, cornstarch and orange juice concentrate. Simmer, stirring constantly, until mixture is clear and slightly thickened. Add liqueur and cherries and simmer a few minutes more. Turn hens breast side up and bake an additional 30 minutes. Baste with half of the cherry sauce and cook an additional 20 to 25 minutes, basting frequently. Remove hens to a serving platter. Heat remaining sauce and serve on the side.

✦ 6 servings.

APRICOT CORNISH HENS

4 (1½ pound) Cornish hens
3 tablespoons pareve margarine,
   softened
salt and pepper
1 (6 ounce) can frozen orange juice
   concentrate, thawed
1½ cups apricot preserves
1 ounce brandy, optional
1 (16 ounce) can apricot halves,
   drained
1 (16 ounce) can whole cranberry
   sauce

Note: Perfect for Shabbat dinner.

✦ Place hens, breast side up, in a shallow roasting pan which has been coated with nonstick vegetable spray. Rub with margarine and bake in preheated 325° oven for one hour, uncovered. While hens are baking, combine orange juice, apricot preserves and salt and pepper to taste in a small saucepan. Bring to a boil over low heat. Pour most of drippings off hens and top with apricot mixture. Bake an additional 30 minutes. Turn hens over, baste and bake 30 minutes more. Turn breast up, baste, and bake 15 minutes more. Add brandy, if desired, and baste well.
✦ Place apricot halves on a baking sheet and fill with cranberries. Heat under broiler. Place hens on warm serving platter and garnish with apricot halves. Spoon any remaining apricot sauce over hens. Serve with rice.
✦ 4 servings.

COPPER MOUNTAIN TURKEY CHILI

2 tablespoons vegetable oil
1 large onion, chopped
4 cloves garlic, minced
8 mushrooms, sliced
1 pound ground turkey
1 large red bell pepper, seeded and
   diced
3 tablespoons chili powder
1 teaspoon hot pepper sauce
1 teaspoon ground cumin
2 (14½ ounce) cans Italian-style
   stewed tomatoes
1 (8 ounce) can tomato sauce
1 (15 ounce) can kidney beans,
   undrained

✦ Heat oil over medium-high heat in a Dutch oven. Add onion, garlic and mushrooms and sauté until onions are soft. Add meat and brown, stirring to break up any large pieces. Add remaining ingredients except beans. Bring to a boil, reduce heat and simmer 30 minutes. Add beans and cook an additional 15 minutes.
✦ 6 servings.

POULTRY

MINERS' TURKEY BURGERS WITH BLACK BEAN SALSA

Meat

3 tablespoons olive oil, divided
½ small red onion, minced
1 carrot, finely chopped
1 stalk celery, finely chopped
1 pound ground turkey
1 slice white bread, crumbled
1 (4 ounce) can chopped mild green
　　chiles, drained
½ teaspoon salt

Black Bean Salsa:
2 tablespoons lime juice
¼ teaspoon coarsely ground pepper
1 tablespoon olive oil
½ teaspoon salt
1 large tomato, seeded and diced
1 avocado, diced
1 (15 ounce) can black beans, rinsed
　　and drained
1 (8¾ ounce) can whole kernel corn,
　　drained
4 (8-inch) flour tortillas, hamburger
　　buns or pita breads
1 head Boston lettuce

✦ Heat 1 tablespoon oil in a large skillet over medium heat. Sauté onion, reserving 1 tablespoon onion. Add 1 tablespoon oil to skillet with carrot and celery. Sauté until very tender, about 10 minutes. Remove from heat and place in a mixing bowl. Add turkey, bread crumbs, chiles and salt. Combine well and shape into 4 (¾-inch) thick patties. Heat 1 tablespoon oil in same skillet over medium heat. Cook patties about 10 minutes or until thoroughly cooked and lightly browned on both sides.
✦ For salsa, mix lime juice, pepper, oil and salt. Stir in tomato, avocado, black beans, corn and reserved onion.
✦ To serve, heat tortillas, buns or pita breads. Top with lettuce leaves and turkey patty. Spoon salsa over patties.
✦ 4 servings.

DIJON TURKEY BREAST

Meat

3 onions, sliced
1 (5 to 6 pound) turkey breast

Dijon Sauce:
3 tablespoons Dijon mustard
3 tablespoons soy sauce
3 tablespoons sherry
3 tablespoons honey
1 teaspoon garlic powder
1 teaspoon ground ginger
½ teaspoon pepper

✦ Place slices of one onion in bottom of a 9 x 13-inch baking pan which has been coated with nonstick vegetable spray. Place turkey over onion. Combine all sauce ingredients and pour over turkey. Top with remaining onion slices. Tent with foil and bake in preheated 325° oven for 3 to 3½ hours, basting frequently. Remove foil and bake an additional 30 minutes. Let rest 10 minutes before slicing.
✦ 8 servings.

Note: Turkey can be marinated in sauce overnight before baking.

PLUM CREEK TURKEY BREAST

1 large clove garlic
4 green onions
2 tablespoons soy sauce
1 teaspoon dried sage
1 teaspoon dried thyme
1 teaspoon dried marjoram
salt
¼ teaspoon pepper
½ cup fresh lemon juice
1½ cups dry white wine
1 (5 to 6 pound) turkey breast

Hint: Double marinade if you wish to have sauce to serve with the turkey.

✦ Mince garlic and onion in a food processor. Add remaining ingredients except turkey and blend well. Pour into a large ziplock bag. Add turkey, seal and turn to coat. Refrigerate overnight, turning bag occasionally.
✦ The following day, remove turkey from marinade and place in a foil pan. Cover with marinade. Cook turkey on a grill until meat thermometer reaches 170°, about 2½ hours, or bake in preheated 325° oven about 2½ hours. Baste frequently and add water if necessary.

JERK TURKEY BURGERS

1 pound ground turkey
⅓ cup bulgur wheat
¼ cup water
2 teaspoons garlic powder
1 teaspoon dried thyme
1 teaspoon curry powder
½ teaspoon ground cumin
½ teaspoon ground allspice
½ teaspoon ground ginger
½ teaspoon salt
¼ teaspoon pepper
¼ teaspoon paprika
⅛ teaspoon cayenne pepper

✦ Combine all ingredients and shape into patties. Pan fry or broil. Grilling is not recommended, as turkey tends to get too dry.
✦ 4 servings.

P
O
U
L
T
R
Y

ALMOND CRUSTED TROUT

Pareve

2 cups almonds
1 cup flour, divided
2 large trout fillets, with skin
salt and pepper
3 large egg whites, well-beaten
1 tablespoon pareve margarine
1 tablespoon oil
lemon slices
parsley sprigs

✦ Combine almonds and 1 tablespoon flour in food processor. Process, but do not grind too fine. Transfer to a plate. Place remaining flour on another plate. Season fish with salt and pepper to taste. Dip fish into flour to coat, and shake off excess. Brush flesh side with egg white. Place fillet, egg-white-side down, on almonds and press to coat. Melt margarine and oil in a large heavy skillet over medium-high heat. Place fillets, almond-side down in skillet and cook until crust is golden and crisp, about 2 minutes per side or until opaque in the center. Serve immediately, garnished with lemon and parsley.

✦ 4 servings.

✦ Instead of using a roasting rack, make a grid of carrot and celery sticks and place the poultry, fish or meat on top. One less item to wash up, and tastier drippings for gravy.

CASHEW TROUT CORTEZ

Dairy

4 trout fillets, rinsed and patted dry
salt and pepper
½ cup flour
3 tablespoons clarified butter*
4 tablespoons fresh lime juice
1 cup pareve chicken-flavored broth
1 cup chopped cashews
5 tablespoons unsalted butter,
   cut into small pieces and softened
¼ cup chopped cilantro
cilantro sprigs

✦ Remove any small bones from fish. Sprinkle fish with salt and pepper and lightly dust with flour. Shake off any excess flour. Heat clarified butter in a sauté pan. Add fillets skin side down and cook 3 to 5 minutes. Turn and cook an additional 2 to 3 minutes. Remove skin and season with additional salt and pepper. Place trout, browned-side up, in an ovenproof serving dish and place in 200° oven to keep warm. Drain grease from sauté pan and add lime juice and chicken broth. Reduce broth over high heat by three-quarters, approximately 15 minutes. Add cashews and turn off heat. Whisk in butter a piece at a time. When butter is incorporated add cilantro. Pour over fish. Garnish with cilantro sprigs.
✦ Serves 4.

✦ To clarify butter, melt over low heat in small heavy saucepan. Remove from heat and set aside for 5 minutes. Remove and discard foamy white butter fat that has risen to top. Pour off clear liquid, which is clarified butter. Discard remaining solids.

GRILLED HALIBUT WITH LEMON BASIL VINAIGRETTE

Pareve

2½ tablespoons fresh lemon juice
2 tablespoons extra virgin olive oil
2 cloves garlic, crushed
½ teaspoon grated lemon peel
3 tablespoons thinly sliced fresh basil
   or 1 tablespoon dried
2 teaspoons drained capers
salt and pepper
4 (6 ounce) halibut fillets

✦ Whisk lemon juice, olive oil, garlic and lemon peel in a small bowl. Stir in basil and capers. Season to taste with salt and pepper. Sprinkle fillets with salt and pepper. Brush with 1 tablespoon vinaigrette. Grill fish until cooked through, about 4 minutes per side. Transfer fish to a serving dish. Whisk vinaigrette again and pour over fish.
✦ 4 servings.

F
I
S
H

SEA BASS WITH ROASTED GARLIC SAUCE

5 large corn husks
1 Anaheim chile, roasted, peeled, seeded and chopped
¼ pound fresh mushrooms, sliced
½ cup diced red bell pepper
2 tablespoons butter, cut in small pieces
salt and pepper
4 (6 ounce) sea bass, halibut or any firm white fish fillets

Roasted Garlic Sauce:
3 heads garlic
1 cup dry white wine
3 tablespoons chopped shallots
¼ cup fresh lime juice
1 cup fish or vegetable stock
1 cup heavy cream
salt and freshly ground pepper

Garnish:
2 avocados, halved and cut into fans

✦ Soak corn husks in water for 1 hour. Remove from water and shake off any excess water. Toss chile, mushrooms, red pepper, butter and salt and pepper together in a medium bowl. Pat onto surface of fillets. Place each fillet on a corn husk. Tear remaining husk into 8 strips. Gather ends of husks and tie with strips, leaving a gap down the middle to allow steam to evaporate. Place in a baking pan and bake in preheated 375° oven until fish flakes, about 12 minutes.

✦ For Roasted Garlic Sauce, trim top quarter off heads to expose cloves. Sprinkle with olive oil and wrap in foil. Bake in preheated 450° oven for 45 minutes or until cloves are tender. Squeeze cloves from skins into a noncorrosive saucepan. Add wine, shallots and lime juice and bring to a boil. Continue cooking until liquid is reduced to ¼ cup. Add stock and reduce to ½ cup. Add cream and reduce to 1 cup. Strain through a fine mesh strainer and season with salt and pepper.

✦ To serve, divide sauce among 4 warm dinner plates. Center wrapped fish on sauce and garnish with avocado fans.

✦ 4 servings.

COUNTRY STYLE SEA BASS Pareve

1½ tablespoons olive oil
4 (7 ounce) sea bass or halibut fillets,
    rinsed and patted dry
salt and pepper

Potato Puree:
1 pound large red potatoes,
    cut into ½-inch cubes
2 teaspoons salt
2 tablespoons olive oil

Zucchini-Tomato Sauce:
¼ cup olive oil
1 tablespoon red wine vinegar
1 tablespoon sherry
1 cup zucchini, cut into ½-inch cubes
12 ounces vine-ripened tomatoes,
    peeled, seeded and cut into ¼-inch
    pieces
2 tablespoons minced shallots
salt to taste
2 tablespoons shredded fresh basil
    leaves

✦ Pour oil in bottom of a shallow baking pan large enough to hold fillets in one layer without touching. Heat in preheated 425° oven for 3 minutes. Season fillets with salt and pepper. Place in hot pan and roast in middle of oven 7 to 10 minutes or until fish is cooked through.

✦ For Potato Puree, place potatoes in a saucepan and cover with 2 inches of cold water. Bring to a boil. Add salt and simmer 15 minutes or until potatoes are very soft. Reserve ¾ cup cooking water. Drain potatoes in a colander. Coarsely mash potatoes in a bowl. Add oil, ½ cup reserved water and salt to taste. Beat with electric mixer until smooth. Add remaining cooking water if necessary to make puree soft. Keep warm.

✦ For Zucchini-Tomato Sauce, combine all ingredients except basil in a small saucepan. Bring to a bare simmer. Heat just until zucchini is translucent. Remove from heat and stir in basil.

✦ To serve, divide potato puree among 4 plates and top with fillet. Spoon sauce over fillet and around puree.

✦ 4 servings.

CHINESE COWBOY SEA BASS

1 large onion, chopped
6 cloves garlic, chopped
1 tablespoon chopped fresh ginger
1 fresh poblano, pacilla or other mild
  green chile, stemmed, seeded, and
  julienned
8 mushrooms, thinly sliced
⅔ cup dry white wine
¼ cup soy sauce
2 tablespoons black bean sauce
1 tablespoon orange marmalade
1 tablespoon fresh lime juice
4 (8 ounce) sea bass fillets,
  1 inch thick
2 tablespoons chopped fresh cilantro,
  optional

✦ Coat a large nonstick skillet with nonstick vegetable spray. Place over medium-high heat and add onion, garlic and ginger. Sauté until golden. Add chile and mushrooms. Sauté an additional minute. Stir in wine, soy sauce, black bean sauce, marmalade and lime juice. Bring to a boil. Season fish with salt and pepper. Add to skillet and reduce heat to medium-low. Cover and simmer until fish is just cooked through, about 5 minutes per side. Transfer fish to plates. Spoon sauce around fish and sprinkle with cilantro, if desired. Serve with rice.

✦ 4 servings.

✦ Nutritional information per serving

Calories: 308.2	Saturated Fat: 1.3g	Calories from Fat: 17.1%
Protein: 44.7g	Cholesterol: 93mg	Calories from Carbohydrate: ... 18.5%
Carbohydrate: 12.9g	Dietary Fiber: 1.6g	Calories from Protein: 64.4%
Total Fat: 5.3g	Sodium: 1,224mg	

Shortly after my family arrived in Denver speaking only Greek, my 16 year old brother appeared at our door with his classmates and teachers from high school. With my limited English I welcomed them all and looked at my brother, who was hesitant to explain to us in Greek what was going on. They had brought a veritable feast, ready to be cooked, from turkey to pies, even a pumpkin and canned goods. When my father protested that we could not accept charity, the teacher told us the story of the first American Thanksgiving. She said that my brother's classmates wanted to help us celebrate our coming to America, just like the Pilgrims did! Our grandchildren love this story of our first Thanksgiving in America.

TERIYAKI TUNA
WITH ASIAN SLAW

1 cup teriyaki sauce
2 tablespoons dry sherry
2 tablespoons fresh lemon juice
2 tablespoons minced fresh ginger
2 cloves garlic, minced
1 teaspoon pepper
4 (¾-inch thick) tuna steaks

Asian Slaw:
2 tablespoons fresh lime juice
2 tablespoons vegetable oil
1 tablespoon teriyaki sauce
1 tablespoon honey
1 teaspoon sesame oil
1 jalapeño, minced
¼ teaspoon salt
4 cups shredded Savoy cabbage
2 carrots, shredded
1 red bell pepper, seeded and thinly
  sliced
¾ cup chopped cilantro
¼ cup chopped peanuts

Garnish:
toasted sesame seeds
thinly sliced scallion
pickled sushi ginger

✦ Combine teriyaki sauce, sherry, lemon juice, ginger, garlic and pepper in a 9 x 13-inch glass baking dish. Add tuna and turn to coat. Chill 1 hour. Drain tuna and place on oiled grill rack 5 inches from medium-hot coals. Cook 2 minutes per side for rare. Remove to serving platter and garnish with sesame seeds, scallions and ginger. Serve with Asian Slaw.
✦ For Asian Slaw, combine lime juice, vegetable oil, teriyaki sauce, honey, sesame oil, jalapeño and salt in a large bowl. Add remaining ingredients and toss.
✦ 4 servings.

GRILLED TUNA WITH MANGO SALSA

2 tablespoons fresh lime juice
2 tablespoons fresh lemon juice
2 tablespoons orange juice
1 tablespoon soy sauce
1 tablespoon rice vinegar
1 teaspoon chopped garlic
2 teaspoons chopped onion
4 (1-inch thick) tuna steaks, skin
   removed

Mango Salsa:
1 mango, chopped (1½ cups)
½ to 1 small jalapeño, chopped,
   to taste
¼ cup chopped red onion
¼ cup chopped red bell pepper
2 tablespoons fresh lime juice
1 tablespoon chopped cilantro

Note: If fresh mango is not available, mango in a jar works well.

✦ Combine juices, soy sauce, vinegar, garlic and onion in a small bowl. Pour over tuna and refrigerate 30 minutes. Remove from marinade and grill 3 to 5 minutes per side. Gently combine all salsa ingredients and serve with fish.
✦ 4 servings.

✦ **Nutritional information per serving**

Calories: 303.3	Saturated Fat: 2.2g	Calories from Fat: 25.7%
Protein: 40.9g	Cholesterol: 65mg	Calories from Carbohydrate: ... 20.0%
Carbohydrate: 15.1g	Dietary Fiber: 1.6g	Calories from Protein: 54.3%
Total Fat: 8.6g	Sodium: 283mg	

TUNA STEAKS NIÇOISE

¼ cup lemon juice
¼ cup dry vermouth
1 tablespoon minced fresh ginger
¼ teaspoon sugar
freshly ground pepper, divided
2½ tablespoons olive oil
6 (8 ounce) tuna steaks, 1 inch thick
2 cups finely chopped onion
1 tablespoon minced garlic
1 cup tomato sauce
2 tomatoes, peeled, seeded and
    coarsely chopped
¼ cup chopped green olives
3 tablespoons brandy
1 tablespoon chopped fresh basil
pinch dried red pepper flakes
6 pitted green olives, julienned

Note: This is great over pasta.

✦ Combine lemon juice, vermouth, ginger, sugar, 1 tablespoon olive oil and freshly ground pepper in a small bowl. Blend well and pour over tuna. Cover and refrigerate at least 2 hours, turning occasionally. Heat 1 tablespoon olive oil in a medium saucepan. Add onions and garlic. Cover and cook over low heat until softened, stirring occasionally. Add tomato sauce, tomatoes, chopped olives, brandy, basil, red pepper and freshly ground pepper. Cook over very low heat, stirring occasionally, about 20 minutes. Remove from heat. Preheat oven to 400°. Remove tuna from marinade and pour marinade into saucepan. Cook over high heat until slightly thickened, about 5 minutes. Heat remaining olive oil in a large skillet. Add tuna and sear about 2 minutes per side. Transfer tuna to a baking dish and brush with thickened marinade. Reduce oven temperature to 350° and bake tuna 8 to 9 minutes or until done. Reheat tomato sauce and spoon onto 6 plates. Arrange tuna on top and garnish with sliced olives.
✦ 6 servings.

TUNA KEBABS WITH
WASABI DIPPING SAUCE

1 cup mayonnaise
4 teaspoons soy sauce
1½ teaspoons sugar
2 teaspoons fresh lemon juice
4 teaspoons wasabi powder, with
    enough cold water added to form
    a paste
1 (12 ounce) tuna steak, cut into
    1-inch cubes
bamboo skewers soaked in water 30
    minutes
vegetables

✦ Combine mayonnaise, soy sauce, sugar and lemon juice in a medium bowl. Transfer two-thirds of mixture to a small bowl and add wasabi paste. Refrigerate. Add tuna to remaining mayonnaise mixture. Cover and refrigerate at least 1 hour and up to 24 hours. Thread tuna and your favorite shish kebab vegetables on skewers. Grill until just cooked through, 2 to 3 minutes per side. Serve with wasabi mayonnaise on side.
✦ 2 servings.

*Hint: Wasabi powder can be found in the
    Asian section of most supermarkets.*

MEDITERRANEAN TUNA WITH GREEN BEANS AND FENNEL

10 ounces fresh green beans, trimmed
2 (8 ounce) tuna steaks, ¾-inch thick
1 large fennel bulb, trimmed, cored
  and julienned
3 large bunches watercress, stems
  trimmed
1 small radicchio, torn into bite-sized
  pieces
20 pitted Kalamata olives, halved
  lengthwise
salt and pepper
2 tablespoons chopped fresh chives

Dressing:
1¼ cups minced red onion
3 tablespoons red wine vinegar
6 tablespoons olive oil
¼ cup walnut oil
½ teaspoon salt
¼ teaspoon pepper

*Note: Makes a great light dinner served
  with crusty bread and good wine.*

✦ Cook beans in large pot of boiling salted water until crisp-tender, about 4 minutes. Drain and refresh with cold water. Drain and pat dry.

✦ For dressing, place onion and vinegar in a small bowl. Gradually whisk in both oils. Add salt and pepper. Brush 2 tablespoons dressing over one side of tuna steaks. Season with salt and pepper. Grill over high heat or broil, seasoned side down, 2 minutes. Brush with 2 more tablespoons dressing and season with salt and pepper. Turn steaks and cook to desired doneness, 2 minutes for medium-rare. Cut into quarters. Combine beans, fennel, watercress, radicchio and olives in a large bowl. Top with remaining dressing and toss. Adjust seasonings. Divide among 4 large plates. Top with 2 tuna pieces and garnish with chives.

✦ 4 servings.

CHILLED POACHED SALMON WITH CUCUMBER SAUCE

Dairy

Poached Salmon:
1 lemon, sliced
1 onion, sliced
½ teaspoon whole peppercorns
½ cup dry white wine
½ cup water
4 salmon fillets or steaks

Cucumber Grape Sauce:
½ cup sour cream
3 tablespoons mayonnaise
1 tablespoon lime juice
⅓ cup cucumber, peeled, seeded and grated
1 cup seedless grapes, halved
1 teaspoon dill

Cucumber Green Sauce:
⅓ cup mayonnaise
⅓ cup sour cream
3 tablespoons chopped fresh chives
3 tablespoons chopped fresh parsley
2 tablespoons lemon juice
1 clove garlic, minced
¼ teaspoon pepper
1 medium cucumber, peeled, seeded and coarsely chopped

✦ Layer lemon and onion in the bottom of a glass baking dish. Top with peppercorns, white wine and water. Add salmon and cover with waxed paper. Poach in preheated 350° oven for 20 minutes or microwave 4 to 6 minutes per pound at 70% power. Let stand covered 3 to 5 minutes. Remove fish from broth, chill and skin. Serve with either Cucumber Sauce.
✦ Combine all ingredients for Cucumber Grape Sauce and chill.
✦ Mix Cucumber Green sauce ingredients and chill.
✦ 4 servings.

SALMON WITH CITRUS CRÈME FRAÎCHE

½ cup olive oil
1 tablespoon chopped garlic
salt and pepper to taste
4 salmon fillets

Citrus Crème Fraîche:
¾ cup crème fraîche
¼ cup fresh orange juice
1 tablespoon lime juice
1 tablespoon marinated green
   peppercorns, drained

Berry Compote:
1 tablespoon sugar
1 tablespoon balsamic vinegar
⅓ cup fresh raspberries
⅓ cup fresh strawberries, halved
⅓ cup orange sections, membranes
   removed

Garnish:
4 large Belgian endive leaves
12 slices peeled mango
12 strawberries
12 raspberries

Note: Easy to prepare.

✦ Crème Fraîche is available at specialty food stores. To make your own, combine 1 cup heavy cream with 2½ teaspoons buttermilk in a jar. Cover tightly and shake for 1 minute. Let stand at room temperature for at least 8 hours, until thick. Store in refrigerator.

✦ For salmon, combine olive oil, garlic, salt and pepper. Brush on salmon and grill 3 to 4 minutes each side. Chill.

✦ For Citrus Crème Fraîche, combine crème fraîche, orange juice and lime juice in a bowl. Stir in peppercorns. Use at room temperature.

✦ For Berry Compote, dissolve sugar in vinegar. Place berries and orange sections in a bowl and lightly fold in vinegar mixture. Use at room temperature.

✦ To assemble: Divide Citrus Crème Fraîche among 4 plates. Place a salmon fillet in center of each plate. Place an endive leaf perpendicular to the salmon, with its tip resting on rim of plate. Spoon Berry Compote into leaf so that it overflows. Place 3 mango slices on opposite side of salmon, also perpendicular to fish. Alternate 3 strawberries and 3 raspberries around rim of plate.

✦ 4 servings.

SALMON YUCATAN STYLE   Dairy

1 pound salmon fillet
3 tablespoons fresh lime juice,
    divided
1 tablespoon butter, divided
salt and pepper
3 jalapeño peppers, seeded and
    julienned
1 cup sour cream
snipped fresh chives
lime wedges

✦ Place salmon in a buttered baking dish, skin side down. Combine 1 tablespoon lime juice and 1½ teaspoons melted butter. Brush over salmon. Sprinkle with salt and pepper and let stand 15 minutes. Bake in preheated 500° oven until fish is opaque, about 9 minutes per inch of thickness. Melt remaining butter in a small saucepan over medium-low heat. Add jalapeños and cook until tender, about 3 minutes, stirring occasionally. Add sour cream and stir until heated through, but do not boil. Stir in remaining lime juice, and add salt and pepper to taste. Transfer fish to serving platter and top with sauce. Sprinkle with chives and garnish with lime wedges.
✦ 2 servings.

SALMON PECAN   Dairy or Pareve

4 (6 ounce) salmon fillets
⅛ teaspoon salt
⅛ teaspoon pepper
2 tablespoons Dijon mustard
2 tablespoons butter or pareve
    margarine, melted
1 tablespoon honey
¼ cup bread crumbs
¼ cup chopped pecans
2 teaspoons chopped parsley
parsley sprigs
lemon slices

✦ Sprinkle salmon with salt and pepper. Place skin side down in a lightly greased 9 x 13-inch baking pan. Combine mustard, butter and honey. Brush on fillets. Combine bread crumbs, pecans and parsley. Spoon evenly on top of each fillet. Bake in preheated 450° oven for 10 minutes or until fish flakes easily.
✦ 4 servings.

✿ See Pareve Food Preparation, page 30

SALMON WITH ISLAND SALSA

Island Salsa:
1 small papaya, peeled, seeded and diced
1 large kiwi, peeled and diced
½ cup diced red bell pepper
½ cup diced yellow bell pepper
2 large jalapeño peppers, seeded and diced
¼ cup chopped cilantro
3 tablespoons lemon juice
2 tablespoons lime juice
1 tablespoon sugar

Salmon:
1 tablespoon olive oil
¼ teaspoon cayenne pepper
6 salmon steaks, rinsed and patted dry

Note: This salsa is great on other fish too.

✦ For salsa, combine all ingredients and mix gently. Cover and chill up to 4 hours.
✦ Combine oil and cayenne in a shallow dish. Dip salmon to coat lightly. Grill until opaque, about 5 minutes per side. Serve with salsa.
✦ 6 servings.

✦ **Nutritional information per serving**

Calories: 270.1	Saturated Fat: 1.3g	Calories from Fat: 28.1%
Protein: 35.1g	Cholesterol: 88mg	Calories from Carbohydrate: ... 19.6%
Carbohydrate: 13.2g	Dietary Fiber: 2.0g	Calories from Protein: 52.3%
Total Fat: 8.4g	Sodium: 120mg	

SALMON ORANGERIE

4 oranges
2 lemons
¼ cup minced fresh mint leaves
½ cup thawed frozen orange juice
    concentrate
1 tablespoon butter or pareve
    margarine
4 (6 ounce) salmon fillets,
    1-inch thick, with skin
mint sprigs, optional

✦ Grate enough orange peel to make 1 tablespoon. Peel oranges and remove white membrane. Divide into segments and drain in a colander. Grate enough lemon peel to make 1 tablespoon. Combine orange and lemon peel with mint leaves in a small bowl. Squeeze lemons and mix juice with orange juice concentrate. Melt butter in a large ovenproof skillet over medium-high heat. When butter sizzles, add salmon, skin side down. Cook until skin is well-browned and crisp, about 7 minutes. To remove skin, gently slide a spatula under skin of each fillet, leaving fish in place. Brush with one-fourth of lemon juice mixture. Broil 4 inches from heat 3 to 4 minutes, or until salmon is just barely opaque. Transfer to a serving plate and keep warm. Stir remaining lemon juice mixture into skillet and return to broiler just until sauce bubbles, about 4 minutes. Pour over salmon and sprinkle with mint mixture. Arrange orange segments around fish and garnish with mint sprigs, if desired.
✦ 4 servings.

✡ See Pareve Food Preparation, page 30

✦ **Nutritional information per serving**

Calories: 306.0	Saturated Fat: 2.8g	Calories from Fat: 24.0%
Protein: 37.1g	Cholesterol: 96mg	Calories from Carbohydrate: ... 34.1%
Carbohydrate: 30.2g	Dietary Fiber: 3.6g	Calories from Protein: 41.9%
Total Fat: 9.4g	Sodium: 150mg	

THAI SALMON

4½ teaspoons peanut oil
2¼ teaspoons minced garlic
2¼ teaspoons minced fresh ginger
1 tablespoon curry powder
1 tablespoon Thai red curry base
1 tablespoon paprika
½ teaspoon whole coriander seeds,
   lightly crushed
1 teaspoon ground cumin
2½ cups unsweetened coconut milk
⅓ cup tomato puree
3 tablespoons soy sauce
3 tablespoons golden brown sugar
6 (8 ounce) salmon fillets,
   ¾-inch thick
2 tablespoons olive oil
½ cup chopped peanuts

Thai Slaw:
6 cups shredded green cabbage
1 cup matchstick-sized peeled
   cucumber strips, peeled and seeded
¾ cup chopped cilantro
¾ cup coarsely chopped fresh mint
3 tablespoons rice vinegar
1½ tablespoons soy sauce

✦ Heat peanut oil in heavy saucepan over medium heat. Add garlic and ginger and sauté until light brown, about 2 minutes. Add curry powder, curry base, paprika, coriander and cumin. Reduce heat to low and sauté until fragrant, about 1 minute. Add coconut milk, tomato puree, soy sauce and brown sugar. Bring almost to a simmer, whisking constantly, but do not boil. Cover and chill. Can be made one day ahead. Sprinkle salmon with salt and pepper. Heat olive oil in a heavy skillet over high heat. Sauté fish until opaque, about 4 minutes per side. Place in center of serving plate. Ladle sauce around fish, top with Thai Slaw and sprinkle with peanuts.

✦ For Thai Slaw, toss all ingredients in a bowl and season with salt and pepper. Can be made up to 2 hours ahead.

✦ 6 servings.

✦ When recipes call for a small amount of tomato paste, freeze the rest in a plastic bag.

HERBED SALMON IN PARCHMENT WITH BEURRE BLANC SAUCE

Dairy

4 (18-inch) squares cooking parchment
butter
3 shallots, minced
4 (6 ounce) salmon fillets, skin removed
8 cherry tomatoes, halved
8 large mushrooms, quartered
2 zucchini or summer squash, julienned
¾ cup baby carrots, blanched and julienned
dry white wine
salt and pepper
1 tablespoon chopped fresh tarragon or dill

Beurre Blanc Sauce:
1 tablespoon finely minced shallot
2 tablespoons white wine vinegar
1½ tablespoons dry vermouth
1½ tablespoons fresh lemon juice
½ cup heavy whipping cream
1 cup unsalted butter, chilled
salt and pepper

✦ Fold parchment squares in half diagonally. Butter entire bottom half. Divide shallots among the pieces and place 1 fillet on top of the shallots. Surround each fillet with the vegetables. Sprinkle each portion with wine, herbs and salt and pepper. Fold upper triangle of parchment over fish and vegetables and seal the 2 open edges with a triple foldover, being careful to seal completely. Place in a baking dish and bake in preheated 450° oven for 10 to 15 minutes. Serve immediately with the Beurre Blanc Sauce.

✦ For Beurre Blanc Sauce, combine shallots, vinegar, vermouth and lemon juice in a small saucepan. Cook over high heat until almost evaporated, about 1 to 2 minutes. Add cream and cook over medium heat until slightly reduced, about 2 minutes. Remove from heat and set aside. Just before serving, reheat in double boiler over hot water. Whisk in chilled butter, 1 tablespoon at a time, until butter emulsifies. Season to taste with salt and pepper. Serve immediately.

✦ 4 servings.

FISH

SALMON IN PHYLLO WITH PESTO AND RED PEPPER SAUCE

8 phyllo dough sheets
4 tablespoons butter
8 (6 ounce) salmon fillets
salt and pepper

Pesto:
2 cups packed fresh basil leaves
2 tablespoons pine nuts
½ cup grated Parmesan cheese
2 cloves garlic
1 teaspoon salt
1 tablespoon olive oil

Red Pepper Sauce:
3 large red bell peppers
¾ cup dry white wine
½ cup sour cream

✦ Lay one sheet of phyllo on work surface. Brush half of sheet with butter. Fold in half and brush again. Place a salmon fillet in center of one long edge of sheet. Spread with 1 tablespoon pesto and season with salt and pepper. Roll phyllo in a cylinder and crimp the ends or gather up into a knot on top. Brush top with butter. Repeat with remaining dough and salmon. Place on a baking sheet and bake in preheated 400° oven until browned, about 15 to 20 minutes.
✦ For Pesto, place basil, pine nuts, Parmesan cheese, garlic and salt in food processor. Pulse until evenly blended. With machine running, drizzle olive oil into mixture.
✦ For Red Pepper Sauce, roast peppers over flame or broil until black. Place in a paper bag until cool. Peel and seed. Puree peppers with wine in a blender or food processor. Simmer in a saucepan for 5 minutes. Add sour cream and simmer another 5 minutes, stirring until smooth. Divide between individual serving plates and top with phyllo rolls.
✦ 8 servings.

F
I
S
H

SALMON STUFFED PORTOBELLO MUSHROOMS WITH SPINACH AND CHEESE

2 large portobello mushrooms
1 tablespoon olive oil
salt and pepper
2 tablespoons chopped scallions
½ pound salmon, skinned and
　chopped by hand
lemon juice
4 cups chopped fresh spinach
4 tablespoons cream cheese, softened
3 tablespoons crumbled feta cheese
3 tablespoons shredded mozzarella
　cheese
2 tablespoons shredded Parmesan
　cheese

✦ Stem and clean underside of mushrooms. Brush with oil and season with salt and pepper. Broil in a baking dish, hollow side up, for 3 minutes. Sprinkle with scallions. Season salmon with salt, pepper and lemon juice. Fill mushrooms with salmon. Microwave spinach on high for 1 minute. Add cheeses and stir to combine. Pile over salmon. Place in preheated 375° oven for 20 minutes.
✦ 2 servings.

SALMON BURGERS WITH GINGER SAUCE

Pareve

¾ pound salmon fillet, skinned
1 tablespoon Dijon mustard
2 teaspoons finely chopped fresh
　ginger
1 teaspoon soy sauce
salt and pepper
2 teaspoons vegetable oil
sliced sweet onion
sliced tomato
lettuce leaves
soft hamburger buns

Ginger Sauce:
2 tablespoons mayonnaise
1½ teaspoons Dijon mustard
¾ teaspoon finely grated fresh ginger
½ teaspoon soy sauce

✦ Coarsely chop salmon by hand. Add mustard, ginger, soy sauce and salt and pepper to taste. Form into two 2-inch thick patties. Heat oil in a nonstick skillet until hot but not smoking. Sauté patties 4 minutes per side or until cooked through. Combine all Ginger Sauce ingredients in a small bowl. Place patties on hamburger buns and top with onions, tomato, lettuce and sauce.
✦ 2 servings.

KIT CARSON FAJITAS

Salsa:
1 papaya, peeled, seeded and
  cut into ½-inch pieces
¼ fresh pineapple, peeled, cored and
  cut into ½-inch pieces
¼ red bell pepper, finely chopped
1 tablespoon finely chopped
  red onion
1 kiwi, peeled and diced
2 tablespoons fresh lime juice
1 tablespoon fresh lemon juice
½ fresh jalapeño pepper, seeded and
  finely chopped

Fajitas:
2 tablespoons fresh lime juice
½ teaspoon lemon pepper
¼ ground cumin
1½ pounds snapper filets, skinned
  and cut into ½-inch strips
1 tablespoon vegetable oil
1 cup vertically sliced red onion
½ cup red bell pepper strips
½ cup green bell pepper strips
½ cup yellow bell pepper strips
1 medium zucchini, cut into strips
fajita-size flour tortillas

✦ For Salsa, combine all ingredients and refrigerate 4 or more hours.
✦ For Fajitas, combine lime juice, lemon pepper, cumin and fish in a zip-lock bag. Shake well to coat fish. Marinate in refrigerator for 20 minutes. Do not over-marinate. Heat oil in a nonstick skillet over medium-high heat. Sauté onions, peppers and zucchini until crisp-tender. Set aside and keep warm. Arrange fish in a single layer on a broiler pan coated with nonstick vegetable spray and broil 4 minutes on each side or until fish flakes easily. Serve "Self-Serve" style with vegetable mixture, salsa and warmed tortillas.
✦ 6 servings.

PORTOBELLO MUSHROOM FAJITAS

 Dairy | Lighter

3 tablespoons water
1 tablespoon olive oil
2 tablespoons lime juice
½ teaspoon cumin powder
¼ teaspoon oregano
3 cloves garlic, minced
salt and pepper
1 pound portobello mushrooms,
   thinly sliced
1 large red onion, thinly sliced
1 red bell pepper, thinly sliced
1 green bell pepper, thinly sliced
6 flour tortillas
lime wedges
salsa
sour cream, optional

✦ Combine water, oil, lime juice, cumin, oregano, garlic and salt and pepper in a small bowl. Place all vegetables in a large zip lock bag. Pour marinade over, seal and turn to coat well. Let sit at room temperature for 30 minutes. Heat a large skillet over medium-high heat. Sprinkle with water. When droplets sizzle, add vegetables and cook until soft, about 10 minutes. While vegetables are cooking, wrap tortillas in foil and warm in 350° oven. To serve, place vegetables in center of tortilla, roll up and garnish with lime, salsa and sour cream, if desired.

✦ 6 servings.

V E G E T A R I A N

✦ **Nutritional information per serving**

Calories: 347.6	Saturated Fat: 1.5g	Calories from Fat: 26.1%
Protein: 10.7g	Cholesterol: 0mg	Calories from Carbohydrate: ... 62.1%
Carbohydrate: 55.9g	Dietary Fiber: 6.2g	Calories from Protein: 11.8%
Total Fat: 10.5g	Sodium: 345mg	

ZUCCHINI BURRITOS

3 medium zucchini
1 large onion
1 tablespoon olive oil
1 clove garlic, minced
1 (4 ounce) can mild chopped green
   chiles
½-1 jalapeño, chopped
1 teaspoon dried basil
½ teaspoon dried oregano
¼ teaspoon ground cumin
¼ teaspoon salt
⅔ cup shredded Monterey Jack cheese
6 large flour tortillas at room
   temperature
1 teaspoon canola oil, optional
sour cream
salsa

✦ Shred zucchini and onion in a food processor. Heat olive oil in a skillet over medium heat. Add zucchini, onion, garlic, chiles, jalapeño, basil, oregano, cumin and salt. Sauté until vegetables are soft, about 5 minutes. Drain vegetables. Add cheese and mix gently. Spoon equal portions of cheese mixture into center of tortillas and roll up. Heat canola oil in a large skillet. Place burritos seam-side down in skillet and fry until heated through, turning once. Burritos will burn easily, so watch carefully. Serve immediately, with sour cream and salsa.
✦ 6 servings.

✦ Nutritional information per serving

Calories: 205.7	Saturated Fat: 3.1g	Calories from Fat: 40.8%
Protein: 7.3g	Cholesterol: 11mg	Calories from Carbohydrate: ... 45.2%
Carbohydrate: 23.6g	Dietary Fiber: 2.4g	Calories from Protein: 14.0%
Total Fat: 9.4g	Sodium: 417mg	

PICNIC POLENTA TORTE

4 cloves garlic, minced
½ teaspoon olive oil
1 (14 ounce) can vegetable broth
2½ cups water
salt and pepper
1½ cups yellow cornmeal
⅓ cup Neufchâtel or lite cream
  cheese, softened
3½ ounces goat cheese, softened
1 egg white
1 cup thinly sliced zucchini
1 cup thinly sliced yellow squash
1 tablespoon fresh thyme leaves
2 tablespoons grated Parmesan
  cheese

✦ Sauté garlic in olive oil in a large saucepan over medium heat until golden, about 3 minutes. Add broth, water, and salt and pepper to taste. Bring to a boil. Gradually stir in cornmeal and cook until very thick, stirring constantly, about 5 to 10 minutes. Spread in bottom of a greased 9-inch springform pan. Combine Neufchâtel cheese, goat cheese and egg white in a food processor. Blend until smooth. Spread over polenta. Top with zucchini and squash arranged alternately in concentric circles. Sprinkle with thyme and Parmesan and bake in preheated 400° oven for 15 minutes or until lightly browned. Serve warm or at room temperature.

✦ 8 servings.

VEGETARIAN

*When my husband's father was very young, in the "old country,"
he was sort of a mama's boy — always hanging on, always underfoot.
This was difficult for his mother, especially when she was preparing for
the holidays, and she devised a way to make him feel needed and yet get him out
from under foot. She would tell him that she wanted him to go across the village
to borrow a "milchig" pot that she needed. It was a long way to go across the
village and back, and when he returned about an hour and a half later, his
mother contritely apologized and told her son that she had made a mistake —
she needed a "fleishig" pot, but she had already found one to use, so would he
please return the "milchig" pot? It worked, and her preparations were
accomplished without too much interruption. This story lives on in our
family after all these years, and when our children or grandchildren get under foot, we threaten to send them
"across the village to get a 'milchig' pot"! It has become
one of our treasured traditions.*

SPICY TAMALE PIE

Dairy

1 large yellow onion, chopped
1 (4 ounce) can chopped green chiles
1 (4 ounce) can chopped jalapeño
   peppers
1 (14½ ounce) can chopped tomatoes
1 (12 ounce) package frozen yellow corn,
   thawed
1½ teaspoons garlic, minced
1 teaspoon dried basil
½ teaspoon dried oregano
½ teaspoon cumin powder
1 teaspoon salt
1-2 teaspoons sugar
2 tablespoons chili powder
2 cups skim milk
1½ cups cornmeal
2 eggs, lightly beaten
grated cheese, sour cream, salsa, optional

Note: This dish freezes well.

✦ Coat a large saucepan with nonstick vegetable spray. Add onion and sauté until soft, about 5 minutes. Stir in chiles, jalapeños, tomatoes, corn, garlic and seasonings. Reduce heat and simmer, stirring occasionally, 2-3 minutes. Pour milk into a medium saucepan. Heat to a simmer and gradually add cornmeal. Cook, stirring constantly, until mixture begins to thicken. Slowly add beaten eggs and heat for 1 minute, then remove from heat. Add to corn mixture and stir gently. Pour into a 9 x 13-inch baking dish which has been coated with nonstick vegetable spray. Bake in preheated 350° oven for 1 hour. If desired, sprinkle with cheese during the last 5 minutes of cooking. Let stand 5 minutes before serving. Serve with sour cream and salsa.

✦ 8 servings.

MUSHROOM AND LEEK EMPANADAS

Dairy

2 large leeks
1½ teaspoons olive oil
1 pound mushrooms, chopped
3 roasted green or red peppers,
   chopped
2 tablespoons whipping cream
¼ cup dry sherry
3 tablespoons seasoned bread crumbs
salt and pepper
1 package frozen puff pastry, thawed
1 egg, lightly beaten with
   1 tablespoon water

Note: This dish freezes well and can go directly from freezer to oven without defrosting. Add 5 minutes to cooking time.

✦ Chop white and green parts of leeks. Heat oil in a large skillet and sauté leeks until beginning to soften, about 3 minutes. Add mushrooms and peppers and sauté 2 minutes. Stir in cream and sherry. Bring to a boil and continue cooking until all liquid has evaporated, about 10 minutes. Remove from heat and stir in bread crumbs and salt and pepper to taste. Roll out 1 sheet of puff pastry on a floured surface until thin. Cut into 16 squares. Place 1 tablespoon mushroom mixture in center of each square. Fold 1 corner over to make a triangle. Crimp edges with a fork to seal and place on greased baking sheet. Repeat with second pastry sheet. Brush empanadas with egg wash and bake in preheated 375° oven for 25 to 30 minutes or until lightly browned.

✦ 8 servings (32 empanadas).

RATATOUILLE TART

Dairy

2 tablespoons olive oil, divided
6 large cloves garlic, minced
1 large onion, chopped
1 medium green bell pepper, seeded and chopped
1 medium red bell pepper, seeded and chopped
1 pound Japanese eggplants, cut in ½-inch rounds
1 teaspoon dried thyme
salt and pepper
¼ cup golden raisins, optional
3 tablespoons tomato paste
12 sheets phyllo dough
4 tablespoons plus 1 teaspoon grated Parmesan cheese, divided
¾ cup grated provolone cheese
6 plum tomatoes, sliced ¼-inch thick
2 medium zucchini, sliced ¼-inch thick
1 egg white, lightly beaten
fresh thyme leaves

✦ Heat 1½ teaspoons oil in a large skillet over medium-high heat. Sauté garlic and onion for 3 minutes. Add bell peppers and eggplant. Sprinkle with 1½ teaspoons oil and thyme. Season with salt and pepper and sauté 10 minutes. Reduce heat to low. Add raisins, if desired, cover and cook until eggplant is tender, about 10 minutes. Uncover and stir in tomato paste. Continue cooking 5 minutes, then transfer to a large strainer to allow excess liquid to drain.

✦ Coat a 9-inch springform pan with non-stick vegetable spray. Press one sheet phyllo into pan, allowing it to extend above rim of pan. (Cover remaining sheets of phyllo with a damp towel.) Brush with some of remaining oil and sprinkle with 1 teaspoon Parmesan. Top with another sheet of phyllo, oil and 1 teaspoon cheese. Repeat with remaining sheets, adjusting sheets so entire rim is covered. Spoon eggplant mixture into shell, sprinkle with provolone and lay tomato and zucchini slices in overlapping circles on top. Brush with remaining oil, season with salt and pepper and sprinkle with remaining Parmesan. Fold overhanging sheets of phyllo decoratively along edges of pan and brush with beaten egg white. Bake in pre-heated 350° oven until zucchini is tender and tart is set, about 1 hour. Cool, sprinkle with fresh thyme, remove from pan and cut in wedges. Serve at room temperature.

✦ 6 servings.

VEGETARIAN

✦ Brush a little oil on the grater before you start grating, and the cheese will wash off easily.

VAIL VALLEY
VEGETABLE STRUDEL

1½ tablespoons olive oil, divided
1 large yellow onion, sliced thin
8 cloves garlic, minced
1 red bell pepper, seeded and cut into strips
1 green bell pepper, seeded and cut into strips
1 yellow bell pepper, seeded and cut into strips
3 Japanese eggplants, cubed
1 medium zucchini, cubed
1 medium summer squash, cubed
2 tablespoons minced fresh thyme
salt and pepper
¼ cup pine nuts or sliced almonds
⅓ cup golden raisins
12 Kalamata olives, chopped
16 sheets phyllo dough
½ cup light butter spread, melted
5 ounces part skim milk mozzarella cheese, thinly sliced and cut into strips

Note: May be prepared 1 day in advance. Stop before brushing tops with butter and baking. Wrap tightly and refrigerate. Let stand at room temperature for 30 minutes before brushing tops and baking.

✦ Place 1½ teaspoons olive oil in a large skillet over medium-high heat. Add onions and garlic and sauté until soft, about 10 minutes. Remove from skillet and set aside. Add 1½ teaspoons oil to skillet and sauté peppers until beginning to soften, about 5 minutes. Add remaining vegetables and oil and sauté until tender, about 15 minutes. Remove from heat. Stir in thyme, salt and pepper to taste, pine nuts, raisins and olives. Lay one phyllo sheet on work surface. Cover remaining with a damp towel. Brush phyllo with butter and top with another sheet. Brush with butter and repeat until 8 sheets have been stacked. Spread half of onion mixture on long side of sheet, leaving a 3-inch border on bottom and a 2-inch border on each side. Top with half of pepper mixture. Layer half of cheese over pepper mixture. Fold the 3-inch border over filling, then fold in each end and roll completely. Place seam-side down on a nonstick baking sheet. Repeat process with remaining phyllo and filling. Brush strudel tops with remaining butter. Bake in preheated 375° oven until golden brown, about 30 minutes. Let stand 5 minutes before slicing diagonally.

✦ 12 servings.

SAN LUIS VEGETABLE POT PIE

Dairy or Pareve | **Lighter** | ✡

15 pearl onions, peeled
2 russet potatoes, peeled and cubed
2 sweet potatoes, peeled and cubed
1 red bell pepper, seeded and cut in eighths
1 green bell pepper, seeded and cut in eighths
10 ounces mushrooms, chopped
1 rutabaga, peeled and cubed
1 turnip, peeled and cubed
10 baby carrots
1 tablespoon olive oil
2 teaspoons herbes de Provence
1 cup frozen peas, thawed
2 (14 ounce) cans vegetable broth, divided
1 cup red wine, divided
1 tablespoon cornstarch
1¼ cups water
1½ cups cornmeal
1 tablespoon grated Parmesan cheese, optional

✦ Blanch pearl onions in boiling water for 2 minutes. Drain. Place potatoes, sweet potatoes, peppers, mushrooms, rutabaga, turnip and carrots in a large plastic bag. Add oil and herbes de Provence and toss. Spread on 2 baking sheets coated with nonstick vegetable spray. Bake in preheated 425° oven for 45 minutes or until tender. Transfer to a 9 x 13-inch baking dish and top with pearl onions and peas. Season with salt and pepper to taste and mix well.

✦ While vegetables are roasting, combine 1 can broth and ¾ cup wine in a saucepan. Bring to a simmer. Mix remaining wine with cornstarch in a small bowl until smooth. Add to saucepan and stir until thickened, about 5 minutes. Pour over vegetables in baking dish and toss well to coat.

✦ For crust, combine 1 can broth with 1¼ cups water in a large saucepan. Bring to a boil. Gradually stir in cornmeal and continue stirring until very thick, about 10 minutes. Spread over vegetables. Reduce oven temperature to 350° and bake 15 minutes, or until heated through. Sprinkle with cheese, if desired, and place under broiler for 5 minutes.

✦ 8 servings.

✡ See Pareve Food Preparation, page 30

VEGETARIAN

✦ **Nutritional information per serving**

Calories: 330.9	Saturated Fat: 0.8g	Calories from Fat: 12.0%
Protein: 9.2g	Cholesterol: 1mg	Calories from Carbohydrate: ... 76.5%
Carbohydrate: 61.2g	Dietary Fiber: 9.2g	Calories from Protein: 11.5%
Total Fat: 4.3g	Sodium: 941mg	

GARBANZO BEAN LASAGNA

2 (15 ounce) cans garbanzo beans,
   rinsed and drained
4 tablespoons dry vermouth, divided
1 (28 ounce) can plum tomatoes,
   undrained
4 teaspoons dried parsley
¼ large green bell pepper, chopped
1 large sweet onion, chopped
2 scallions, chopped
4 cloves garlic, crushed
¼ cup water
⅔ cup dry sherry or dry red wine
1 tablespoon minced fresh oregano
½ teaspoon salt
1 teaspoon honey
½ teaspoon pepper
½ teaspoon ground cumin
2 cups 2% fat cottage cheese
2 eggs, lightly beaten
1 tablespoon ground coriander
⅓ cup fat-free ricotta cheese
½ teaspoon crushed red pepper
12 lasagna noodles, cooked and
   drained according to package
   directions
oil
2 cups shredded mozzarella cheese

✦ Place 1 can garbanzo beans in food processor. Pulse briefly, add remaining beans and 2 tablespoons vermouth and pulse until beans are chopped, but not pureed. Remove to a bowl. Puree tomatoes in food processor. Add parsley and green pepper and chop for 10 seconds. Remove to a bowl. Place onions, scallions, garlic, remaining vermouth and ¼ cup water in a large skillet. Sauté until vegetables are soft, about 5 minutes. Add sherry and simmer until liquid has almost evaporated, about 10 minutes. Add bean mixture, tomato mixture, oregano, salt, honey, pepper and cumin. Cover and simmer 1 hour.

✦ Meanwhile, combine cottage cheese, eggs, coriander, ricotta and red pepper. Whip lightly. When ready to assemble, lightly coat a 9 x 13-inch baking pan with oil. Arrange 4 lasagna noodles in bottom. Top with a third of cheese mixture, then a third of bean and sauce mixture. Sprinkle with a third of mozzarella. Repeat 2 more times. Bake in preheated 375° oven for 45 minutes or until golden brown on top. Let stand 5 minutes before serving.

✦ 8 servings.

✦ Nutritional information per serving

Calories: 862.6	Saturated Fat: 4.8g	Calories from Fat: 13.5%
Protein: 45.1g	Cholesterol: 74mg	Calories from Carbohydrate: ... 64.7%
Carbohydrate: 133.8g	Dietary Fiber: 12.5g	Calories from Protein: 21.8%
Total Fat: 12.5g	Sodium: 564mg	

ROASTED VEGETABLE NAPOLEON

2 medium baking potatoes
2 medium sweet potatoes
2 medium red onions
1 medium summer squash
1 medium zucchini
1 medium eggplant
4 plum tomatoes
4 teaspoons garlic olive oil, divided
salt and pepper
¾ cup ricotta cheese
1 teaspoon dried thyme
½ pound mozzarella cheese, cut in 12
  slices
6 rosemary sprigs

✦ Slice all vegetables diagonally: potatoes and onions in 6 pieces, squash and eggplant in 12 pieces, tomatoes in 3 pieces. Place potatoes and squash in a large plastic bag. Add 1 teaspoon oil and salt and pepper to taste. Toss to coat and turn onto a baking sheet which has been coated with nonstick vegetable spray. Spread in a single layer and bake in preheated 450° oven for 15 minutes or until tender and lightly browned. Repeat with eggplant and tomatoes, then with onions.

✦ Combine ricotta, thyme and salt and pepper to taste. Lay eggplant evenly on baking sheet and spread each slice with 1 tablespoon ricotta mixture. Layer with 1 slice each of baking potato, sweet potato, zucchini, summer squash, onion, mozzarella and tomato. Continue making stacks until all vegetables are used. Gently pick up one stack and invert it on another, so that stack begins and ends with eggplant. Skewer with a toothpick, remove toothpick and insert rosemary sprig to hold stack together. Repeat with remaining stacks. Reduce oven temperature to 400°, return baking sheet to oven and bake 5 minutes, or until mozzarella is melted. Serve warm or at room temperature.

✦ 6 servings.

VEGETARIAN CASSOULET

1 onion, diced
8 cloves garlic, minced
4 cups chopped assorted fresh
  vegetables
1 (28 ounce) can chopped tomatoes
pepper
1 teaspoon dried thyme
½ teaspoon crushed red pepper,
  optional
1 tablespoon tamari sauce
2 cups cooked lentils
2 cups cooked white beans
¾ cup grated mozzarella cheese

✦ Cook onions and garlic in 2 tablespoons water in a covered pan until tender, about 10 minutes. Add assorted vegetables, tomatoes, pepper, thyme, red pepper and tamari sauce. Cook an additional 10 minutes. Add lentils and beans and heat briefly. Pour into a greased casserole dish and sprinkle with cheese. Bake in preheated 350° oven for 35 minutes or until cheese is melted and golden.
✦ 8 servings.

✦ Nutritional information per serving

Calories: 179.8	Saturated Fat: 1.3g	Calories from Fat: 12.2%
Protein: 13.2g	Cholesterol: 6mg	Calories from Carbohydrate: ... 59.8%
Carbohydrate: 28.1g	Dietary Fiber: 8.2g	Calories from Protein: 28.0%
Total Fat: 2.6g	Sodium: 239mg	

VEGETARIAN KISHKA

1 box traditional onion crackers
1 medium onion, quartered
1 stalk celery, quartered
1 medium carrot, quartered
1 egg, beaten
½ cup pareve margarine, melted
salt, pepper and garlic powder

Note: May be frozen. To reheat, defrost and heat in a 375° oven for 6 to 8 minutes.

✦ Place crackers in a food processor and chop into crumbs. Pour into a medium bowl. Place onion, celery and carrot in processor and pulse until finely chopped. Add to crumbs. Add egg and mix well. Pour margarine over mixture and season to taste. Mold into 2 long narrow logs. Place each log on a piece of aluminum foil which has been coated with nonstick vegetable spray. Roll up and seal ends. Place on baking sheet and bake in preheated 350° oven for 45 minutes. Remove from oven, carefully unroll foil and slice each log into ½-inch slices. Serve hot.
✦ 12 servings as appetizer, 6 as side dish.

RUGGED VEGETABLE RAGOUT

1 teaspoon olive oil
1 cup coarsely chopped onion
1 tablespoon minced garlic
1½ cups thickly sliced zucchini
2 (15 ounce) cans yellow hominy, drained
1 (17 ounce) can unsalted corn, drained
1 (14 ounce) can low-sodium tomatoes, chopped and undrained
2 cups pareve chicken-flavored broth
1 (15 ounce) can unsalted pinto beans, drained
1 teaspoon cumin powder
1 teaspoon dried oregano
1 teaspoon dried basil
1 tablespoon chili powder
3 cups cooked couscous
no-fat sour cream, optional

✦ Coat a large saucepan with nonstick vegetable spray. Add olive oil and place over medium heat. Add onion and garlic and sauté 3 minutes. Add zucchini and sauté 2 more minutes. Add remaining ingredients except couscous. Bring to a boil, cover and reduce heat. Simmer until zucchini is soft, about 20 minutes. Spoon ½ cup couscous into individual serving bowls, top with zucchini mixture and sour cream, if desired, and serve.

✦ 6 servings.

✡ See Pareve Food Preparation, page 30

V E G E T A R I A N

✦ **Nutritional information per serving**

Calories: 407.9	Saturated Fat: 0.8g	Calories from Fat: 9.6%
Protein: 18.6g	Cholesterol: 1mg	Calories from Carbohydrate: ... 72.6%
Carbohydrate: 75.3g	Dietary Fiber: 11.2g	Calories from Protein: 17.9%
Total Fat: 4.4g	Sodium: 770mg	

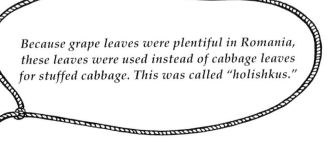

Because grape leaves were plentiful in Romania, these leaves were used instead of cabbage leaves for stuffed cabbage. This was called "holishkus."

VEGETARIAN CABBAGE ROLLS

1 head cabbage, cored
1 pound frozen mixed vegetables,
  thawed
½ cup uncooked rice
1 onion, diced
1 (10 ounce) jar apricot preserves
1 (28 ounce) can tomatoes
½ cup firmly packed brown sugar
½ cup sugar
salt and pepper
1 (12 ounce) can tomato sauce
lemon juice
brown sugar

✦ Place cabbage in a large pot, cover with water and bring to a boil. Cook until leaves begin to fall off. Remove from heat and drain. Combine mixed vegetables and rice in a large bowl. Lay one cabbage leaf flat on work surface. Place 3 tablespoons vegetable mixture in center, fold ends in and roll up. Repeat with 11 more leaves. Spread diced onion in bottom of a baking dish which has been coated with nonstick vegetable spray. Place cabbage rolls seam-side down over onion. Combine apricot preserves, tomatoes, brown sugar, sugar and salt and pepper to taste in a food processor or blender. Process until smooth and pour over rolls. Bake rolls, uncovered, in preheated 350° oven until sauce begins to boil. Add tomato sauce and lemon juice and additional brown sugar to taste. Continue baking, covered, until cabbage is soft and rolls are slightly browned, about 2½ to 3 hours.

✦ 6 servings.

✦ **Nutritional information per serving**

Calories: 280.3	Saturated Fat: 0.2g	Calories from Fat: 2.8%
Protein: 6.4g	Cholesterol: 0mg	Calories from Carbohydrate: ... 88.6%
Carbohydrate: 66.1g	Dietary Fiber: 5.5g	Calories from Protein: 8.6%
Total Fat: 0.9g	Sodium: 410mg	

1.
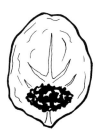

2.
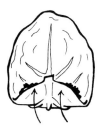

3.

4.

5.

PASTA AND GRAINS

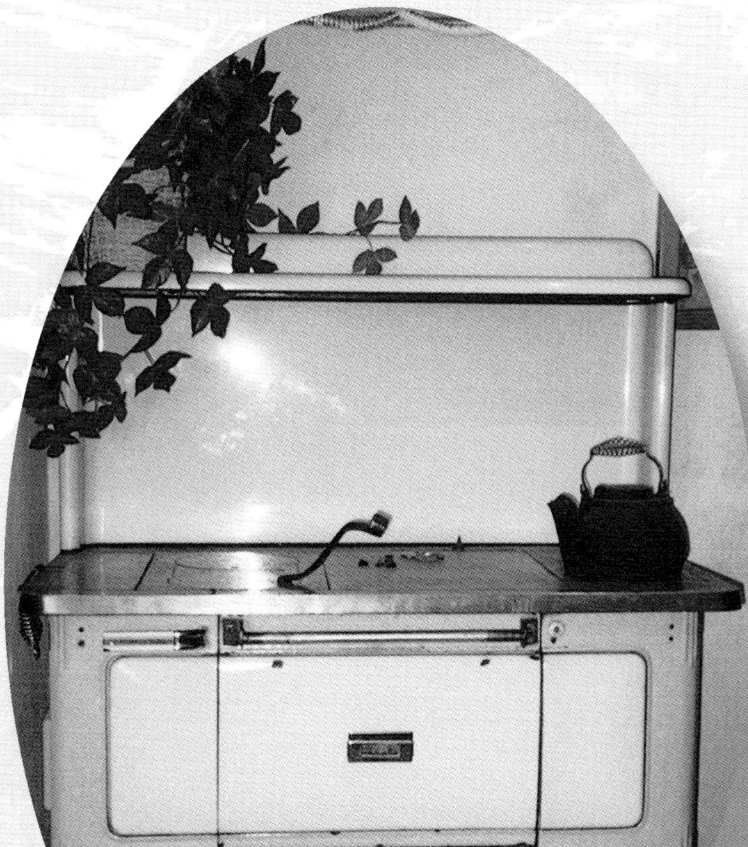

PASTA AND GRAINS INDEX

ROASTED GARLIC SPAGHETTI SAUCE

1 head garlic
2 tablespoons extra virgin olive oil, divided
1 pound very lean ground chuck
1½ teaspoons garlic powder
½ teaspoon oregano
1 teaspoon onion powder
salt and pepper
1 pound mushrooms, sliced
1 medium onion, chopped
1 large bunch fresh basil, chopped
1 Anaheim green chile, seeded and chopped
2½ pounds fresh Italian tomatoes, peeled
4 cups tomato sauce
1 (6 ounce) can tomato paste
1½ tablespoons sugar
½ teaspoon crushed red pepper

Hint: To skin tomatoes easily, drop into boiling water for 30 seconds, then run under cold water. The skin will slip off easily.

✦ Trim ¼ inch from top of garlic head to expose cloves. Place on square of foil and drizzle with 1 tablespoon olive oil. Wrap tightly and bake in preheated 375° oven for 45 minutes, until soft. Remove from oven and set aside. Brown beef in a 4-quart saucepan. Add garlic powder, oregano, onion powder and salt and pepper to taste. Cook over moderately-high heat until meat is brown, stirring occasionally. Remove from pan. Add remaining oil to same pan and sauté onion and mushrooms until onion is translucent. Return meat to pan and stir. Chop basil in a food processor. Add chile and fresh tomatoes. Squeeze roasted garlic from skins into processor. Process until chopped and add to meat mixture. Add remaining ingredients, bring to a boil, reduce heat and simmer, covered, 1 hour, stirring occasionally. Serve over your choice of pasta.

✦ 8 servings.

P A S T A

My mother-in-law makes wonderful food. As long as she has known me, I have been on a diet. Being a good Jewish mother, she can't stand to see me not eat everything she makes. Therefore, no matter what she makes, she always prefaces serving me with "there's nothing in it"! She then goes on to list the ingredients, saying "there's only a little sugar, only a cube of margarine..." Of course I always eat it. That's why I am always on a diet!

SZECHUAN NOODLES WITH PEANUT SAUCE

10 ounces dry oriental-style noodles,
   cooked according to package
   directions
1¾ teaspoons dark sesame oil,
   divided
½ cup plain yogurt
4 tablespoons peanut butter
4 tablespoons rice wine vinegar
3 tablespoons low-sodium soy sauce
2 teaspoons sugar
1½ teaspoons crushed red pepper
½ teaspoon minced garlic

Garnish:
½ cup chopped scallions
½ cup diced red bell pepper
½ cup chopped roasted peanuts

✦ Drain and rinse cooked noodles thoroughly. Toss with 1½ teaspoons sesame oil and refrigerate until chilled. Combine remaining ¼ teaspoon sesame oil with remaining ingredients in a food processor and blend until smooth. To serve, place 1 cup noodles on individual serving plate. Top with ¼ cup sauce and garnish with scallions, red peppers and peanuts.
✦ 4 servings.

FRESH BASIL MARINARA SPAGHETTINI

5 large cloves garlic
1½ ounces fresh basil leaves
2 (28 ounce) cans Italian crushed
   tomatoes, with juice
¼ cup extra virgin olive oil
1 teaspoon salt
½ teaspoon freshly ground pepper
sugar
½ teaspoon crushed red pepper,
   optional
½ cup Parmesan cheese, optional
1 pound spaghettini, cooked
   according to package directions

✦ Chop garlic in food processor. Add basil leaves and pulse briefly to chop coarsely. Remove to a saucepan. Add tomatoes, olive oil, salt and pepper. Bring to a boil, reduce heat and simmer 20 minutes. Add sugar if sauce tastes acidic. Cook an additional 5 minutes. Serve over pasta, sprinkled with crushed red pepper and Parmesan, if desired.
✦ 6 servings.

✿ See Pareve Food Preparation, page 30

PASTA WITH TURKEY SAUSAGE

2 tablespoons olive oil
3 cloves garlic, minced
⅓ cup chopped red onion
1 (28 ounce) can crushed Italian tomatoes
½ teaspoon crushed dried rosemary
1 teaspoon crushed dried basil, or more
1 (4 ounce) can sliced black olives, drained
¼ teaspoon freshly ground pepper
4 tablespoons tomato paste
¾ cup water
1 to 2 teaspoons sugar, to taste
1 pound turkey sausage (see following recipe)
1 pound bowtie pasta, cooked according to package directions
crushed red pepper, optional

✦ Heat olive oil in a large saucepan. Sauté garlic and onion until soft, about 4 minutes. Add tomatoes, rosemary, basil, olives, pepper, tomato paste and water. Stir to combine. Cook over medium heat for 10 minutes. Add sugar if sauce tastes acidic. Add turkey sausage. Reduce heat and simmer 30 minutes. Serve over pasta, sprinkled with red pepper, if desired.

✦ 6 servings.

✦ **Nutritional information per serving**

Calories: 514.1	Saturated Fat: 2.9g	Calories from Fat: 25.6%
Protein: 25.2g	Cholesterol: 60mg	Calories from Carbohydrate: ... 54.8%
Carbohydrate: 70.8g	Dietary Fiber: 4.2g	Calories from Protein: 19.5%
Total Fat: 14.7g	Sodium: 262mg	

P
A
S
T
A

TURKEY SAUSAGE

1 pound ground turkey
½ teaspoon each basil, thyme and sage
¼ teaspoon each cumin, marjoram, pepper, oregano, cayenne pepper, garlic powder, nutmeg and ground ginger
1 tablespoon matzo meal

✦ Combine all ingredients in a large bowl. Form into patties or logs. Brown thoroughly in a skillet which has been coated with non-stick vegetable spray.

GEORGETOWN PASTA

Marinade:
2 tablespoons chopped fresh basil,
    or 2 teaspoons dried
2 tablespoons olive oil
2 tablespoons red wine vinegar
2 tablespoons balsamic vinegar
¼ teaspoon salt
¼ teaspoon crushed red pepper
1 clove garlic, minced
2 pounds boneless, skinless chicken
    breasts, rinsed and patted dry
1 pound angel hair or penne pasta,
    cooked according to package
    directions
fresh parsley

Sauce:
4 cups chopped fresh tomatoes
2 tablespoons chopped fresh basil,
    or 2 teaspoons dried
3 tablespoons sliced Kalamata olives
2 tablespoons olive oil
2 tablespoons red wine vinegar
2 tablespoon balsamic vinegar
¼ teaspoon salt
¼ teaspoon crushed red pepper
2 cloves garlic, minced
2 teaspoons capers, optional
¼ to ½ cup chicken broth, optional

*Variation: For a delicious dairy meal,
omit chicken and chicken broth
and add ⅓ cup crumbled feta
cheese.*

✦ Mix basil, olive oil, vinegars, salt, red pepper and garlic in a large zip-lock bag. Add chicken, seal and turn to coat. Marinate chicken for at least 30 minutes, then remove from marinade and grill until cooked through. Slice.

✦ Combine all sauce ingredients in a bowl and stir well. Let stand at least 10 minutes. Transfer to a saucepan and heat gently. If more sauce is needed, add chicken broth. To serve, place chicken on pasta, top with sauce and garnish with parsley.

✦ 6 servings.

✦ **Nutritional information per serving**

Calories: 560.6	Saturated Fat: 2.0g	Calories from Fat: 19.9%
Protein: 46.9g	Cholesterol: 88mg	Calories from Carbohydrate: ... 46.2%
Carbohydrate: 64.0g	Dietary Fiber: 3.2g	Calories from Protein: 33.9%
Total Fat: 12.3g	Sodium: 544mg	

SILVER CREEK
CHICKEN PASTA

Meat

3 tablespoons bottled Italian dressing
3 tablespoons teriyaki sauce
3 tablespoons soy sauce
2 tablespoons balsamic vinegar,
  divided
⅛ teaspoon crushed red pepper
1½ pounds boneless, skinless chicken
  breasts, rinsed and patted dry
1 bunch green onions, chopped
1 shallot, chopped
3 large cloves garlic, minced
⅓ cup chopped fresh parsley
1 jalapeño, chopped
2 tablespoons pareve margarine
2 tablespoons olive oil
1 teaspoon dried basil
1 (10 ounce) can condensed chicken
  broth
1 tomato, chopped
6 oil-packed sun-dried tomatoes,
  drained and chopped
½ red bell pepper, seeded and sliced
salt and pepper
1 pound linguini, fettuccini or angel
  hair pasta, cooked according to
  package directions

✦ Combine salad dressing, teriyaki sauce, soy sauce, 1 tablespoon balsamic vinegar and crushed red pepper in a large zip-lock bag. Add chicken, seal and turn to coat. Marinate chicken at least 30 minutes and up to 4 hours.

✦ Sauté green onions, shallots, garlic, parsley and jalapeño in margarine and olive oil in a medium saucepan until soft. Add basil and broth and simmer until reduced by one quarter. While broth is reducing, remove chicken from marinade and grill. When chicken is almost done, add tomatoes, red peppers and remaining balsamic vinegar to sauce. Heat gently. Slice chicken across grain and add to sauce. Serve over pasta.

✦ 6 servings.

GRILLED SALMON PESTO
WITH ANGEL HAIR PASTA

Dairy or Pareve ✿

1½ pounds salmon
salt and pepper
lemon juice
1 (28 ounce) jar marinara sauce
1 (8 ounce) jar pesto
1 pound angel hair pasta, cooked
  according to package directions
shredded Parmesan cheese, optional

✦ Season salmon with salt and pepper to taste and sprinkle with lemon juice. Grill. Heat marinara to a simmer and stir in pesto. Pour over pasta and top with sliced salmon. Sprinkle with Parmesan, if desired.

✦ 6 servings.

✿ See Pareve Food Preparation, page 30

**P
A
S
T
A**

CHILLED SESAME NOODLES

2 tablespoons peanut or canola oil
2 tablespoons sesame oil
½ teaspoon crushed red pepper, or to taste
½ cup sliced pea pods
¼ cup chopped roasted peanuts
¼ cup chopped green onions
2 tablespoons honey
2 tablespoons soy sauce
2 tablespoons chopped cilantro
1 tablespoon toasted sesame seeds
1 teaspoon salt
½ teaspoon hot chili sauce
½ pound thin spaghetti, cooked according to package directions

✦ Combine oils and red pepper in a medium bowl. Microwave until hot, about 1 minute. Add remaining ingredients except pasta and blend well. Add pasta and toss to coat. Refrigerate at least one hour.
✦ 4 servings.

Hint: *To toast sesame seeds, microwave 1 to 2 minutes until lightly browned, or bake in a 350° oven 3 to 5 minutes. Watch carefully.*

CREAMY ANGEL HAIR PASTA

1 teaspoon chopped fresh rosemary or ¼ teaspoon dried
1 teaspoon chopped fresh thyme or ¼ teaspoon dried
2 tablespoons chopped fresh basil
½ to 1 tablespoon minced garlic
½ teaspoon salt
¼ teaspoon freshly ground pepper
¼ cup extra virgin olive oil
4 cups chopped tomatoes
1 pound angel hair pasta
1 (4 ounce) carton light garlic and herb cream cheese

✦ Combine rosemary, thyme, basil, garlic, salt and pepper in a large bowl. Whisk in olive oil and add tomatoes. Toss and let sit at room temperature for 1 hour. Cook pasta according to package directions, drain and add to tomato mixture. Crumble cheese over top and toss until cheese melts. Serve immediately.
✦ 6 servings.

PASTA PUTTANESCA

2 tablespoons olive oil
4 large cloves garlic, minced
1 cup chopped fresh parsley
1½ ounces capers, drained
1 cup sliced, pitted Kalamata olives
¼ teaspoon crushed red pepper
4 cups chopped tomatoes
1 (4 ounce) can tomato sauce
2 teaspoons sugar
½ teaspoon salt
¼ teaspoon freshly ground pepper
1 pound linguini or thin spaghetti,
    cooked according to package
    directions

◆ Heat oil in a large saucepan over medium-high heat. Sauté garlic, parsley, capers, olives and red pepper for a few minutes. Add remaining ingredients except pasta. Bring to a boil, reduce heat and simmer, uncovered, for 1 hour. Serve over pasta.

◆ 6 servings.

◆ Nutritional information per serving

Calories: 448.7	Saturated Fat: 1.6g	Calories from Fat: 25.2%
Protein: 13.6g	Cholesterol: 0mg	Calories from Carbohydrate: ... 62.9%
Carbohydrate: 72.2g	Dietary Fiber: 4.5g	Calories from Protein: 11.8%
Total Fat: 12.9g	Sodium: 1,082mg	

WARM ZITI PASTA

1 (14½ ounce) can diced tomatoes
3 tablespoons olive oil
1½ tablespoons balsamic vinegar
1 clove garlic, minced
½ cup marinated sun-dried tomatoes,
    drained and chopped
⅓ cup chopped Greek olives
½ cup chopped red bell pepper
⅓ cup chopped fresh basil or 2
    teaspoons dried basil
½ teaspoon freshly ground pepper
1½ cups Italian 6 cheese blend or ¼
    cup each shredded mozzarella,
    provolone, Parmesan, romano,
    fontina and asiago
8 ounces ziti pasta, cooked according
    to package directions

◆ Combine all ingredients except pasta in a large bowl and toss well. Add pasta and toss again. Heat briefly in microwave, but do not melt cheese.

◆ 8 servings.

P
A
S
T
A

LODO LINGUINI

½ pound Brie cheese
4 very large tomatoes, chopped
1 cup fresh basil, julienned
3 cloves garlic, minced
¼ cup olive oil
½ teaspoon salt
½ teaspoon freshly ground pepper
8 ounces linguini pasta

Note: Delicious and very easy.

✦ Remove rind from Brie and cut into small pieces. Place in a large bowl and add remaining ingredients, except pasta. Let stand at room temperature for at least 2 hours. Cook pasta according to package directions, drain and immediately toss with tomato mixture.
✦ 4 main dish servings; 6 side dish servings.

✦ A few teaspoons of cooking oil added to water when boiling rice or pasta will prevent boiling over.

UPSIDE DOWN KUGEL

12 ounces medium wide noodles, cooked according to package directions
4 eggs, lightly beaten
1 cup sour cream
1 cup cottage cheese
½ cup sugar
1 tablespoon vanilla
1 tablespoon cinnamon
pinch of salt
¼ cup butter or margarine
1 cup firmly packed brown sugar
1 cup pecan halves

Note: This recipe can be prepared in advance and frozen. It can also be baked in a ring mold or bundt pan.

✦ Rinse noodles in cold water and drain. Place in a large bowl. Add eggs, sour cream, cottage cheese, sugar, vanilla, cinnamon and salt. Mix well. Place butter in a 9 x 13-inch baking pan. Heat in preheated 350° oven until butter melts. Sprinkle brown sugar over butter and press pecans into the sugar. Pour noodle mixture into pan and bake for 1 hour. Cool in pan for 10 minutes, run knife around edge and invert onto serving platter.
✦ 10 servings.

PUCKER UP
LEMON KUGEL

8 ounces wide noodles, cooked
  according to package directions
½ cup unsalted butter, melted
2 cups sour cream
juice of 3 lemons
5 ounces cream cheese, softened
1 cup sugar
5 eggs
1 cup golden raisins

✦ Rinse noodles in cold water and drain. Place butter, sour cream, lemon juice, cream cheese, sugar and eggs in a food processor. Process until well blended. Transfer to a large bowl and fold in noodles and raisins. Pour into a greased 9 x 13-inch pan. Bake in preheated 350° oven for 1 hour.
✦ 12 servings.

Note: This very lemony kugel is delicious with fish.

HOMESTEAD SWEET
NOODLE KUGEL

Dairy or Pareve | Traditional | Lighter ✡

8 ounces wide noodles, cooked
  according to package directions
2 large eggs
¼ cup sugar
¼ teaspoon cinnamon
¼ cup butter or pareve margarine,
  melted
3 tablespoons fine bread crumbs
¾ cup firmly packed brown sugar
1 (8 ounce) can pineapple slices,
  drained
1 (12 ounce) can pitted Bing cherries,
  drained

✦ Rinse noodles in cold water and drain. Beat eggs in a large bowl. Add sugar and cinnamon and mix well. Fold in noodles, butter and bread crumbs. Coat a ring mold or bundt pan with nonstick vegetable spray. Pat brown sugar in bottom. Place pineapple and cherries in a design on top of brown sugar. Add noodle mixture and bake in preheated 375° oven for 45 minutes. Unmold to a serving platter.
✦ 8 servings.

✡ See Pareve Food Preparation, page 30

**P
A
S
T
A**

✦ **Nutritional information per serving**

Calories: 299.2	Saturated Fat: 4.3g	Calories from Fat: 25.0%
Protein: 6.4g	Cholesterol: 95mg	Calories from Carbohydrate: ... 66.6%
Carbohydrate: 50.9g	Dietary Fiber: 1.7g	Calories from Protein: 8.4%
Total Fat: 8.5g	Sodium: 103mg	

FAVORITE NOODLE PUDDING

12 ounces fine noodles, cooked according to package directions
4 eggs, separated
4 tablespoons butter, softened
¾ cup sugar
1 (8 ounce) package cream cheese, softened
2 teaspoons vanilla
1 (16 ounce) carton sour cream
1 tablespoon lemon juice
1 tablespoon grated lemon peel

Topping:
2 tablespoons sugar
1 teaspoon cinnamon
¾ cup slivered almonds

✦ Rinse noodles in cold water and drain. Beat egg yolks in a small bowl until thick and lemon-colored. Cream butter, sugar, cream cheese and vanilla in a large bowl. Add egg yolks, sour cream and noodles. Mix well. Beat egg whites in a separate bowl until stiff. Fold in lemon juice and peel. Fold egg white mixture into noodle mixture. Pour into a 9 x 13-inch pan which has been coated with nonstick vegetable spray. For topping, combine sugar and cinnamon. Sprinkle over noodle mixture. Top with almonds. Bake in preheated 350° oven for 40 minutes.
✦ 12 servings.

Hint: Low fat cream cheese and sour cream may be used.

KASHA WITH VARNISHKES

Meat or Pareve **Traditional** **Lighter** ✡

2 tablespoons vegetable oil
1 onion, chopped
½ pound fresh mushrooms, sliced
1 cup medium-grain kasha (buckwheat)
1 egg, beaten
2 cups pareve beef- or chicken-flavored broth
2 cups bowtie noodles, cooked according to package directions
pepper and seasoning salt

✦ Heat oil in a skillet over medium-high heat. Sauté onions and mushrooms until onions are soft and mushrooms are lightly browned. Add kasha, brown a little more and stir in egg to coat. Stir over high heat until egg has dried and kernels have separated, 3 to 5 minutes. Cool slightly. Add broth and seasonings and cover tightly. Steam 10 minutes. Add noodles, mix well and correct seasonings. Cook a few minutes more, stirring well.
✦ 6 servings.

Note: Delicious served with brisket gravy.

✡ See Pareve Food Preparation, page 30

✦ Nutritional information per serving

Calories: 198.4	Saturated Fat: 1.0g	Calories from Fat: 26.8%
Protein: 6.8g	Cholesterol: 36mg	Calories from Carbohydrate: . 60.1%
Carbohydrate: 31.0g	Dietary Fiber: 1.7g	Calories from Protein: 13.2%
Total Fat: 6.1g	Sodium: 495mg	

ORZO AND TOASTED BARLEY PILAF

Meat or Pareve ✿

1 teaspoon vegetable oil
1 cup quick-cooking barley
1 large clove garlic, minced
3 cups chicken broth or pareve
 chicken-flavored broth
1 cup orzo
1 tablespoon chopped fresh thyme
 or 1 teaspoon dried
salt and freshly ground pepper
¼ cup chopped chives or scallion
 greens
½ cup toasted chopped pecans

✦ Heat oil in large skillet over medium-high heat. Sauté barley until golden and toasted, about 5 minutes. Add garlic and sauté 2 minutes more. Pour in chicken stock and bring to a boil. Add orzo, thyme and salt and pepper to taste. Stir, reduce heat to low, cover and simmer 10 minutes. Remove from heat and let rest 5 minutes to absorb any remaining liquid. Stir in chives or scallions and pecans. Correct seasonings and serve.
✦ 6 servings.

✿ See Pareve Food Preparation, page 30

ORZO WITH RED PEPPERS AND PINE NUTS

Pareve

2 teaspoons olive oil
⅓ cup pine nuts
1 medium red bell pepper, diced
1 medium green bell pepper, diced
1 medium onion, diced
2 cloves garlic, minced
2¼ cups cooked orzo
½ teaspoon salt
freshly ground pepper
⅛ teaspoon cayenne pepper or to taste
1 medium plum tomato, chopped
2 tablespoons snipped fresh chives

✦ Heat oil in a medium skillet over medium heat. Add pine nuts and cook until light brown and fragrant, stirring often. Remove pine nuts with a slotted spoon and set aside. Increase heat to medium-high. Add bell peppers, onion and garlic and sauté until tender, about 5 minutes, stirring occasionally. Add orzo, salt, pepper to taste and cayenne. Heat for 1 minute. Just before serving, add pine nuts, tomato and chives. Adjust seasonings to taste.
✦ 6 servings.

GRAINS

MIDDLE EASTERN COUSCOUS

Meat or Pareve ✡

2 cups chicken broth or pareve
  chicken-flavored broth
¼ cup margarine or pareve margarine
1 cup couscous
½ cup slivered almonds
¼ cup raisins
3 tablespoons honey
¼ teaspoon cinnamon
¼ teaspoon ground ginger
¼ teaspoon cumin powder
⅛ teaspoon pepper

✦ Bring broth and margarine to a boil in a medium saucepan. Stir in couscous. Remove from heat and let stand, covered, for 5 minutes. Stir in remaining ingredients. Spoon into a greased 1½-quart casserole dish. Bake, uncovered, in preheated 375° oven for 20 minutes.

✦ 6 servings.

✡ See Pareve Food Preparation, page 30

COUSCOUS WITH ASPARAGUS, LEEKS, CARROTS AND PINE NUTS

Pareve

1 (10 ounce) box couscous
2 tablespoons olive oil
1 large leek, white part only, sliced
1 clove garlic, minced
½ pound asparagus, cut in 1½-inch
  pieces
⅔ cup chopped carrots, parboiled
  for 2 minutes
½ cup lightly toasted pine nuts
salt and pepper

✦ Cook couscous according to package directions, keeping warm until ready to serve. Heat olive oil in a large skillet over medium-high heat. Sauté leek and garlic until soft, about 3 minutes. Add asparagus and carrots and sauté 2 more minutes. Add pine nuts and salt and pepper to taste. Heat through. Mound couscous on a platter and make a hole in center of mound. Arrange vegetables in center and serve.

✦ 8 servings.

LUSCIOUS LENTIL RICE

Pareve Lighter

1 tablespoon olive oil
1 onion, coarsely chopped
1 cup chopped celery
1½ cups sliced carrots
1 large clove garlic, minced
1 cup pareve long grain/wild rice mix
½ cup dried lentils
3 cups water or vegetable broth
½ teaspoon curry powder or to taste
½ cup chopped fresh parsley
salt and pepper

✦ Heat oil in a large skillet over medium-high heat. Sauté onions until they begin to soften. Add celery, carrots and garlic and sauté 2 more minutes. Add rice and lentils. Add water or broth, bring to a boil, then reduce heat to medium-low. Cover and cook until liquid is absorbed, 15 to 20 minutes. Stir in curry powder, parsley and salt and pepper to taste.
✦ 4 servings.

Note: This dish freezes well and is delicious with grilled chicken.

✦ Nutritional information per serving

Calories: 334.3	Saturated Fat: 0.8g	Calories from Fat: 14.4%
Protein: 13.1g	Cholesterol: 0mg	Calories from Carbohydrate: 70.3%
Carbohydrate: 60.5g	Dietary Fiber: 12.1g	Calories from Protein: 15.3%
Total Fat: 5.5g	Sodium: 218mg	

ALMOND RICE

Meat

1 cup long grain white rice
¼ pound fresh mushrooms, sliced
2 tablespoons pareve margarine, melted
2 cups chicken broth
½ cup toasted slivered almonds
3 scallions, chopped
⅛ teaspoon pepper

✦ Sauté mushrooms and rice in margarine until lightly brown. Combine with remaining ingredients in a 3-quart casserole dish. Cover tightly and bake in preheated 350° oven for 1 hour. Stir to fluff before serving.
✦ 4 servings.

FRONT RANGE RICE

3 tablespoons pareve margarine
1 tablespoon olive oil
½ cup chopped onion
1 cup jasmine or white rice
2 cups chicken broth
½ teaspoon salt
¼ teaspoon pepper
⅓ cup raisins
2 tablespoons chopped fresh parsley
½ cup toasted slivered almonds

✦ Heat margarine and olive oil in a skillet over medium-high heat. Sauté onions until tender. Add rice and cook over low heat, stirring constantly, until rice is golden. Add broth, salt and pepper. Bring to a boil, then cover and reduce heat. Simmer for 20 minutes. Remove from heat and stir in raisins and parsley. Let stand, covered, until all liquid is absorbed. Add almonds, stir and serve.

✦ 6 servings.

RISOTTO WITH ARTICHOKES AND PEAS

1 tablespoon margarine
2 tablespoons olive oil
½ cup chopped onion
2 cloves garlic, minced
1½ cups Arborio rice
4 cups pareve chicken-style broth, divided
1 (14 ounce) can artichoke hearts, drained and quartered
1 tablespoon grated lemon peel
⅔ cup frozen peas, thawed
1½ tablespoons lemon juice
1 tablespoon chopped fresh dill
¼ cup chopped fresh parsley
salt and pepper to taste
½ cup grated Parmesan cheese

✦ Heat margarine and oil in a large skillet over medium heat. Sauté onion and garlic until soft. Add rice and cook for 2 minutes, stirring constantly. Slowly stir in 1 cup chicken broth. Cover and reduce heat to low. Let cook until liquid is absorbed, about 10 minutes. Stir in second cup of broth and repeat procedure. Uncover rice and add artichoke hearts and lemon peel. Add third cup of broth slowly. Cover and cook 10 minutes, as before. Add peas, lemon juice, dill, parsley and salt and pepper to taste. Gradually stir in remaining broth, cover and cook until liquid is absorbed. Rice should be creamy but al dente in the middle. Stir in Parmesan just before serving. Serve immediately.

✦ 6 servings.

VEGETABLE INDEX

SAUTÉED LEEKS AND ASPARAGUS

Dairy or Pareve ✿

¾ tablespoon butter or pareve margarine
¾ tablespoon olive oil
1 large leek, coarsely chopped
1 pound asparagus, cut in 1-inch pieces
1 tablespoon fresh thyme leaves or 1 teaspoon dried
1½ tablespoons dry white wine
¾ tablespoon fresh lemon juice
salt and pepper

✦ Heat butter or margarine and oil in a large skillet. Add leeks and sauté until soft, about 5 minutes. Add asparagus, thyme and white wine. Cover and cook 5 minutes. Add lemon juice and salt and pepper to taste.
✦ 4 servings.

✿ See Pareve Food Preparation, page 30

V E G E T A B L E S

AWESOME ASPARAGUS

Pareve

1 pound asparagus
2 teaspoons olive oil
salt and pepper

✦ Place asparagus in a single layer on heavy duty foil. Sprinkle with oil and salt and pepper to taste. Fold foil and crimp edges to seal. Bake in preheated 350° oven for 20 minutes. Remove from oven and let rest 5 minutes before serving. May be served warm or cold.
✦ 4 servings.

BOULDER BROCCOLI CASSEROLE

Dairy

1 tablespoon flour
¼ cup margarine, melted
2 eggs, lightly beaten
1 (16 ounce) carton 2% fat cottage cheese
1 (16 ounce) package frozen chopped broccoli, thawed
4 ounces sharp cheddar cheese, grated
salt and pepper

✦ Blend flour and margarine in a large bowl. Beat in eggs, then add remaining ingredients and stir to blend. Pour into greased casserole and bake in preheated 350° oven for 55 to 60 minutes, or until lightly browned. Let rest 5 minutes before serving.
✦ 6 servings.

CLASSIC CARROT RING

1¼ cups flour
1 teaspoon baking soda
1 teaspoon baking powder
pinch of salt
cinnamon, optional
nutmeg, optional
1 cup vegetable shortening
½ cup firmly packed brown sugar
1 egg
1½ cups grated carrots
2 tablespoons lemon juice

Note: This can be made ahead and warmed before serving or frozen and reheated before serving.

✦ Sift flour, baking soda, baking powder, salt and cinnamon and nutmeg, if desired, together in a small bowl. Cream shortening and brown sugar together in a large bowl. Add egg and beat until well blended. Stir in carrots. Add half of flour mixture and beat until combined. Add lemon juice. Add remaining flour mixture and beat until well blended. Pour into an 8-cup ring mold which has been coated with nonstick vegetable spray. Bake in preheated 325° oven for 1 hour or until golden brown and a toothpick inserted in center comes out clean.

✦ 12 servings.

APPLE GLAZED CARROTS

✡

1 tablespoon butter or pareve
   margarine
1 (16 ounce) package fresh baby
   carrots
¾ cup unsweetened apple juice
1 teaspoon honey
salt and pepper
1½ teaspoons chopped parsley

✦ Melt butter or margarine over medium-high heat in a large skillet. Add carrots and cook 3 minutes or until just beginning to brown. Pour juice over carrots and stir in honey. Bring to a boil, then reduce heat to low and continue cooking until liquid has evaporated and glazed the carrots. Remove from heat, add salt and pepper to taste and sprinkle with parsley.

✦ 4 servings.

✡ See Pareve Food Preparation, page 30

✦ Mushrooms will stay fresh longer
when refrigerated in a brown paper bag.

A DILLY OF A CARROT

Pareve

6 medium carrots, peeled and sliced
   diagonally
2 tablespoons chopped fresh dill
4 teaspoons apple cider vinegar
2 tablespoons frozen apple juice
   concentrate, thawed

✦ Bring 1 inch of water to a boil in a medium saucepan. Place carrots in a steamer basket and set in pan. Sprinkle with dill, cover and steam until tender, about 10 minutes. Place in a bowl, toss with vinegar and juice and serve.
✦ 4 servings.

GRILLED CORN ON THE COB

Dairy

4 ears corn, husks and silk removed
1 lemon, quartered
pepper

✦ Place each ear of corn on a square of aluminum foil. Rub with a lemon quarter and sprinkle with pepper to taste. Tightly fold foil over corn and grill over moderate coals about 10 minutes, turning every 2 minutes to cook evenly. Serve with your choice of spread.

Chili Butter:
✦ Melt ½ cup unsalted butter or margarine. Stir in 1½ teaspoons chili powder and 1 tablespoon chopped parsley.

Curry Butter:
✦ Melt ½ cup unsalted butter or margarine. Stir in 1 teaspoon curry powder and 1½ teaspoons lime juice.

Herb Butter:
✦ Melt ½ cup unsalted butter or margarine. Stir in 2 tablespoons chopped chives, 1 tablespoon chopped parsley, ¼ teaspoon white pepper and ½ teaspoon lime juice.
✦ 4 servings.

VEGETABLES

CHEYENNE CORN PIE

½ cup butter, softened
¾ cup sugar
3 eggs
1 (4 ounce) can chopped green chiles, drained
½ cup shredded Monterey Jack cheese
½ cup shredded cheddar cheese
1 (15 ounce) can creamed corn
1 cup yellow cornmeal
1 tablespoon baking powder
¼ teaspoon salt
1 cup flour

✦ Cream butter and sugar in a large mixing bowl. Add eggs one at a time, beating well after each addition. Mix in chiles, corn and cheese. Stir in remaining ingredients. Pour into a greased 9-inch pie plate and bake in preheated 350° oven for 1 hour or until golden brown. Serve warm or at room temperature.
✦ 8 servings.

Note: For muffins, fill muffin tins two-thirds full and bake in a preheated 350° oven for 30 to 35 minutes.

CAPONATA WITH PINE NUTS

5 tablespoons olive oil, divided
6 Japanese eggplants, sliced ¼-inch thick
6 large cloves garlic, minced
3 medium onions, coarsely chopped
1 (28 ounce) can peeled Italian tomatoes, chopped, undrained
3 stalks celery, chopped
⅓ cup red wine vinegar
2 tablespoons sugar
¼ cup toasted pine nuts
⅓ cup capers, drained
½ cup green olives, halved, optional
¼ teaspoon crushed red pepper
salt and pepper

✦ Heat 2 tablespoons oil in a large skillet over medium heat. Sauté half of eggplant until lightly browned, about 10 minutes. Remove to a bowl and repeat with remaining eggplant and 2 tablespoons oil. Remove. Heat 1 tablespoon oil in same skillet. Add garlic and cook for 15 seconds. Add onions and cook until soft, about 10 minutes. Add tomatoes and celery. Cover, reduce heat to low and cook 10 minutes. Combine vinegar and sugar in a small bowl. Stir to dissolve sugar. Add to tomato mixture, stir, then add eggplant. Cover and cook over low heat until vegetables are tender, about 30 minutes. Add remaining ingredients. Serve warm or at room temperature.
✦ 10 servings.

Hint: To toast pine nuts, bake on a baking sheet in a preheated 350° oven for 5 minutes, stirring frequently.

EGGPLANT OLÉ!

1 eggplant
vegetable oil
1 (15 ounce) can tomato sauce
1 (4 ounce) can green chiles
½ cup sliced green onions
½ teaspoon ground cumin
½ teaspoon garlic salt
1 (12½ ounce) can pitted ripe olives,
   chopped
grated cheddar cheese, optional

✦ Slice eggplant ½-inch thick. Brush both sides with oil and place on baking sheet. Bake in preheated 350° oven until soft, about 20 minutes. While eggplant is baking, combine tomato sauce, chiles, green onion, cumin and garlic salt in a saucepan. Bring to a boil, then reduce heat to low and simmer 10 minutes. Place half of eggplant in bottom of a greased 9 x 13-inch baking dish. Top with half of sauce. Sprinkle with half of olives and layer with cheese, if desired. Repeat. Bake in 350° oven for 25 minutes, until lightly browned.
✦ 6 servings.

✿ See Pareve Food Preparation, page 30

**V
E
G
E
T
A
B
L
E
S**

ROSEMARY GREEN BEANS WITH HAZELNUTS

1 pound green beans
2 tablespoons butter or pareve
   margarine
2 large shallots, chopped
1 tablespoon chopped fresh rosemary
salt and pepper
¼ cup chopped toasted hazelnuts

✦ Cook beans in boiling water until crisp tender, about 5 minutes. Drain, refresh under cold water and pat dry. Melt butter or margarine in a large skillet over medium-high heat. Sauté shallots for 2 minutes, add rosemary and cook until shallots are tender, about 5 more minutes. Add green beans and toss until heated through. Season with salt and pepper to taste. Sprinkle with hazelnuts.
✦ 4 servings.

✿ See Pareve Food Preparation, page 30

HIGH COUNTRY HERBED PEAS

2 tablespoons pareve margarine
2 tablespoons dried onion flakes
¾ teaspoon garlic powder
1 teaspoon dried oregano
¼ teaspoon pepper
2 (10 ounce) packages frozen peas

✦ Place all ingredients except peas in a large microwave bowl. Microwave on high until butter is melted. Stir and mix in peas. Microwave until peas are cooked, 5 to 6 minutes. For stove top, cook peas according to package directions and drain. Add butter and spices and stir until butter melts.
✦ 8 servings.

SPINACH WITH ROASTED GARLIC BUTTER

1 head garlic
1½ teaspoons extra virgin olive oil
3 tablespoons light butter spread or pareve margarine
2 pounds spinach, washed and trimmed
salt and pepper

✦ Trim ¼ inch from top of garlic to expose cloves. Place on square of foil and drizzle with oil. Seal foil tightly and bake in preheated 400° oven until soft, about 20 to 30 minutes. Cool. Melt butter or margarine in a large skillet. Squeeze garlic cloves from skins into pan and mash slightly. Add spinach and toss until coated with butter. Cover and cook until spinach wilts. Season with salt and pepper to taste.
✦ 4 servings.

✡ See Pareve Food Preparation, page 30

LOUISVILLE SPINACH PARMESAN

Dairy

4 (10 ounce) packages frozen chopped spinach
1 cup grated Parmesan cheese
½ cup finely chopped onion
⅓ cup whipping cream
¼ cup butter, melted
½ teaspoon salt
½ teaspoon pepper
lemon wedges

✦ Cook spinach according to package directions. Drain and squeeze out excess moisture. Place in a large bowl and add remaining ingredients except lemon wedges. Mix well and pour into an 8-inch square glass baking dish which has been coated with nonstick vegetable spray. Bake in preheated 350° oven for 20 minutes. Garnish with lemon wedges.
✦ 8 servings.

STUFFED ACORN SQUASH

Pareve **Lighter**

2 acorn squash
1 cup peeled, chopped apples
½ cup raisins
½ cup chopped pecans
½ cup fresh cranberries
    or ¼ cup dried
2 tablespoons sugar
1 teaspoon lemon juice
¼ teaspoon cinnamon
¼ teaspoon nutmeg

✦ Wash and dry squash. Slice off and reserve tops. Scoop out seeds. Combine remaining ingredients in a large bowl. Stuff into squash and replace tops. Place on a baking sheet which has been coated with nonstick vegetable spray. Bake in preheated 350° oven until tender, about 1 hour and 45 minutes. Serve hot or cold.
✦ 4 servings.

✦ Nutritional information per serving

Calories: 272.6	Saturated Fat: 0.9g	Calories from Fat: 28.7%
Protein: 3.4g	Cholesterol: 0mg	Calories from Carbohydrate: ... 66.7%
Carbohydrate: 50.0g	Dietary Fiber: 2.6g	Calories from Protein: 4.6%
Total Fat: 9.6g	Sodium: 9mg	

VEGETABLES

SUMMER SQUASH SOUFFLÉ

1 tablespoon butter
1¾ cups milk
2 eggs, lightly beaten
½ cup flour
¼ cup sugar
¼ teaspoon cinnamon
2 summer squash, sliced ¼-inch thick

✦ Place butter in an 8-inch square glass baking dish and heat in preheated 350° oven until melted. Whisk milk and eggs together in a medium bowl. Add flour, sugar and cinnamon and blend well. Gently fold in squash. Pour into prepared dish and bake until firm and golden brown, about 1 hour. Let stand 5 minutes before serving.
✦ 6 servings.

ROUNDUP BAKED PUMPKIN

1 (10 to 12-inch) pumpkin
8 Granny Smith apples, cored and thinly sliced
1 (15 ounce) package golden raisins
1 cup chopped pecans
½ cup firmly packed brown sugar
1 teaspoon cinnamon
½ cup plum wine

✦ Cut top off pumpkin and scoop out and discard seeds. Place apples in a large bowl and add remaining ingredients. Toss to combine. Stuff into pumpkin. Place pumpkin in a shallow pan with 2 inches of water in bottom. Bake in preheated 350° oven for 2 to 2½ hours, until pumpkin is soft. Add more water to cover the bottom if pan dries out during cooking. Serve warm or at room temperature.
✦ 8 servings.

✦ Nutritional information per serving

Calories: 245.5	Saturated Fat: 0.8g	Calories from Fat: 31.9%
Protein: 2.2g	Cholesterol: 0mg	Calories from Carbohydrate: ... 64.7%
Carbohydrate: 42.7g	Dietary Fiber: 4.8g	Calories from Protein: 3.4%
Total Fat: 9.4g	Sodium: 9mg	

MAPLE ROASTED SQUASH AND PUMPKIN

Dairy or Pareve | Lighter ✡

1 large acorn squash
1 small pumpkin
¾ cup pure maple syrup
2 tablespoons pareve margarine or butter
¼ teaspoon salt

✦ Cut squash and pumpkin into 8 sections each. Remove and discard seeds. Place in a 9 x 13-inch baking dish which has been coated with nonstick vegetable spray. Drizzle with maple syrup, dot with margarine or butter and sprinkle with salt. Bake in preheated 400° oven for 45 minutes or until tender, basting occasionally. Syrup should bubble and almost glaze squash and pumpkin when done.
✦ 8 servings.

✡ See Pareve Food Preparation, page 30

✦ **Nutritional information per serving**

Calories: 127.8	Saturated Fat: 1.8g	Calories from Fat: 19.8%
Protein: 0.6g	Cholesterol: 8mg	Calories from Carbohydrate: ... 78.4%
Carbohydrate: 26.4g	Dietary Fiber: 0.3g	Calories from Protein: 1.8%
Total Fat: 3.0g	Sodium: 100mg	

PECAN CRUMBLE SWEET POTATOES

Pareve

½ cup flour
½ cup firmly packed brown sugar
½ teaspoon allspice
3 pounds sweet potatoes, peeled and thinly sliced
¼ cup margarine, melted
⅓ cup chopped pecans
½ cup pure maple syrup

✦ Combine flour, brown sugar and allspice in a small bowl. Place a third of potatoes in bottom of a greased 8 or 9 inch square pan. Pour a third of margarine over potatoes and top with a third of flour mixture and a third of pecans. Drizzle with a third of syrup. Repeat 2 more times. Tightly cover with foil and bake in preheated 350° oven until tender, about 1½ hours. Remove foil last 10 minutes of baking.
✦ 6 servings.

VEGETABLES

GLENWOOD SWEET POTATO DELIGHT

3 cups cooked yams (one 29 ounce
    [large] can or 3 fresh)
1 teaspoon vanilla
⅓ cup firmly packed brown sugar
½ teaspoon salt
2 egg whites, lightly beaten
⅓ cup skim milk
2 tablespoons butter
¼ cup flour
½ cup firmly packed brown sugar
⅓ cup chopped pecans

✦ Mash yams with vanilla, ⅓ cup brown sugar, salt, milk and egg whites in a large bowl. Mix until smooth. Pour into a 2-quart casserole which has been coated with non-stick vegetable spray. Cut butter into flour and ½ cup brown sugar in a small bowl. Add pecans and sprinkle over yams. Bake in preheated 350° oven until top is brown and bubbly and yams are set, about 30 minutes. Let stand 5 minutes before serving.
✦ 8 servings.

SOUTHWESTERN SWEET POTATOES

✿

3 pounds sweet potatoes, peeled and
    shredded
½ cup pareve margarine or unsalted
    butter
¼ cup lime juice
3 tablespoons sugar
⅔ cup tequila

Note: Yes, you really do use that much
    tequila!

✦ Sauté potatoes in margarine or butter in a large skillet for 5 minutes. Add remaining ingredients and cook until al dente. Serve.
✦ 8 servings.

✿ See Pareve Food Preparation, page 30

MASHED POTATOES
AND BUTTERNUT SQUASH

Pareve **Lighter**

8 large cloves garlic, unpeeled
1 teaspoon olive oil
2½ pounds russet potatoes, peeled
   and cubed
2½ pounds butternut squash, peeled
   and cubed
¼ cup pareve margarine
pinch of nutmeg
salt and pepper

✦ Place garlic cloves on a square of aluminum foil, drizzle with oil and seal foil to make a packet. Roast in preheated 400° oven until tender, about 30 minutes. Bring 1 inch of water to a boil in a large pot. Place potatoes and squash in a steamer rack and set over water. Cover and steam until tender, about 20 to 30 minutes, adding more water if necessary. Transfer vegetables to a large bowl. Squeeze garlic out of skins into bowl. Add margarine and mash until smooth. Season with nutmeg and salt and pepper to taste.

✦ 8 servings.

✦ **Nutritional information per serving**

Calories: 236.0	Saturated Fat: 1.1g	Calories from Fat: 23.5%
Protein: 4.6g	Cholesterol: 0mg	Calories from Carbohydrate: ... 69.1%
Carbohydrate: 43.2g	Dietary Fiber: 2.3g	Calories from Protein: 7.4%
Total Fat: 6.5g	Sodium: 81mg	

ANYTIME POTATOES

Dairy or Pareve

3 pounds potatoes, peeled and thinly
   sliced
1 onion, finely chopped
salt and pepper
½ cup butter or pareve margarine,
   thinly sliced

✦ Spread half of potatoes in an ungreased 9 x 13-inch glass baking dish. Sprinkle with half of onions and salt and pepper. Dot potatoes with half of the butter or margarine. Repeat with remaining ingredients. Cover tightly and bake in preheated 350° oven for 1 hour. Uncover and bake an additional 30 minutes.

✦ 8 servings.

✿ See Pareve Food Preparation, page 30

POTATO KNISH

Dairy or Pareve | Traditional | ✡

2 pounds potatoes
2 medium onions, chopped
4 tablespoons vegetable oil
2 tablespoons butter or pareve
  margarine
1 teaspoon salt
½ teaspoon pepper
1 package frozen puff pastry, thawed
1 egg beaten with 1 tablespoon water

Note: Can be frozen, baked or unbaked, for a month. Use plastic wrap between layers, making sure knishes do not touch each other.

✦ Peel and cube potatoes. Cover with water in a large saucepan. Bring to a boil, cover and reduce heat to low. Simmer until tender. While potatoes are cooking, sauté onions in oil in a large skillet until golden brown. Drain potatoes, add butter or margarine and mash. Add onions and salt and pepper. Beat until smooth. Roll one pastry sheet on floured board until 16 x 18 inches. Cut into 18 squares. Place 1½ tablespoons potato mixture, rolled into a ball, in center of each pastry square. Brush edges of square with egg wash and pinch edges together on top to seal. Flatten slightly and brush with egg wash. Place on a baking sheet which has been coated with nonstick vegetable spray. Repeat with remaining pastry sheet. Bake in preheated 425° oven until golden brown, about 15 to 20 minutes.
✦ Yields 3 dozen knishes.

✡ See Pareve Food Preparation, page 30

One of my pleasant childhood culinary memories is of my Bubbie Ruthel's potato knishes and challah. Every Friday Zaidy would proudly deliver large brown paper bags filled with chicken fat-loaded potato knishes and beautifully browned challah.... (B.C.P. — Before Cholesterol and Plastic Wrap).

POTATO KUGEL

6 large potatoes
½ teaspoon salt
2 tablespoons flour
4 eggs
1 large onion, cut in eighths
½ teaspoon garlic salt
salt and pepper
1 teaspoon instant pareve, beef, or
    chicken granules
¼ cup matzo meal
¼ cup cold water
¼ cup vegetable oil

*Variation: For muffins, coat muffin tins
with nonstick vegetable spray
and place 1 teaspoon oil in
each tin. Fill two-thirds full
with batter and bake in preheated 375° oven for one hour.*

✦ Peel and cut potatoes in eighths. Combine salt and flour with enough water to
cover potatoes in a large bowl. Stir to dissolve. (Omit flour during Passover.) Add
potatoes, cover and refrigerate overnight.
This will keep the potatoes very white.

✦ The following day, drain potatoes. Place a
third of potatoes, 1 egg and a third of onion
in food processor. Process until finely
grated, scraping down sides of processor
twice while processing. Remove to a large
bowl and repeat with remaining potatoes,
eggs and onions. Add fourth egg while processing the final batch. Add garlic salt, salt
and pepper, instant granules, matzo meal
and cold water. Blend well. Pour oil into 9 x
13-inch glass baking dish. Place in preheated 425° oven until very hot, 1 to 2 minutes. Pour potato mixture into dish and
bake 15 minutes. Reduce oven temperature
to 375° and bake until browned, about 1
hour.

✦ 12 servings.

✡ See Pareve Food Preparation, page 30

POTATO LATKES

4 pounds potatoes
2 tablespoons flour
3 eggs
1 large onion, cut in eighths
3 tablespoons matzo meal
salt and pepper
vegetable oil

*Hint: Latkes can be frozen. Freeze in
single layers with plastic wrap in
between. To reheat, defrost and
place in single layer on baking
sheets. Bake in preheated 350° oven
for 15 to 20 minutes, until crisp.*

✦ Peel and cut potatoes in eighths. Place in a
large bowl and cover with cold water. Add
flour and stir to dissolve. Cover and refrigerate overnight. This will keep the potatoes
very white.

✦ The following day, drain potatoes. Place a
third of potatoes, 1 egg and a third of onion
in food processor. Process until finely
grated. Remove to a large bowl and repeat
with remaining potatoes, eggs and onions.
Add matzo meal and salt and pepper to
taste. Blend well. Heat a quarter inch of oil
in a large skillet or electric frying pan to a
temperature of 375°. Spoon potato mixture
in scant ⅓ cups into oil. Fry until golden on
both sides and drain on paper towels. Add
oil as needed.

✦ Yields 2 dozen latkes.

VEGETABLES

FULL UP SPUD

4 large baking potatoes
4 large cloves garlic, unpeeled
½ teaspoon olive oil
1 large onion, diced
butter or margarine
1 cup low-fat cottage cheese
½ cup buttermilk
⅓ cup grated Parmesan cheese
salt and pepper
paprika
4 tablespoons chopped green onions

✦ Bake potatoes in preheated 400° oven until tender, about 1 hour. Cool slightly. While potatoes are baking, place garlic cloves on a square of aluminum foil, drizzle with olive oil and seal foil tightly to make a packet. Roast in oven with potatoes for about 20 minutes, or until tender. Cool. Melt a small amount of butter or margarine in a medium skillet. Sauté onions until soft.

✦ Cut a thin slice from top of each potato. Scoop out pulp into a large bowl, leaving skin intact. Squeeze garlic cloves from skins into potato pulp. Mash thoroughly. Add cottage cheese, buttermilk, Parmesan and salt and pepper to taste. Blend thoroughly. Stir in onions. Stuff each skin with potato mixture and sprinkle with paprika. Reduce oven temperature to 350° and bake until warmed through, about 15 minutes. Garnish with green onions.

✦ 4 servings.

✦ Nutritional information per serving

Calories: 191.0	Saturated Fat: 1.9g	Calories from Fat: 16.7%
Protein: 13.7g	Cholesterol: 9mg	Calories from Carbohydrate: ... 54.8%
Carbohydrate: 26.4g	Dietary Fiber: 2.5g	Calories from Protein: 28.5%
Total Fat: 3.6g	Sodium: 531mg	

✦ Keep potatoes white for your kugels and latkes
by peeling and quartering them the night before,
placing them in a bowl, covering them with cold water
into which 2 heaping tablespoons of white flour
have been added. Refrigerate overnight, drain and use.

RED ROCKS POTATOES

1 large jewel yam
1 large sweet potato
1 large garnet yam
1 large baking potato
1 large red potato
2 teaspoons dried rosemary
2 tablespoons olive oil
salt and pepper

Note: Any combination of yams and sweet potatoes may be used.

✦ Peel and cut potatoes into 1-inch dice. Place in a large zip-lock bag. Add remaining ingredients and turn to coat well. Spread potatoes evenly on a baking sheet which has been coated with nonstick vegetable spray. Bake in preheated 400° oven until browned and crispy, about 45 minutes to 1 hour, turning occasionally.
✦ 4 servings.

TANGY LEMON PARMESAN POTATOES

4 large potatoes, peeled and cubed
¼ cup margarine or butter, melted
6 tablespoons lemon juice
2 tablespoons grated Parmesan cheese
1 tablespoon grated Romano cheese
2 green onions, chopped
1 teaspoon garlic salt
¼ teaspoon freshly ground pepper

✦ Heat 1 inch water (salted, if desired) to boiling in a 3-quart saucepan. Add potatoes and return to a boil. Cover and reduce heat. Simmer 20 to 25 minutes or just until tender. Drain. Combine remaining ingredients in a small bowl. Pour over potatoes and toss to coat.
✦ To grill, spoon potato mixture onto 14 x 20-inch piece of double thickness heavy-duty aluminum foil. Seal securely and place on grill set 4 inches above coals. Grill 30 minutes, turning once.
✦ To bake, place potato mixture in a greased 9 x 13-inch pan. Bake in preheated 350° oven for 30 minutes. If necessary, broil for a few minutes to brown.
✦ 8 servings.

VEGETABLES

LEMON DILL GLAZED WINTER VEGETABLES

12 small new potatoes, halved
2 rutabagas, peeled and cubed
2 turnips, peeled and cubed
1 parsnip, peeled and sliced
2 cups baby carrots
1 onion, cut in wedges
3 tablespoons pareve margarine
½ cup firmly packed brown sugar
4 teaspoons cornstarch
1 cup water
½ cup plus 1 tablespoon lemon juice
2 teaspoons shredded lemon peel
5 tablespoons fresh snipped dill
salt and pepper

✦ Place potatoes and rutabagas in a large saucepan. Cover with water and bring to a boil. Cover and reduce heat. Cook 10 minutes, then add remaining vegetables and cook until tender, about 15 minutes. Drain. While vegetables are cooking, melt margarine in a small saucepan over low heat. Add brown sugar and cornstarch and stir until smooth. Add water, lemon juice, lemon peel and dill. Cook until thick and bubbly, stirring occasionally. Pour over vegetables and toss gently to coat. Serve warm or at room temperature.
✦ 8 servings.

✦ Heat vegetables in the least amount
of water possible, and use the
vitamin-enriched water in soups or gravies.

BALSAMIC VINEGAR GLAZED VEGETABLES

1 tablespoon garlic olive oil
1 red onion, thinly sliced
1 red bell pepper, seeded and cut into
   strips
1 yellow bell pepper, seeded and cut
   into strips
1 green bell pepper, seeded and cut
   into strips
2 zucchini, cut in ½-inch rounds
2 summer squash, cut in ½-inch
   rounds
2 tablespoons balsamic vinegar
salt and pepper

✦ Heat oil over medium heat in a large skillet. Add onions and sauté 2 minutes. Add peppers and sauté until beginning to soften, about 5 minutes. Add squash and sauté until all vegetables are tender, about 10 minutes. Pour vinegar over vegetables and bring to a boil. Continue boiling until vinegar glazes vegetables. Season with salt and pepper to taste.
✦ 6 servings.

ORANGE SAUCE

1 cup orange juice
1½ tablespoons butter or pareve
   margarine
1 tablespoon sugar
1 teaspoon grated orange peel

✦ Combine all ingredients in a small sauce-pan and bring to a boil. Reduce heat and simmer until slightly thickened. Serve over broccoli, snap peas or asparagus.
✦ 4 servings.

✡ See Pareve Food Preparation, page 30

LEADVILLE LEMON ZING!

⅓ cup chopped fresh chives
2 tablespoons butter or pareve
   margarine, softened
1 tablespoon grated lemon peel
salt and pepper to taste

✦ Combine all ingredients in a small bowl. Add to hot vegetable of choice and stir until butter melts and coats vegetables.
✦ 4 servings.

✡ See Pareve Food Preparation, page 30

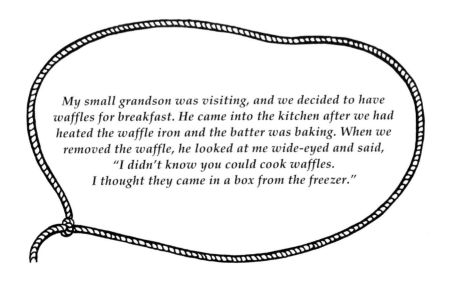

My small grandson was visiting, and we decided to have waffles for breakfast. He came into the kitchen after we had heated the waffle iron and the batter was baking. When we removed the waffle, he looked at me wide-eyed and said, "I didn't know you could cook waffles. I thought they came in a box from the freezer."

ROASTED GARLIC DRESSING

10 cloves garlic, unpeeled
1 teaspoon olive oil
¼ cup balsamic vinegar
2 tablespoons sour cream
1 tablespoon Dijon mustard
1 teaspoon Worcestershire sauce
1 teaspoon hot pepper sauce
salt and pepper to taste

✦ Place garlic cloves on a square of aluminum foil. Drizzle with olive oil and seal foil tightly to make a packet. Bake in preheated 400° oven until soft, about 20 to 25 minutes. Cool. Squeeze cloves from skins into food processor. Add remaining ingredients and process until smooth. Pour over green beans or broccoli and toss to coat.
✦ 4 servings.

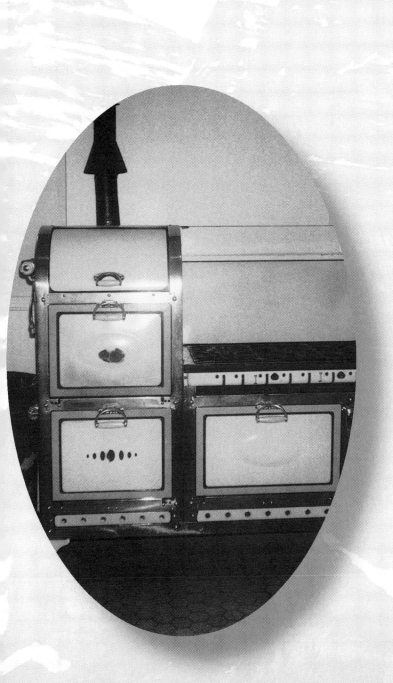

DESSERTS

DESSERT INDEX

(Quick breads appear in Brunch section)

FABULOUS FUDGE CAKE

Pareve

12 ounces pareve semisweet chocolate
5 tablespoons brewed strong coffee
2 cups sugar
2 sticks pareve margarine, softened
6 eggs, separated
1 cup flour
powdered sugar

✦ Preheat oven to 350°. Place chocolate and coffee in a small saucepan. Heat over low heat, stirring often, until chocolate is melted. Cool slightly. Beat egg whites in a bowl until stiff. Fold one-quarter of whites into chocolate mixture, then fold chocolate mixture into remaining whites.

✦ Cream sugar and margarine in a separate bowl. Add egg yolks, one at a time, beating well after each addition. Add flour and blend.

✦ Add chocolate mixture to flour mixture and fold gently to combine. Pour batter into a lightly greased and floured 10-inch springform pan. Bake in center of oven until top is crusty and cracked, but middle is slightly moist, about 1 to 1¼ hours. Cool; remove from pan. Sprinkle cooled cake with powdered sugar. Chill before serving.

DENVER CHOCOLATE CAKE

Dairy

2 sticks butter, softened
3 cups firmly packed brown sugar
4 eggs
2 teaspoons vanilla
¾ cup unsweetened cocoa
1 tablespoon baking soda
½ teaspoon salt
3 cups flour
1⅓ cups sour cream
1⅓ cups boiling water

Frosting:
1½ sticks butter, softened
1½ cups unsweetened cocoa
2 teaspoons vanilla
5½ cups powdered sugar
⅔ cup milk

✦ Preheat oven to 350°. Cream butter and sugar in mixing bowl. Add eggs, one at a time, beating well after each addition. Add vanilla, cocoa, soda and salt. Blend. Alternately add flour and sour cream, then water. Batter will be stiff. Coat 3 9-inch cake pans with nonstick vegetable spray. Dust with flour and shake out any excess. Divide batter among pans and bake for 20 to 25 minutes, or until a toothpick inserted in center comes out clean. Cool on wire racks.

✦ For frosting, cream butter in mixer. Add cocoa and mix well. Add vanilla. Alternately add powdered sugar and milk. Beat well. Add additional milk if necessary to achieve spreading consistency. Spread between cooled cake layers and cover entire cake. Some frosting will be left over.

C A K E

PAWNEE PEAR CAKE

1 stick unsalted butter, softened, divided
½ cup vanilla sugar* or sugar, divided
1½ pounds ripe pears
2 eggs, room temperature
2 tablespoons pear brandy, divided
¾ cup sifted cake flour
crème fraîche, optional

*Hint: To make vanilla sugar, seal 3 cups sugar and 1 split vanilla bean in a tightly fitting jar for 1 week. Keeps indefinitely. Replenish sugar as needed.
Note: Crème fraîche is available in specialty food stores.

✦ Preheat oven to 325°. Grease a 10-inch springform or tart pan with removable bottom with 1 tablespoon butter. Sprinkle with 1 tablespoon sugar. Peel, core and quarter pears, then cut into 4 slices per quarter. Arrange in circle just inside outer edge of pan, slightly overlapping. Working in concentric circles, fill interior with overlapping slices. Sprinkle with 1 tablespoon pear brandy. Cream remaining butter and sugar in mixing bowl. Add eggs, one at a time, beating well after each addition. Add flour and mix until just combined. Stir in remaining brandy. Spoon batter over pears. Bake until firm and nicely browned, about 45 minutes. Serve garnished with crème fraîche, if desired.

LIMON LEMON CAKE

2 sticks unsalted butter, softened
2 cups sugar
3 eggs
3 cups flour
½ teaspoon baking soda
½ teaspoon salt
1 cup buttermilk
2 tablespoons grated lemon rind
2 tablespoons fresh lemon juice

Lemon Glaze:
1½ cups sifted powdered sugar
4 tablespoons unsalted butter, melted
1½ teaspoons grated lemon rind
¼ cup warm lemon juice

✦ Preheat oven to 350°. Cream butter and sugar in mixing bowl. Add eggs one at a time, beating well after each addition. Sift flour, baking soda and salt together. Add to creamed mixture alternately with buttermilk, beginning and ending with flour mixture. Mix in lemon rind and juice. Pour into a 10-inch tube pan which has been coated with nonstick vegetable spray. Bake until a toothpick inserted in center comes out clean, about 1 hour and 15 minutes. Cool in pan for 45 minutes, then invert onto a tray. Combine all glaze ingredients and pour over cake. Remove to a serving dish when set.

CARROT CAKE

Dairy

2 cups sugar
1½ cups vegetable oil
4 eggs
2 cups plus 2 tablespoons flour
1 teaspoon cinnamon
1 teaspoon baking soda
1 teaspoon salt
3 cups well-packed shredded carrots
½ cup shredded coconut
½ cup chopped nuts

Cream Cheese Frosting:
1 (8 ounce) package cream cheese,
    softened
1½ cups powdered sugar
½ teaspoon vanilla
⅛ teaspoon lemon juice

✦ Preheat oven to 375°. Combine cake ingredients in a large bowl in order listed. Mix well. Pour batter into two 9-inch cake pans which have been coated with nonstick vegetable spray. Bake until toothpick inserted in center comes out clean, 30 to 35 minutes. Cool on wire rack. Beat cream cheese in large mixing bowl until smooth. Sift in sugar and beat until well blended. Add vanilla and lemon juice. Frost cooled cake and refrigerate.

Note: Light cream cheese may be used in frosting.
Hint: To bake in bundt pan, reduce oven temperature to 350° and bake 50 to 60 minutes.

HONEY CAKE

Pareve Traditional

2 cups honey
2 cups brewed strong coffee
6 eggs
2 cups sugar
1 cup vegetable oil
4 cups flour
1 teaspoon baking soda
1 tablespoon baking powder
¾ teaspoon salt
1½ teaspoons cinnamon
2½ teaspoons nutmeg
½ teaspoon ground cloves
1 teaspoon ground ginger
1 cup chopped pecans or walnuts,
    optional
powdered sugar

✦ Preheat oven to 350°. Combine honey and coffee in a medium saucepan. Heat, stirring, until honey is melted. Cool. Beat eggs, sugar and oil in a mixing bowl. Sift flour, baking soda, baking powder, salt and spices together. Add to egg mixture alternately with honey mixture. Add nuts, if desired. Pour batter into greased 10 x 15½-inch baking pan. Bake until toothpick inserted in center comes out clean, about 45 minutes. Sprinkle cooled cake with powdered sugar.

C
A
K
E

ROCKY MOUNTAIN CHOCOLATE ZUCCHINI CAKE

1 stick margarine, softened
½ cup oil
1¾ cups sugar
2 eggs
1 tablespoon vanilla
½ cup sour milk* or buttermilk
2½ cups flour, sifted
4 tablespoons cocoa
1 teaspoon baking soda
½ teaspoon salt
½ teaspoon cinnamon
½ teaspoon nutmeg
2 cups finely chopped zucchini
¼ cup chocolate chips
¼ cup chopped nuts

✦ Preheat oven to 350°. Cream margarine, oil and sugar in a mixing bowl. Add eggs one at a time, mixing well after each addition. Add vanilla. Combine milk and vinegar or lemon juice. Sift together flour, cocoa, baking soda, salt and spices. Add to sugar mixture alternately with sour milk/buttermilk. Fold in zucchini. Pour batter into greased and floured 9 x 13-inch baking pan. Sprinkle with chips and nuts and bake until toothpick inserted in center comes out clean, about 45 minutes.

*Sour milk: Combine 1½ teaspoons vinegar or lemon juice with plain milk.

CRIPPLE CREEK CHEESECAKE

Dairy

Crust:
1 stick unsalted butter, softened
1¾ cups graham cracker crumbs
¼ cup finely chopped pecans
1 tablespoon water
½ teaspoon cinnamon

Filling:
3 eggs
2 (8 ounce) packages cream cheese, softened
1 cup sugar
¼ teaspoon salt
1 teaspoon almond extract
2 teaspoons vanilla
3 cups sour cream

✦ Preheat oven to 375°. Combine butter and graham cracker crumbs. Add remaining crust ingredients and mix well. Reserve 1 rounded tablespoon of crumb mixture. Press remainder into bottom and 1 inch up sides of 10-inch springform pan. Bake for 10 minutes. Let cool while preparing filling.
✦ Beat eggs at medium speed in large mixing bowl until pale yellow. Reduce speed to low and add cream cheese. Blend. Add sugar, salt and extracts. Beat until smooth. Add sour cream and beat until blended. Pour into crust and sprinkle with reserved crumbs. Bake 35 to 40 minutes.

Variation: Substitute lemon extract or liqueur for almond extract.

LOW-FAT NEW YORK CHEESECAKE

Crust:
1 cup graham cracker crumbs
2 tablespoons sugar
3 tablespoons margarine, softened

Filling:
½ cup plain low fat yogurt
2 tablespoons flour
4 (8 ounce) packages fat free cream cheese, softened
1 cup sugar
¾ cup egg substitute
½ teaspoon grated lemon rind
2 teaspoons lemon juice
2 teaspoons vanilla

Topping:
1 (8 ounce) carton low fat sour cream
1 tablespoon sugar

Strawberry Sauce:
1 (10 ounce) carton frozen strawberries, sweetened

✦ Preheat oven to 300°. Combine crust ingredients and mix well. Press evenly into a 9-inch springform pan which has been coated with nonstick vegetable spray. Combine yogurt and flour in a large mixing bowl. Beat at low speed until well blended. Add cream cheese and beat at medium speed until smooth. Add sugar, egg substitute, lemon rind and vanilla. Beat well. Spoon over crust and bake for one hour. Center will be soft. Turn off oven and partially open oven door. Leave cheesecake in oven for 30 minutes.

✦ While cake is resting in oven, combine sour cream and sugar. Spread over cake and return to oven. Let cool an additional 30 minutes with door ajar. Remove from oven and cool to room temperature on a wire rack. Cover and chill for 8 hours. Partially thaw strawberries and puree in food processor. Chill. Serve with cheesecake.

✦ Serves 14.

**C
A
K
E**

✦ **Nutritional information per serving**

Calories: 217.9	Saturated Fat: 0.8g	Calories from Fat: 16.9%
Protein: 14.3g	Cholesterol: 14mg	Calories from Carbohydrate: ... 57.0%
Carbohydrate: 31.3g	Dietary Fiber: 0.5g	Calories from Protein: 26.1%
Total Fat: 4.1g	Sodium: 485mg	

PUMPKIN COGNAC CHEESECAKE

Dairy

Crust:
1 cup graham cracker crumbs
3 tablespoons sugar
3 tablespoons butter, melted

Filling:
4 (8 ounce) packages cream cheese, softened
1½ cups sugar
4 eggs
½ cup sour cream
2 teaspoons vanilla
1 cup canned pumpkin
½ teaspoon cinnamon
½ teaspoon nutmeg
½ teaspoon allspice
1½ ounces cognac

Topping:
1 cup sour cream
¼ cup sugar
1 teaspoon vanilla

✦ Preheat oven to 325°. For crust, combine cracker crumbs and sugar in a small bowl. Stir in butter. Press into bottom and up sides of a 9-inch springform pan which has been coated with nonstick vegetable spray.
✦ For filling, beat cream cheese and sugar in a large mixing bowl. Add eggs, one at a time, beating well after each addition. Stir in sour cream and vanilla. Beat well. Spoon half of mixture over crust. Combine pumpkin, spices and cognac. Add to remaining cheese mixture and blend well. Spread gently over mixture in pan. Bake for 1½ hours. Turn off oven and leave cheesecake in oven for 30 minutes more. Combine topping ingredients and spread over cheesecake. Chill before serving.

CHOCOLATE TURTLE PIE

Dairy

Cookie Crust:
2 cups chocolate cookie wafer crumbs (about 18 cookies)
½ stick butter or margarine, melted

Caramel Filling:
1 cup chewy caramel candies
¼ cup whipping cream
2 cups pecan pieces

Topping:
¾ cup semisweet chocolate chips
¼ cup whipping cream

✦ Preheat oven to 375°. Combine cookie crumbs and butter in a medium bowl. Press evenly on bottom and up sides of 9-inch pie pan. Bake for 10 minutes. Cool on wire rack. For filling, melt caramels in heavy saucepan over low heat, stirring constantly. Stir in cream and remove from heat. Add pecans. Spread evenly over crust. Refrigerate until set, at least 10 minutes.
✦ For topping, melt chocolate in double boiler over simmering water. Stir in cream. Drizzle over filling and refrigerate at least 1 hour before serving.

PUEBLO PECAN PIE

3 eggs, lightly beaten
1 cup light or dark corn syrup
½ cup sugar
2 tablespoons pareve margarine,
    melted
1 teaspoon vanilla
⅛ teaspoon salt
1 cup pecans
1 unbaked 9-inch deep dish
    or 10-inch regular pie crust

*Note: If crust starts to get too brown,
    cover edges with foil.*

✦ Preheat oven to 450°. Combine eggs, syrup, sugar, margarine, vanilla and salt in a medium bowl. Fold in pecans. Pour into pie crust and bake for 10 minutes. Reduce temperature to 350° and continue baking until knife inserted in center comes out clean, about 45 minutes. Cool.

CHOCOLATE MACADAMIA NUT PIE

3 eggs
1 cup plus 1 tablespoon sugar
½ teaspoon salt
1 stick butter, melted
¾ cup dark corn syrup
1½ cups macadamia nuts
1 cup chopped dark chocolate or
    semisweet chocolate chips
1 unbaked 9-inch deep dish pie crust
1 jar caramel sauce

✦ Preheat oven to 350°. Beat eggs, sugar and salt until light and lemon-colored. Blend butter and corn syrup and add to egg mixture. Sprinkle nuts and chocolate over pie crust. Top with blended mixture and bake until set and golden brown, 50 to 60 minutes. Chill. Drizzle with caramel sauce to serve.

**P
I
E
S**

Le Petit Gourmet

PEACHY CUSTARD PIE

Dairy Lighter

Crust:
1½ cups flour
½ cup sugar
¼ teaspoon salt
½ cup butter, softened
2 tablespoons sour cream

Filling:
5 peaches, peeled, sliced and drained
⅓ cup sour cream
3 egg yolks
¼ teaspoon salt
1 cup sugar
¼ cup flour

✦ Preheat oven to 350°. Mix all crust ingredients with a pastry blender. Press into a 10-inch pie plate. Bake until brown, about 10 minutes. Cool. Arrange peach slices over crust. Combine remaining ingredients and pour over peaches. Bake until a knife inserted in center comes out clean, 45 minutes to 1 hour. Serve same day at room temperature.
✦ Serves 8.

✦ Nutritional information per serving

Calories: 325.0	Saturated Fat: 5.9g	Calories from Fat: 29.1%
Protein: 4.8g	Cholesterol: 101mg	Calories from Carbohydrate: ... 65.1%
Carbohydrate: 53.8g	Dietary Fiber: 1.3g	Calories from Protein: 5.8%
Total Fat: 10.7g	Sodium: 202mg	

✦ To roll out pastry, pies and cookies without sticking, use a pastry cover for your rolling pin. Flour it lightly and keep it floured during the rolling process. A lightly floured pastry cloth on the rolling surface will also prevent sticking.

CARAMEL APPLE CHEESE TART

Crust:
1¼ cups flour
¼ cup sugar
1¼ teaspoons cinnamon
½ cup butter, softened

Filling:
1 (8 ounce) package cream cheese, softened
1¼ teaspoons vanilla
½ cup sugar
1 tablespoon flour
1 egg, beaten

Topping:
½ cup chopped pecans
3 Granny Smith apples, peeled and diced
¾ cup caramel topping
½ teaspoon cinnamon

✦ Preheat oven to 375°. For crust, combine flour, sugar and cinnamon in a medium bowl. Cut butter into flour mixture with a fork or pastry blender until mixture resembles coarse meal. Reserve ⅓ cup mixture for topping. Press remaining pastry into bottom and up sides of 11-inch tart pan. Pierce all over with a fork and bake until golden, 15 to 20 minutes.
✦ For filling, beat cream cheese and vanilla in medium mixing bowl until smooth. Gradually beat in sugar and flour, then egg. Pour into hot crust and spread evenly. Return to oven and bake until set, about 15 minutes.
✦ For topping, combine nuts and reserved crumb mixture. Place apples in another bowl and coat with caramel topping and cinnamon. Working quickly, arrange apples on top of hot tart. Spoon any remaining caramel over apples and sprinkle with pecan mixture. Bake until apples are tender, 20 to 25 minutes. Cool before serving.

Thanksgiving has always been a favorite holiday of mine. As a child it meant sharing the celebration with two of my favorite adults — my father's sister and my best friend's mother. Thanksgiving dinner at my aunt's was a child-friendly affair, involving my younger cousins, their magical hiding places and a large meal overflowing with many of my favorite dishes. At my friend's house the taste of the holiday lingered throughout the following week in a refrigerator crammed with succulent leftovers, including a seemingly bottomless turkey carcass.

**P
I
E
S**

APPLE TART WITH MAPLE SAUCE

Dairy

1 cup plus 3 tablespoons flour
½ teaspoon salt
1½ tablespoons sugar
7 tablespoons cold unsalted butter
1 large egg yolk
1 to 2 tablespoons cold water

Filling:
¼ cup unsalted butter
6 Granny Smith apples, peeled and
    sliced
½ cup sugar
1 tablespoon cinnamon
2 tablespoons bourbon, optional
½ cup chopped walnuts
¼ cup raisins

Topping:
½ cup flour
½ cup sugar
½ cup chopped walnuts
¼ cup unsalted butter, softened

Sauce:
¾ cup pure maple syrup
¾ teaspoon vanilla
½ cup vanilla ice cream, softened

✦ Sift flour, salt and sugar into a bowl. Blend in butter, using fingers, until mixture resembles coarse meal. Add yolk and 1 tablespoon water. Toss and add more water if needed to form a dough. Shape into a ball, dust with flour and wrap in waxed paper. Refrigerate at least 2 hours. Preheat oven to 350°. Roll dough on a lightly floured board to a 13-inch round. Fit into lightly buttered 12-inch tart pan with removable rim. Crimp edges and prick dough all over with fork. Bake until golden, about 20 minutes.

✦ For filling, combine all ingredients in a large heavy metal pot. Cook over medium heat, stirring, until apples are softened, about 20 minutes. Spoon into crust. Combine all topping ingredients in a medium bowl and blend until mixture resembles coarse meal. Sprinkle over filling. Bake until golden and apples are tender, about 30 minutes. Heat maple syrup in a saucepan over low heat for 5 minutes. Whisk in vanilla and ice cream until smooth. Spoon over tart slices.

✦ Some of the recipes in this section call for butter only.
This means that they have not been tested using
margarine. You can try using margarine if you wish.

TELLURIDE APPLE PIE

Dairy

Crust:
1 stick salted butter, softened
4 ounces cream cheese, softened
1½ cups flour
2 teaspoons sugar

Filling:
7 cups cored, peeled and sliced
Granny Smith or MacIntosh apples
¾ cup sugar
¼ teaspoon cinnamon
2 teaspoons fresh lemon juice
3 tablespoons tapioca

Note: This dough also makes a wonderful
strudel crust.

✦ Place butter and cream cheese in food processor and pulse until blended. Add flour and sugar and process until dough forms a ball. Divide dough in half and shape into balls. Flatten and place in zip-lock bags. Refrigerate for at least 4 hours and up to 3 days.
✦ Preheat oven to 400°. When ready to assemble, roll one piece of dough into circle large enough to fit an 8 or 9-inch pie pan with one inch hanging over. Carefully arrange in pan. Combine all filling ingredients in a large bowl and place over crust. Roll out remaining dough and lay over filling with one inch hanging over edge. Press edges together and flute. Cut several slits in top. Bake for 10 minutes, then reduce heat to 350° and bake until brown, about 45 minutes. Cool on rack.

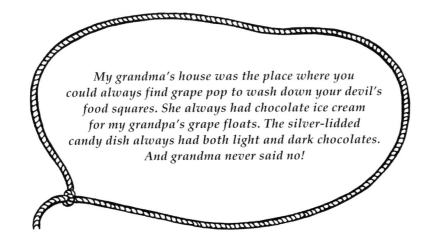

My grandma's house was the place where you could always find grape pop to wash down your devil's food squares. She always had chocolate ice cream for my grandpa's grape floats. The silver-lidded candy dish always had both light and dark chocolates. And grandma never said no!

P
I
E
S

COCONUT LEMON ICE CREAM PIE

Dairy

Crust:
2½ cups shredded coconut
1 stick plus 5 tablespoons margarine
   or butter, divided

Filling:
½ cup fresh lemon juice
grated rind of 1 lemon
¼ teaspoon salt
1⅓ cups sugar
3 whole eggs
3 egg yolks

Meringue:
3 egg whites
⅓ cup sugar
1 quart vanilla ice cream or frozen
   yogurt, softened

✦ Sauté coconut in 4 tablespoons butter until brown. Press into bottom of 10-inch springform pan and chill. Melt remaining butter in saucepan over very low heat. Add lemon rind, lemon juice, salt and 1⅓ cups sugar. Separate 3 eggs. Place 3 egg yolks plus 3 whole eggs in a medium bowl and beat until thick and yellow. Add to lemon mixture and cook until smooth and very thick, stirring constantly. Cool. Spread half of softened ice cream over crust. Top with half of lemon mixture. Freeze until hard. Repeat with remaining ice cream and lemon mixture and refreeze. Beat egg whites until soft peaks form. Continue beating while gradually adding sugar. Beat until stiff, but not dry. Spread over frozen pie, sealing edges. Broil until browned and serve immediately.

✦ Butter your knife before cutting a meringue pie —
you'll get a clean cut without damaging the meringue.

THE BEST SWEET POTATO PIE

Dairy or Pareve

2 large sweet potatoes or yams
½ cup firmly packed brown sugar
¼ cup sugar
2 tablespoons cornstarch
1 egg, lightly beaten
3 tablespoons butter or pareve
   margarine, melted
¼ teaspoon salt
½ teaspoon cinnamon
⅓ cup chopped pecans
1 unbaked 9-inch pie crust

*Note: 2 cups canned sweet potatoes or
yams may be substituted for fresh.*

✦ Preheat oven to 425°. Bake potatoes one hour. Cool enough to handle. Scoop pulp into a large bowl. Add sugars, cornstarch, egg, butter, salt and cinnamon. Mix well and spoon into pie crust. Sprinkle with pecans and bake in preheated 350° oven until top is browned and bubbly, 45 to 50 minutes.

✿ See Pareve Food Preparation, page 30

TROPICAL FRUIT TART

Dairy

Crust:
1 cup flour
6 tablespoons cold butter, cut into pieces
2 tablespoons sugar
1 egg yolk
1 tablespoon cold water
⅛ teaspoon salt

Filling:
1 (8 ounce) package cream cheese, softened
½ cup sugar
1 egg
dash of salt
½ teaspoon vanilla
1 teaspoon almond extract
1 teaspoon amaretto liqueur
1 cup sour cream

Topping:
sliced fresh fruit (peaches, kiwi, strawberries)
½ cup apple jelly
1 tablespoon lemon juice
1 tablespoon amaretto liqueur

✦ Preheat oven to 425°. For crust, combine all ingredients in food processor and pulse for 5 seconds. Continue processing until mixture forms a ball. Remove and roll between 2 sheets of waxed paper into a 12-inch circle. Coat a 9-inch tart pan with removable bottom with nonstick vegetable spray. Fit dough into pan and trim any excess. Pierce all over with a fork. Bake for 10 to 12 minutes. Cool on wire rack before filling.

✦ For filling, place all ingredients in food processor and mix until smooth. Pour into tart shell and bake in 350° oven until set, about 20 minutes. Remove from oven and cool on wire rack. Refrigerate overnight.

✦ The following day, arrange fruit over filling in concentric circles, covering entire top. Combine jelly, juice and liqueur in a small saucepan and heat, stirring, until smooth. Cool slightly and brush over fruit.

Variation: *For a raspberry tart, arrange 3 cups raspberries over filling. Combine ¼ cup seedless raspberry jam with 1 tablespoon water in a small saucepan. Heat over moderate heat, stirring constantly, until melted and smooth. Cool slightly, then brush over raspberries.*

✦ **Honey is sweeter and more liquid than sugar.
For each cup of sugar, substitute ¾ cup honey
and reduce other liquid by ¼ cup.**

P
I
E
S

LOW-GUILT BROWNIES

Dairy Lighter

½ cup flour
3 tablespoons unsweetened cocoa
¼ teaspoon baking powder
1 cup sugar minus 2 tablespoons
⅓ cup low fat or nonfat cream cheese, softened
3½ ounces semisweet chocolate, melted
5 tablespoons vegetable oil
¼ cup liquid egg substitute
2 teaspoons vanilla
1 cup fresh or frozen raspberries, rinsed and patted dry, optional

✦ Preheat oven to 350°. Combine flour, cocoa and baking powder. Cream sugar and cream cheese in mixing bowl until light and fluffy. Beat in melted chocolate and oil. Gradually beat in egg substitute and vanilla. Beat in flour mixture on low speed until smooth. Fold in raspberries, if desired. Spoon batter into an 8-inch square baking pan which has been coated with nonstick vegetable spray. Bake until firm, about 35 minutes. Cool in pan on wire rack and cut into 16 pieces.

✦ When melting chocolate, spray the pot with vegetable spray and the chocolate will slip right out.

WILD WEST RASPBERRY BROWNIES

6 ounces unsweetened chocolate
2 sticks butter
2 cups sugar
4 eggs
2 teaspoons vanilla
1½ cups flour
½ teaspoon baking powder
dash of salt
1 cup chopped or sliced almonds
1 cup milk chocolate or semisweet chocolate chips
1 cup raspberry or strawberry preserves

✦ Preheat oven to 350°. Melt unsweetened chocolate and butter over low heat in a medium saucepan. Cool. Beat sugar, eggs and vanilla in a mixer. Add chocolate mixture and mix well. Add flour, baking powder and salt. Combine well. Fold in almonds and chocolate chips. Spread two-thirds of batter in a 9 x 13-inch buttered baking pan. Heat preserves in microwave for 1 minute. Spread gently over batter. Top with remaining batter and swirl lightly with a spoon. Bake until top is firm and a toothpick inserted in center comes out clean, 30 to 40 minutes. Cool in pan on wire rack before cutting.
✦ Yields 32 brownies.

QUICK AND EASY BROWNIES

Dairy

2 sticks butter
4 ounces unsweetened chocolate
2 cups sugar
4 eggs
1 cup flour
1 teaspoon vanilla
1 cup chopped nuts, optional
powdered sugar, optional

✦ Preheat oven to 350°. Melt butter and chocolate in a saucepan over low heat. Remove from heat. Add sugar and blend. Add eggs, one at a time, blending well after each addition. Stir in flour and vanilla. Add nuts, if desired. Pour into an 8½ x 12-inch baking pan which has been coated with nonstick vegetable spray. Bake until firm and a toothpick inserted in center comes out almost clean, 25 to 30 minutes. Do not overbake. Sprinkle with powdered sugar, if desired.
✦ Yields 2 dozen brownies.

FUDGY CHOCOLATE BROWNIES

Dairy or Pareve

2 sticks unsalted butter or pareve
   margarine
4 ounces unsweetened chocolate or
   pareve chocolate
¼ teaspoon salt
1½ cups sugar
½ cup firmly packed light brown
   sugar
4 eggs, room temperature
1¼ cups flour
1½ teaspoons vanilla
1½ cups chopped pecans or walnuts
raspberry or fruit sauce, optional

✦ Preheat oven to 350°. Grease 9-inch square baking pan and line with foil, leaving 2 inches overhanging. Grease foil. Place butter, chocolate and salt in a 3-quart saucepan over low heat. Stir until melted and smooth. Remove from heat and whisk in sugars until mixture is melted and smooth. Add eggs, one at a time, beating well after each addition. Whisk in flour and vanilla until just blended. Fold in nuts. Pour batter into prepared pan. Bake until toothpick inserted in center comes out almost clean, 25-30 minutes. Cool in pan on wire rack. Cut into 16 pieces and serve with fruit sauce, if desired.
✦ Yields 16.

✿ See Pareve Food Preparation, page 30

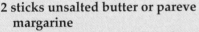
✦ Brown sugar will stay fresh and soft if stored in the refrigerator or freezer in a plastic bag.

PLENTY O' PECANS

1 stick pareve margarine, softened
1½ cups sugar
4 eggs
2 cups sifted flour
½ teaspoon baking powder
3 cups chopped pecans
2 teaspoons vanilla

Topping:
½ cup sugar
2 teaspoons cinnamon

✦ Preheat oven to 350°. Cream margarine and sugar in large mixing bowl. Add eggs, one at a time, beating well after each addition. Add remaining ingredients and blend well. Coat three 4 x 8-inch loaf pans with nonstick vegetable spray. Divide batter evenly among pans. Bake for 35 to 40 minutes. Cool 5 minutes and remove from pans. Wrap in foil and freeze.
✦ When ready to finish, defrost loaves slightly and slice with a serrated knife ¼- to ½-inch thick. Preheat oven to 325°. Combine sugar and cinnamon on a saucer or plate and coat both sides of each piece. Place on baking sheet and bake until brown, 15 to 20 minutes. Turn slices and continue baking until lightly browned.
✦ Yields 5 to 6 dozen.

CHOCOLATE STRUDEL

Dough:
2½ sticks butter, softened
1 cup firmly packed brown sugar
3 cups flour
1 tablespoon vanilla
3-4 tablespoons milk

Filling:
1 (12 ounce) package semisweet
   chocolate chips
1 (14 ounce) can sweetened
   condensed milk
1 tablespoon butter
1 cup chopped pecans
powdered sugar, sifted

Hint: Light condensed milk may be used in filling. To prevent spreading, refrigerate rolls ½ hour before baking.

✦ Cream butter and sugar in large mixing bowl until light and fluffy. Add flour, vanilla and milk and mix until combined. Divide dough into 4 parts, wrap in plastic wrap and refrigerate at least one hour. Preheat oven to 350°. Melt chocolate chips and butter in saucepan over low heat. Stir in condensed milk. Roll each dough section between 2 sheets of well-floured waxed paper to 12 x 18-inch rectangles. Spread with a quarter of chocolate mixture and sprinkle with ¼ cup pecans. Roll up jelly roll style starting from long side. Pinch ends together and place, seam-side down, on a greased baking sheet which has been coated with nonstick vegetable spray. Repeat with remaining dough and filling. Cut steam vents 1 inch apart. Bake until light golden brown, about 25 to 30 minutes. Cool slightly and slice into 1-inch pieces. Sprinkle with powdered sugar when cool.

MELT-IN-YOUR-MOUTH CRESCENT COOKIES

2 sticks butter, softened
3 tablespoons powdered sugar
1 teaspoon vanilla
2 cups flour
1 cup chopped pecans
powdered sugar

✦ Preheat oven to 350°. Cream butter and sugar in mixing bowl on medium speed until light and fluffy. Add vanilla and blend. Slowly add flour and mix on low speed until blended. Stir in pecans. Pinch off about 2 teaspoons of dough at a time and shape into crescents. Place on ungreased baking sheet and bake until golden, about 20 minutes. Roll carefully in powdered sugar while still warm, then repeat when slightly cooled.
✦ Yields 3 dozen.

BONANZA BUTTER COOKIES

4 sticks unsalted butter, softened
1⅓ cups sugar
¾ teaspoon salt
3 egg yolks
2 teaspoons vanilla
4⅔ cups flour

Variation: Chanukah candle cookies: Add 2½ cups toasted and cooled sweetened coconut to half recipe of dough. Divide into 2 pieces and pat each half into a 2½ x 11-inch rectangle on a piece of waxed paper. Using a sharp knife, cut each rectangle into ½ x 2½-inch strips. Place 1 inch apart on an ungreased baking sheet. Bake 10 to 12 minutes and cool. Melt 2 cups chocolate chips. Dip one end of cookie into chocolate and cool on waxed paper.

✦ Cream butter, sugar and salt in large bowl of mixer until light and fluffy. Beat in yolks one at a time, blending well after each addition. Add vanilla and beat until smooth. Add flour gradually, mixing just until dough is combined. Split into two parts. Wrap in plastic wrap and refrigerate until ready to use.
✦ Preheat oven to 350°. Pinch off dough into 1-inch balls. Flatten on ungreased baking sheets. If desired, sprinkle with cinnamon-sugar mixture, top with a whole nut or press ½ teaspoon jam into thumb print indented in center of cookie before baking. Bake 10 to 12 minutes.
✦ Yields 8 to 9 dozen.

COOKIES

VICTORIAN LACE PECAN COOKIES

⅔ cup firmly packed light brown
   sugar
½ cup light corn syrup
½ cup unsalted butter
⅔ cup cake flour
1 cup finely chopped pecans

Hint: *For a fabulous presentation, stand*
fans up on a plate and serve ice
cream and fresh berries on bottom
part of cookie.

✦ Preheat oven to 325°. Combine sugar, syrup and butter in a heavy saucepan. Bring to a boil. Remove from heat and stir in flour and pecans. For large cookies, drop ¼ cup dough onto cookie sheet and bake one cookie at a time. For small cookies, drop 2 tablespoons per cookie and bake 2 cookies at a time. Bake for 12 minutes. Remove from oven and let rest 30 to 45 seconds. Remove from pan and shape over a bottle or prop up at a right angle to fan out.
✦ 6 to 8 large cookies.

LIME TEA COOKIES

2 cups plus 2 tablespoons flour
¼ teaspoon salt
¼ teaspoon nutmeg
¼ teaspoon cinnamon
1 teaspoon baking powder
1 cup sugar
1 stick butter or pareve margarine,
   softened
1 egg
1½ teaspoons finely grated lime peel
3 tablespoons fresh lime juice

Topping:
⅓ cup sugar
¼ teaspoon nutmeg
¼ teaspoon cinnamon

✦ Preheat oven to 350°. Combine flour, salt, nutmeg, cinnamon and baking powder. Cream sugar, butter, egg and lime peel in a large mixing bowl until fluffy and light. Gradually add lime juice. Add flour mixture ½ cup at a time, blending completely after each addition. Combine topping ingredients in a small bowl. Roll dough into 1-inch balls and roll in sugar mixture. Place on a baking sheet which has been coated with nonstick spray. Flatten cookies with bottom of a glass. Bake until golden brown on edges and bottoms, 12 to 18 minutes. Cool. Store in freezer bags or plastic containers.
✦ Yields 3 dozen.

✡ See Pareve Food Preparation, page 30

✦ Nutritional information per serving		
Calories: 79.0	Saturated Fat: 1.6g	Calories from Fat: 30.9%
Protein: 0.9g	Cholesterol: 13mg	Calories from Carbohydrate: ... 64.5%
Carbohydrate: 12.9g	Dietary Fiber: 0g	Calories from Protein: 4.6%
Total Fat: 2.8g	Sodium: 53mg	

MACADAMIA COOKIES

1½ cups firmly packed brown sugar
1 cup white sugar
2 cups pareve butter-flavored
  shortening
2 eggs
2 teaspoons vanilla
2 tablespoons coffee liqueur
4 cups flour
1 teaspoon salt
2 teaspoons baking soda
6 ounces semisweet chocolate chips
6 ounces white chocolate chips
8 ounces macadamia nuts, halved

✦ Preheat oven to 350°. Cream sugars and shortening well in a large mixing bowl. Combine eggs, vanilla and coffee liqueur in a small bowl. Beat until well blended. Stir into sugar mixture. Combine flour, salt and baking soda. Add to creamed mixture until just combined. Fold in remaining ingredients. Drop large teaspoons of dough 2 inches apart onto baking sheets. Bake for 10 to 12 minutes. Loosen and cool on baking sheet before removing to rack.
✦ Yields 3 dozen.

SWISS TARTLETTES

2 sticks butter or pareve margarine,
  softened
⅔ cup sugar
2 cups flour
2 teaspoons orange liqueur
apricot, raspberry, blackberry or
  strawberry jam
powdered sugar

✦ Preheat oven to 325°. Combine butter, sugar, flour and liqueur in a large mixing bowl, blending well. Cover and refrigerate 2 hours. Line muffin tins with cupcake liners and coat with nonstick vegetable spray. Press enough dough into each liner to fill it two-thirds full. Bake until golden, about 30 minutes. While still warm, place a dollop of jam in center of each and sprinkle with powdered sugar.

✡ See Pareve Food Preparation, page 30

✦ Polyunsaturated oils can replace solid fats in some baked goods. Reduce the amount by one third.

COMPANY CHEESE BRAIDS

Dough:
1 cup sour cream
½ cup plus 1 tablespoon sugar, divided
1 teaspoon salt
1 stick butter or margarine, melted
2 packages dry yeast
½ cup warm water
2 eggs, lightly beaten
4 cups flour

Filling:
2 (8 ounce) packages cream cheese, softened
¾ cup sugar
1 egg, lightly beaten
⅛ teaspoon salt
2 teaspoons vanilla

Glaze:
2 cups powdered sugar
¼ cup milk
2 teaspoons vanilla

✦ Heat sour cream in a medium saucepan over low heat. Stir in ½ cup sugar, salt, and butter or margarine. Cool to lukewarm. Sprinkle yeast and remaining sugar over warm water in a large bowl. Stir until yeast and sugar are dissolved. Add sour cream mixture, eggs and flour. Mix well, cover tightly and refrigerate overnight.

✦ The following day, combine all filling ingredients and blend well. Divide dough into 4 parts. Roll out each part on a well-floured board into an 8 x 12-inch rectangle. Spread with a quarter of the filling and roll up jelly roll style, beginning from long side. Pinch ends together and fold slightly under roll. Place seam side down on greased baking sheet. Slit each roll at 2-inch intervals to resemble a braid, cutting two-thirds through the dough. Repeat with remaining dough and filling. Cover and let rise in a warm place for 1 hour. Preheat oven to 375°. Bake for 20 to 25 minutes. Combine all glaze ingredients and spread over braids while still warm.

Toasting nuts
✦ In microwave on high for 1 or 2 minutes —
toss at 30-second intervals. Additional time may be
needed to reach desired doneness. Watch carefully.
In oven, toast at 350°, stirring frequently.
Watch carefully.

HAMANTASHEN

2 sticks butter or pareve margarine, softened, or 1 cup oil
1 cup sugar
3 eggs
grated rind of 1 medium orange (about 2 teaspoons)
scant ¼ cup fresh orange juice
1 teaspoon vanilla
4⅔ cups flour
2 teaspoons baking powder

Prune Filling:
1 pound pitted prunes
1 cup white or dark raisins
¾ cup apricot jam
2 tablespoons honey
1 cup chopped nuts
2 tablespoons orange juice, optional
1 teaspoon grated lemon peel, optional

✦ Cream butter and sugar in mixing bowl until light and fluffy. Add eggs, one at a time, beating well after each addition. Add orange rind, juice and vanilla. Mix in flour and baking powder until thoroughly blended. Divide dough into 4 parts, wrap in plastic wrap and refrigerate several hours or overnight. Preheat oven to 350°. Roll out dough, one part at a time, on a floured board to ¼-inch thickness. Cut 3-inch circles with a cookie cutter. Place a heaping teaspoon of filling in center of each circle and pinch sides up to form a triangle. Place on greased cookie sheet and bake until light brown, about 20 minutes.

✦ For filling, chop prunes and raisins in a food processor. Add jam, honey, nuts, orange juice and lemon peel, if desired. Process until well combined.

✦ Other fillings include strawberry preserves, apricot preserves, milk chocolate chips, or poppy seed filling.

✦ Yields 5 dozen.

✡ See Pareve Food Preparation, page 30

✦ Nutritional information per serving

Calories: 132.0	Saturated Fat: 2.2g	Calories from Fat: 31.3%
Protein: 2.1g	Cholesterol: 19mg	Calories from Carbohydrate: ... 62.7%
Carbohydrate: 21.5g	Dietary Fiber: 1.0g	Calories from Protein: 6.0%
Total Fat: 4.8g	Sodium: 67mg	

1.

2.
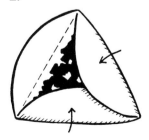

3.

T
R
A
D
I
T
I
O
N
A
L

SOUR CREAM SCHNECKEN

Pecan Rolls:
2 packages yeast
½ cup warm water
½ cup plus 1 teaspoon sugar, divided
4½ cups flour
dash salt
2 sticks butter
3 eggs, beaten well
½ cup sour cream

Filling:
1 stick butter, melted
1⅓ cups raisins
¾ cup sugar
2 tablespoons cinnamon

Topping:
2 cups firmly packed brown sugar
½ cup water
1¼ cups chopped pecans or walnuts

Note: These freeze well and can be made in a food processor.

✦ Dissolve yeast in warm water and add 1 teaspoon sugar. Let stand for 10 minutes, or until yeast begins to foam. Put flour, salt and ½ cup sugar in mixing bowl and cut in butter. Add eggs, sour cream and yeast mixture. Mix until ingredients are fully incorporated. Place in a bowl which has been coated with nonstick vegetable spray. Cover with plastic wrap and refrigerate for several hours or overnight. It should rise to about double in size. Dough can be kept for several days before baking.

✦ When ready to bake, remove from refrigerator and divide into 4 parts on a lightly floured board or pastry cloth. Roll one piece into a ½-inch thick rectangle. Cover remaining pieces until ready to use. Brush with 2 tablespoons melted butter. Sprinkle with a quarter of cinnamon/sugar mixture and ⅓ cup raisins. Starting with long side, roll up jelly roll style. Tuck ends in and cut into 12 slices. Coat 4 12-muffin tins well with nonstick vegetable spray. Combine topping ingredients and place ½ tablespoon in bottom of each tin. Place dough slices over topping. Brush tops with any remaining butter. Cover with a cloth and let rise in a warm place for 1 to 2 hours, or until doubled in size. Bake in preheated 350° oven until deep golden brown, about 15 minutes. Remove from oven and invert immediately on a baking sheet to cool.

✦ Yields 4 dozen rolls.

HUNGARIAN RUGELACH

Dairy Traditional

Dough:
2 cups flour
2 tablespoons powdered sugar
1 egg yolk
1 tablespoon white vinegar
1 cup sour cream
2 sticks butter, softened slightly and
   cut into 10 pieces

Fillings:
preserves and chopped nuts
dots of cream cheese with grated
   lemon rind and white or brown
   sugar
cocoa, cinnamon, nuts, raisins,
   coconut and white or brown sugar
chocolate bits and nuts
almond paste filling

✦ Place flour and powdered sugar in food processor and pulse for 2 seconds. Add egg yolk, vinegar and sour cream and process 2 seconds. Add butter. Process just until butter is the size of peas. Gather dough into a ball, wrap in plastic wrap and refrigerate overnight or up to several days.

✦ When ready to bake, preheat oven to 350°. Divide dough into 6 pieces. Work with one piece at a time, keeping remaining in refrigerator. Roll dough out very thin on a floured board in any of the following ways: roll into a rectangle, sprinkle with filling of choice, roll up jelly roll fashion and cut into 1-inch pieces; or roll into a circle, sprinkle with filling, cut into 16 wedges and roll into crescents, beginning with wide end. Place close together on baking sheets which have been coated with nonstick vegetable spray and bake until bottoms are slightly browned, 22 to 25 minutes.

✦ Yields 7 to 8 dozen.

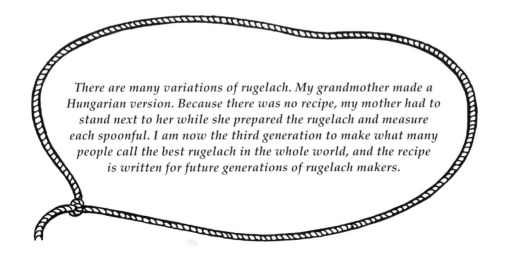

There are many variations of rugelach. My grandmother made a Hungarian version. Because there was no recipe, my mother had to stand next to her while she prepared the rugelach and measure each spoonful. I am now the third generation to make what many people call the best rugelach in the whole world, and the recipe is written for future generations of rugelach makers.

T
R
A
D
I
T
I
O
N
A
L

HOLIDAY RUGELACH

2 sticks butter, softened
1 cup plus 3 tablespoons sugar,
    divided
3 eggs, separated
1 cup sour cream
1 teaspoon white vinegar
1 teaspoon vanilla
1½ packages dry yeast
4 cups flour, sifted

Topping:
1 cup sugar
1 tablespoon cinnamon
1½ cups chopped walnuts or pecans
2 cups raisins
12 ounces apricot preserves

✦ Cream butter and 3 tablespoons sugar in a large mixing bowl. Add egg yolks, sour cream, vinegar and vanilla. Mix and add yeast. Blend well. Add flour gradually and mix well. Cover and refrigerate overnight or up to several days.

✦ The following day, preheat oven to 350°. Divide dough into 6 pieces. Roll each out into a 12-inch circle on a floured board. Beat egg whites until foamy. Gradually add 1 cup sugar and continue beating until stiff peaks form. Spread over each circle. Combine sugar and cinnamon. For raisin rugelach, sprinkle raisins and nuts over dough circles. Top with sugar mixture. For apricot rugelach, spread preserves over dough first, then meringue. Top with nuts and sprinkle with sugar mixture. Cut each circle into 12 wedges with a pizza cutter or sharp knife. Roll up, beginning with wide end, and form into a crescent shape. Place on baking sheets coated with nonstick vegetable spray and sprinkle with remaining sugar mixture. Bake for 20 minutes.

✦ Yields 72 pieces.

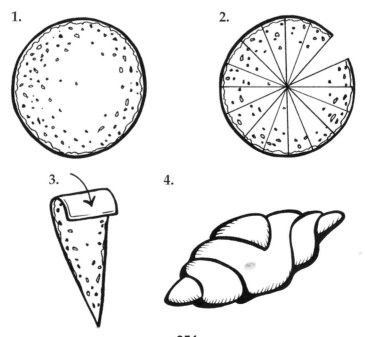

1.

2.

3.

4.

FESTIVE MANDEL BREAD

Pareve | Traditional | Lighter

4 cups flour
4 teaspoons baking powder
½ teaspoon salt
5 eggs, beaten
1⅓ cups sugar
1½ teaspoons almond extract
⅓ cup vegetable oil
¾ cup chopped almonds or pecans
juice of ½ orange
grated rind of 1 lemon
1 cup pareve chocolate chips, optional

Topping:
1 cup sugar
2 tablespoons cinnamon

✦ Sift together flour, baking powder and salt. Combine eggs, sugar, extract, oil and nuts in a large bowl. Add orange juice and lemon rind. Add dry ingredients to egg mixture and blend. Add chocolate chips, if desired. Refrigerate for several hours to make handling easier. Preheat oven to 350°. Lightly oil hands and form dough into 5 logs. Place lengthwise on baking sheets which have been coated with nonstick vegetable spray. Sprinkle with a third of sugar and cinnamon. Bake for 20 minutes. Slice each log into 12 pieces diagonally. Lay slices on baking sheets and sprinkle again with sugar and cinnamon. Bake 10 more minutes, then turn slices and repeat process.
✦ Yields 5 dozen.

✦ Nutritional information per serving

Calories: 102.7	Saturated Fat: 0.9g	Calories from Fat: 30.3%
Protein: 1.8g	Cholesterol: 18mg	Calories from Carbohydrate: ... 62.8%
Carbohydrate: 16.6g	Dietary Fiber: 0.5g	Calories from Protein: 6.8%
Total Fat: 3.6g	Sodium: 48mg	

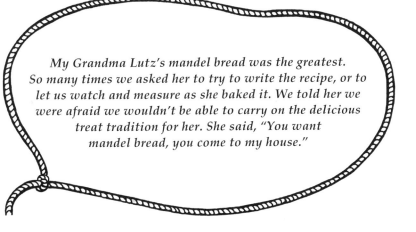

My Grandma Lutz's mandel bread was the greatest. So many times we asked her to try to write the recipe, or to let us watch and measure as she baked it. We told her we were afraid we wouldn't be able to carry on the delicious treat tradition for her. She said, "You want mandel bread, you come to my house."

TRADITIONAL

CRUNCHY MANDEL BREAD

3 eggs, lightly beaten
1 cup sugar
1 cup vegetable oil
1 teaspoon vanilla
1 tablespoon cinnamon
2 teaspoons baking powder
2½ cups flour
¾ cup mini pareve chocolate chips
¾ cup crushed corn flakes
¾ cup shredded coconut

✦ Preheat oven to 350°. Combine eggs, sugar, oil and vanilla in a large bowl. Beat until well blended. Stir in cinnamon, baking powder and flour to make a stiff dough. Add remaining ingredients, mixing by hand. Divide dough into 4 parts and shape into logs. Place logs on baking sheets which have been coated with nonstick vegetable spray. Bake at 350° for 25 minutes. Reduce temperature to 225°. Slice rolls into 1-inch pieces diagonally, return to oven and bake until dry, about 20 more minutes.
✦ Yields 5 dozen.

✦ There is a new prune-based product (or you can use applesauce) to replace butter or oil in baked goods. In moist, soft and chewy baked goods, replace up to half of the butter, oil, margarine or shortening.

CHERRY VISHNIK CORDIAL

4½ cups pitted tart red cherries, fresh or frozen, with juice
6 cups sugar
1⅔ cups bourbon whiskey, 101 proof

Note: Will last for years if stored in a cool, dark place.

✦ Fill wide-mouth gallon jar with alternating layers of cherries and sugar. Put lid on jar and let stand in a cool, dark place for 10 to 14 days. Open jar every 2 days and gently stir sugar into cherries. After 2 weeks, pour in bourbon. Mix gently and store in cool, dark place with lid on for 2 to 4 months. Do not store in refrigerator. When ready to serve, transfer to a crystal decanter and serve in small liqueur glasses.

POPPY SEED MANDEL BREAD

Pareve   Traditional

1 cup sugar
grated rind of 1 medium orange
grated rind of 1 medium lemon
1 cup canola oil
3 eggs
1 teaspoon vanilla
1 teaspoon salt
⅓ cup poppy seeds
3½ cups flour
1 teaspoon baking powder

Topping:
4 tablespoons sugar
1 teaspoon cinnamon

✦ Preheat oven to 325°. Place sugar, orange rind and lemon rind in a food processor and pulse until finely chopped. Turn into a mixing bowl and add oil. Blend. Add eggs, vanilla, salt and poppy seeds and mix well. Slowly add flour and baking powder. Form dough into three 2-inch wide logs and place on a greased baking sheet. Bake until golden brown, 30 to 35 minutes. Remove from oven and cut diagonally into ½-inch slices. Return to baking sheet cut-side down. Combine topping ingredients and sprinkle a very small amount on each slice. Bake until crisp, about 15 to 20 minutes more.
✦ Yields 4 dozen.

TAIGLACH

Pareve   Traditional

6 eggs
1 cup sugar
1 cup oil
1 teaspoon vanilla
5 cups flour
2 teaspoons baking powder
1 (16 ounce) jar honey
1 teaspoon ground ginger
1 cup finely chopped pecans
½ cup coconut, optional

✦ Preheat oven to 350°. Combine eggs, sugar, oil and vanilla in a bowl. Gradually add flour and baking powder. Mix thoroughly. Pinch off small pieces of dough and roll in hands until pencil-thin. Cut into ½-inch pieces and bake on ungreased nonstick baking sheets for 10 to 12 minutes, turning frequently.
✦ Combine honey and ginger in a saucepan. Bring to a boil over high heat, then reduce to medium. Add cookies and stir constantly until all of honey is absorbed. Turn onto a large wooden bread board which has been dampened with cold water. Cool slightly, then pat out with a wet wooden spoon or paddle to ½-inch thickness. Sprinkle with nuts and coconut, if desired, and immediately cut into squares or diamonds.
✦ Yields 4 to 5 dozen.

TRADITIONAL

FLUDIN

¾ cup sugar
1 cup vegetable oil
juice and grated rind of 2 medium
  oranges
3½ cups flour
½ teaspoon cinnamon
1 teaspoon salt
½ teaspoon baking powder
½ teaspoon baking soda
1 tablespoon lemon juice
2 tablespoons cold water

Filling:
plum, apricot-pineapple and
  raspberry jelly
coconut
chopped nuts
cinnamon sugar
lemon juice

*Note: Each layer should have a different
color jelly. A combination of cherry,
apricot-pineapple and plum jellies
is also delicious.*

◆ Preheat oven to 350°. Combine sugar, oil and orange rind in a large bowl. Add flour, cinnamon, salt, baking powder and baking soda. Mix well. Stir in orange juice, lemon juice and water. Mix well. Divide dough into 4 parts. Place one piece of dough between 2 sheets of waxed paper and roll to a 9 x 13-inch rectangle. Place in greased 9 x 13-inch baking pan. Spread with one kind of jelly, then sprinkle with coconut, nuts, cinnamon sugar and lemon juice. Roll out second piece of dough and repeat process, using a different color jelly. Repeat with third piece of dough. Roll out last piece of dough and place on top. Sprinkle with cinnamon sugar and score into 48 sections. Bake until brown on top, about 45 minutes. Slice along scored lines when cooled.

◆ Yields 4 dozen.

I worked in a Sephardic nursing home, where I tasted a delicious cookie and asked for the recipe. It wasn't written — the ingredients were added a small amount at a time, according to the look and feel of the dough. For oil, the measurement was "a half glass." Did that mean a half cup? No, "a half glass." As soon as I arrived home I went into Mom's kitchen where, after looking around, I realized that "a half glass" was a Yahrzeit candle glass! In those days every good Jewish mother and grandmother saved the glasses for reuse when the candles burned down.

SOUR CREAM STRUDEL

Dough:
2 sticks butter, softened
1 cup sour cream
2 cups flour
powdered sugar

Filling:
1 (16 ounce) jar apricot-pineapple jam
1 cup white or dark raisins
1 cup chopped walnuts or pecans
¼ cup flaked coconut
1¼ cups chopped maraschino cherries, well drained
¼ cup lemon juice

✦ Preheat oven to 350°. Combine butter, sour cream and flour thoroughly to make a dough. Divide into 5 parts. Roll each to a 10 x 13-inch rectangle on a board well covered with flour or powdered sugar. Spread with jam and sprinkle with remaining filling ingredients. Roll from long side, jelly roll style. Place seam-side down on a baking sheet which has been coated with nonstick vegetable spray. Cut steam vents 1 inch apart. Bake for 45 minutes. When completely cool sprinkle with powdered sugar.
✦ Yields 5 to 6 dozen.

Grandma made the very best strudel from scratch. One day she and I went to the store, bought all of the ingredients for the strudel, went to her house, and she started the procedure. It took six hours, and the strudel was marvelous. I asked her to dictate the recipe as she made it, and I would write it down so it wouldn't be lost to future generations. She said to remember everything she bought and everything she did — and then go to the bakery and buy strudel.

T
R
A
D
I
T
I
O
N
A
L

259

STRETCH DOUGH STRUDEL

Dough:
2½ cups flour, divided
1 egg
2 tablespoons plus 1 teaspoon
  vegetable oil, divided
½ teaspoon salt
½ teaspoon white vinegar
lukewarm water

Filling:
4 large apples, peeled, cored and
  thinly sliced
water
1 tablespoon lemon juice
1 stick butter or pareve margarine,
  melted
½ cup sugar
1 tablespoon cinnamon
½ cup bread crumbs
1 cup chopped pecans or walnuts
1 cup shredded coconut
1 (16 ounce) jar maraschino cherries,
  drained and chopped
1 cup raisins
1 (16 ounce) jar raspberry preserves
grated rind of 1 lemon

✦ Place 2 cups flour in a medium bowl. Combine egg, 2 tablespoons oil, salt and vinegar in a 1-cup measure. Add enough lukewarm water to measure 1 cup. Whisk well and add to flour. Mix well and turn dough onto a lightly floured board. Knead 3 to 5 minutes, adding enough remaining flour to make a non-sticky dough. Brush top lightly with remaining vegetable oil. Run hot water into a glass bowl to warm it, dry the bowl and place over dough. Let stand 30 minutes. Cover work surface with a heavy cloth. Flour cloth completely. Place dough in center of cloth. Fit rolling pin with a cloth cover and roll dough to a 16-inch circle in all directions. Reach under dough with palms down to lift and ensure that dough is not sticking. Add more flour underneath if necessary to keep from sticking. Stretch dough towards outer edges with knuckles. Carefully continue rolling and stretching until dough measures about 34 x 36 inches. To repair any tears, trim edges with a sharp knife and cut dough to fit over tear. Roll in with rolling pin.

(Continued on next page)

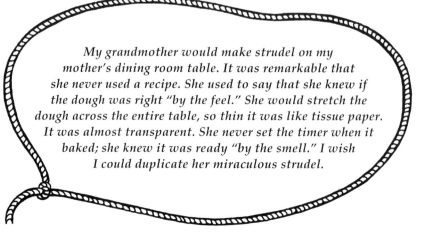

My grandmother would make strudel on my mother's dining room table. It was remarkable that she never used a recipe. She used to say that she knew if the dough was right "by the feel." She would stretch the dough across the entire table, so thin it was like tissue paper. It was almost transparent. She never set the timer when it baked; she knew it was ready "by the smell." I wish I could duplicate her miraculous strudel.

1.

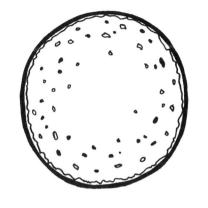

2.

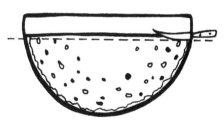

✦ Preheat oven to 350°. Place apple slices in a large bowl and add enough water to cover. Mix in lemon juice to prevent discoloration. Brush dough with melted butter, reserving 1 tablespoon. Combine sugar and cinnamon. Reserve 2 tablespoons. Sprinkle remainder over butter. Top with bread crumbs. Drain apples and pat dry. Layer over bread crumbs. Top with remaining ingredients and press gently. Starting at one end of dough, roll jelly roll fashion halfway up. Cut off with a sharp knife and seal ends. Cut in half diagonally and press seam edge down. Place both rolls seam-side down on a baking sheet which has been coated with nonstick vegetable spray. Repeat with remaining strudel. Brush with reserved melted butter and sprinkle with reserved sugar mixture. Make diagonal slits in tops with a sharp knife, about 1 inch apart. Bake until browned, 50 to 55 minutes. Remove from oven and cut through slices while still warm.

✦ Yields 4 strudels, 50 to 52 pieces.

✡ See Pareve Food Preparation, page 30

3.

4.

TRADITIONAL

PIRESHKES

Dough:
3 eggs
½ cup oil
1 cup sugar
1 teaspoon vanilla
2 tablespoons poppy seeds
juice of ½ orange
4 to 4½ cups flour
pinch of salt
2 teaspoons baking powder

Pineapple Filling:
13 ounces plum or raspberry jam, or a
   combination of both
1 (8 ounce) can crushed pineapple,
   drained
grated rind of 1 lemon
½ cup ground raisins, optional
1 cup chopped pecans
1 cup coconut
½ cup sugar
1 teaspoon cinnamon

Glaze:
2 cups honey
1 tablespoon whiskey
1 tablespoon flour
juice of ½ lemon
¼ cup sugar
poppy seeds
coconut

✦ Combine eggs, oil and sugar in a large bowl. Add vanilla, poppy seeds and orange juice. Add 4 cups flour, salt and baking powder and blend. Add additional flour if necessary to make a smooth dough. Cover and refrigerate 30 minutes. Preheat oven to 350°. Divide dough into 4 balls. Work with 1 ball at a time, refrigerating remaining ones. Roll on a floured board to ⅛-inch thickness. Cut into 1-inch wide strips. Spread with jam and pineapple. Sprinkle with lemon rind, raisins, nuts, coconut and mixture of sugar and cinnamon. Fold each strip over 3 times corner-wise to form a triangle. Cut off from dough. Repeat until all 4 balls are rolled and filled. Place on baking sheets which have been coated with nonstick vegetable spray. Bake until light brown, 30 to 40 minutes. Cool.

✦ For glaze, combine honey, whiskey, flour, lemon juice and sugar in a medium saucepan. Bring to a boil, reduce heat to low and boil 5 minutes. Add 6 pireshkes at a time to pan and stir until glazed. Remove with a slotted spoon to a foil-lined cookie sheet which has been coated with nonstick vegetable spray and sprinkled with poppy seeds and coconut. Sprinkle tops with additional poppy seeds and coconut. Repeat until all pireshkes are glazed.

✦ Yields 5 dozen.

Variation: For peach apple pireshkes, spread dough with 1 (10 ounce) jar peach jam. Top with 2 seeded, peeled and grated apples, 1 cup ground raisins, ¼ cup matzo meal, 1 cup chopped pecans or walnuts and 1 cup coconut.

Note: A Purim alternative to hamantashen.

✦ To keep dried fruits from falling to the bottom
of a cake, coat them lightly with flour.

1.

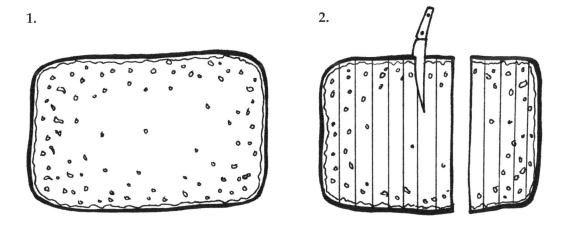

2.

3.

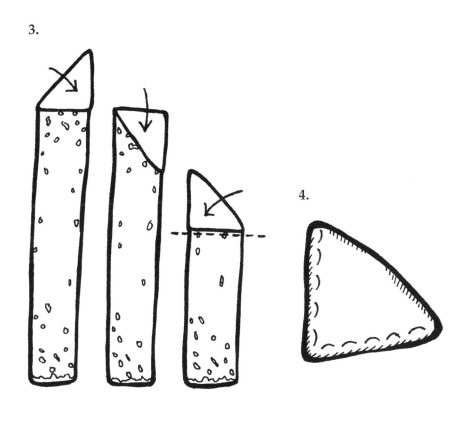

4.

ICEBERG PASS
BERRIES AND CREAM

½ cup sour cream
½ cup frozen whipped topping, thawed
¼ cup firmly packed brown sugar
¼ cup Curaçao, optional
2 tablespoons orange liqueur
1 tablespoon dark or light rum
3 pints assorted berries, washed and patted dry

✦ Combine sour cream and whipped topping. Add remaining ingredients except berries and combine well. Serve over berries.
✦ Serves 8.

✦ **Nutritional information per serving**

Calories: 106.6	Saturated Fat: 2.4g	Calories from Fat: 36.3%
Protein: 1.3g	Cholesterol: 7mg	Calories from Carbohydrate: ... 58.6%
Carbohydrate: 14.6g	Dietary Fiber: 2.7g	Calories from Protein: 5.1%
Total Fat: 4.0g	Sodium: 14mg	

ELEGANT BAKED PEARS

6 Bartlett pears
1 egg white
2 cups hot water
⅔ cup fresh bread crumbs
⅔ cup firmly packed brown sugar
⅓ cup ground almonds
8 teaspoons orange marmalade, divided
2 cups apple juice
frozen vanilla yogurt or whipped cream

✦ Preheat oven to 350°. Peel and core pears, leaving whole. Slice bottom of pears to make a flat surface. Whisk egg white and water together in a large bowl. Add pears. Combine bread crumbs, brown sugar and almonds. Remove pears from water and roll in crumb mixture until well coated. Put 1 teaspoon marmalade in cavity of each pear. Pour apple juice into a glass baking dish. Stand pears upright in dish. (Some of coating will come off.) Bake for 1 hour, then let cool to room temperature before serving. Serve with yogurt or whipped cream.

✦ **Nutritional information per serving**

Calories: 317.3	Saturated Fat: 0.6g	Calories from Fat: 15.2%
Protein: 4.3g	Cholesterol: 0mg	Calories from Carbohydrate: ... 79.7%
Carbohydrate: 66.8g	Dietary Fiber: 5.6g	Calories from Protein: 5.2%
Total Fat: 5.7g	Sodium: 108mg	

CRANBERRY POACHED PEARS

Pareve

1½ cups fresh cranberries
1 cup sugar
½ cup orange juice
2 cups frozen unsweetened
    raspberries or strawberries, thawed
2 tablespoons plus 2 teaspoons fresh
    lemon juice, divided
12 Bartlett pears with stems
2 quarts cranberry/apple juice
6 cloves
2 cinnamon sticks
fresh mint

✦ Combine cranberries, sugar and ½ cup orange juice in a saucepan. Cook over medium heat until cranberries pop, stirring. Add raspberries or strawberries. Remove from heat, cool and puree in blender until smooth. Pour through a sieve into a bowl, pressing down to strain seeds. Stir in 2 teaspoons lemon juice. Cover and refrigerate. Carefully peel pears, leaving stem intact. Slice bottom if needed to make a flat surface. Combine cranberry/apple juice, remaining lemon juice, cloves and cinnamon sticks in a large saucepan. Add pears and bring to a boil. Reduce heat and simmer one hour, uncovered. Cool. Refrigerate in liquid overnight. To serve, drizzle puree onto a plate, stand pear upright in sauce, drizzle with additional puree and garnish with fresh mint.

CHALLAH BREAD PUDDING

Dairy | **Lighter**

1 cup firmly packed brown sugar
4 (1½-inch) thick slices challah,
    buttered
2⅓ cups milk
2 eggs
1 teaspoon vanilla
½ teaspoon nutmeg
½ teaspoon cinnamon
raisins and nuts, optional

✦ Preheat oven to 350°. Spread brown sugar over bottom of an 8-inch square glass baking dish. Tear buttered challah slices into pieces and place on top of sugar. Beat milk, eggs and vanilla together. Stir in nutmeg and cinnamon. Add raisins and nuts, if desired. Pour over bread and sprinkle with additional cinnamon and nutmeg. Bake, uncovered, for 1 hour, or until slightly brown and puffed.

✦ Nutritional information per serving

Calories: 324.8	Saturated Fat: 3.8g	Calories from Fat: 21.6%
Protein: 9.1g	Cholesterol: 103mg	Calories from Carbohydrate: ... 67.3%
Carbohydrate: 55.3g	Dietary Fiber: 0.1g	Calories from Protein: 11.1%
Total Fat: 7.9g	Sodium: 233mg	

BREAD PUDDING WITH CARAMEL MASCARPONE CREAM

Dairy

Pudding:
1 loaf challah, crusts removed,
   cut in ½-inch slices
½ stick unsalted butter, melted
1 cup plus 2 tablespoons sugar,
   divided
2 teaspoons cinnamon, divided
1 vanilla bean or 2 teaspoons extract
2¼ cups whipping cream
2¼ cups milk
6 eggs
⅓ cup raisins soaked in ¼ cup rum
   or favorite liquor

Caramel Mascarpone Cream:
¾ cup sugar
1¼ cups whipping cream, chilled
   and divided
1 cup mascarpone cheese, softened

✦ Preheat oven to 350°. Place bread in a large bowl and toss with melted butter, 1 tablespoon sugar and 1 teaspoon cinnamon. Transfer to a baking sheet and bake until golden brown, 15 to 20 minutes. Combine 1 tablespoon sugar and remaining cinnamon in a small bowl. Sprinkle evenly into a buttered 9 x 13-inch baking dish and tilt to coat sides. Top with toasted bread. If using a vanilla bean, split in half lengthwise. Scrape seeds into a heavy saucepan and add pod or use vanilla extract. Add cream and milk. Heat mixture until just boiling, stirring constantly. Remove from heat. Beat eggs and remaining sugar in a large bowl until light. Strain cream mixture if bean was used. Pour into egg mixture in a stream, beating constantly. Fold in raisins. Pour over bread and let stand 30 minutes. Cover with foil and place into a second pan. Add enough hot water to reach halfway up sides of pudding dish. Bake in middle of preheated 300° oven for 1 hour, remove foil and bake until golden brown and center is barely set, about 30 more minutes.

✦ While pudding is baking, cook ¾ cup sugar in a heavy saucepan over medium-high heat until completely melted and golden, stirring constantly. Add ½ cup of cream, stirring rapidly. Continue stirring until caramel dissolves. Place mascarpone in a large bowl and beat until smooth. Gradually add remaining ¾ cup cream and continue beating until stiff peaks form. Fold in caramel mixture and blend well. If sauce separates, place over warm water in double boiler and whisk until blended.

✦ Cut pudding into squares and serve warm or at room temperature with Caramel Mascarpone Cream.

✦ 12 servings.

PASSOVER

PASSOVER INDEX

(Matzo balls appear in Soup section)

ADAPTING RECIPES FOR PASSOVER

During Passover, you may choose any poultry, meat or fish entrée that meets the dietary requirements. All leavening agents are prohibited. To adapt your favorite recipes for Passover, you can use *Kosher* for *Passover* ingredients, or substitute ingredients as follows:

For:	*Substitute:*
1 cup flour	⅝ cup potato starch, matzo cake meal, or a combination of cake meal and potato starch
Flour for thickening gravy	Half the amount of potato starch, or 1 egg yolk per tablespoon of flour
1 ounce square baking chocolate	3 tablespoons cocoa plus 1 tablespoon shortening, or Passover chocolate, melted, shaved or chopped
Cornstarch	Potato starch
Bread crumbs	Matzo meal
Graham cracker crumbs	Passover cookie or cake crumbs, ground nuts, or ground soup nuts
Extracts	Lemon juice, lemon zest, orange juice, orange zest, Passover brandy, crushed vanilla bean or vanilla sugar *(see page 232)*
1 cup confectioner's sugar	1 tablespoon potato starch and 1 cup granulated sugar, processed in food processor for about 2 minutes. Allow sugar to settle in processor for 1 minute before removing cover.
1 cup sour milk, for baking	1 tablespoon lemon juice plus enough milk to make 1 cup. Let stand 5 minutes.
1 cup light cream, for cooking	⅞ cup milk plus 2 tablespoons melted butter
1 cup heavy cream, for cooking	¾ cup milk plus ⅓ cup melted butter (not for whipping)
Alcoholic beverages, for cooking	Apple, orange or grape juice, Passover wine, or bouillon, in the same amount

P
A
S
S
O
V
E
R

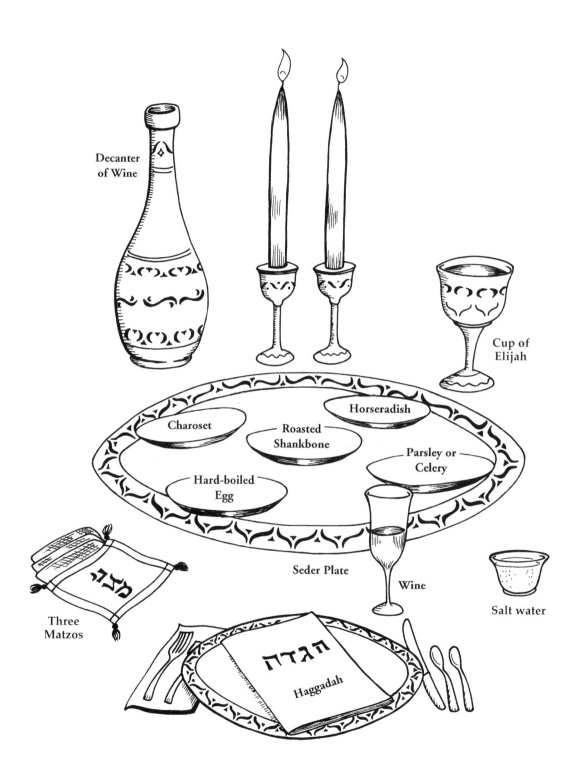

Decanter
of Wine

Cup of
Elijah

Charoset

Horseradish

Roasted
Shankbone

Parsley or
Celery

Hard-boiled
Egg

מצה

Seder Plate

Wine

Salt water

Three
Matzos

הגדה

Haggadah

CHAROSET

Pareve | Traditional

1 cup finely chopped walnuts or
  pecans
4 apples, peeled, cored and grated
1 teaspoon cinnamon
3 tablespoons sugar
7 tablespoons sweet red wine

✦ Combine all ingredients.
✦ 8 servings.

My grandfather was a man of the old school — he virtually never set foot in the kitchen. Once a year, however, he became the director of a major culinary production — the making of the charoset for the Passover seder. My mother procured the ingredients, and my sisters and I spent hours cracking the nuts. The morning of the first seder, my grandfather rolled up his sleeves, tucked his tie into his shirt and took over one corner of the kitchen. He ground the nuts, using a manual meat grinder, and then mixed the ingredients in a large bowl. Every year our family still uses "Papa's recipe," and the flavor always reminds me of his afternoons in the kitchen.

SEPHARDIC CHAROSET

Pareve | Traditional

½ pound dried dates
½ pound dried figs
1 cup dried apricots
¾ cup golden raisins
1 cup coconut
1½ teaspoons cinnamon
1 teaspoon ground cloves
1 cup plum preserves
1 cup sweet grape wine
½ cup orange juice
½ cup chopped pecans, toasted

✦ Chop dates, figs and apricots into ¼ to ½-inch dice. Place in saucepan and add remaining ingredients except pecans. Simmer over low heat, covered, for 30 minutes. Check occasionally while cooking, adding water if it becomes too thick. Cool, then add pecans. Serve at room temperature.
✦ 10 to 12 servings.

Note: Recipe can be made several days ahead and refrigerated.

P
A
S
S
O
V
E
R

PASSOVER SOUP NOODLES

6 eggs
1 cup cold water
pinch of salt
1 tablespoon vegetable oil
6 tablespoons potato starch
vegetable oil or pareve margarine for
    skillet

*Note: These pancakes can also be used for
    blintzes.
    Noodles can be frozen for up to one
    month.*

✦ Place eggs, cold water, salt, 1 tablespoon oil and potato starch in a food processor. Blend until smooth. Let rest in refrigerator, covered, for one hour. Heat vegetable oil or margarine in a medium skillet until hot but not smoking. Stir batter and ladle ¼ cup into skillet to make thin pancakes. Lightly brown on both sides. Repeat with remaining batter, stirring frequently. Cool pancakes, roll up and cut into ¼-inch slices for noodles.
✦ Makes 27 to 30 pancakes.

PASSOVER CHICKEN WITH FARFEL

2 small chickens, halved
1 medium onion, chopped
1 cup sliced celery
½ pound mushrooms, sliced
2 tablespoons pareve margarine
4 cups matzo farfel
salt, pepper, garlic powder and
    seasoning salt to taste
2 eggs, lightly beaten
2 (10 ounce) cans chicken broth
2 teaspoons paprika

*Variation: The farfel mixture also makes a
    great stuffing for a 14 to 18-
    pound turkey.*

✦ Melt margarine in a large skillet. Sauté onion and celery until soft. Add mushrooms and sauté until limp. Add farfel and cook until lightly toasted. Remove from heat. Add eggs and 1½ cans chicken broth; mix well. Season well and cool slightly. Place mixture in a greased 9 x 13-inch pan. Season chicken to taste and place on top of farfel. Cover and bake in preheated 350° oven for 1 hour. Uncover and baste chicken with remaining broth. Sprinkle well with paprika and bake 30 minutes more, or until chicken is done.
✦ 6 servings.

TZIMMES

Meat Traditional

1 large onion, chopped
3 short ribs, well-trimmed
salt and pepper
3 medium sweet potatoes, peeled
   and cut into large cubes
5 medium red potatoes, peeled and
   cut into large cubes
½ cup golden raisins
¼ to ½ cup honey
1 (12 ounce) package prunes with pits

✦ Make a bed of onions in a large Dutch oven. Place ribs over onions and salt and pepper to taste. Cover meat with water and bring to a boil on top of stove. Cover pot and cook 30 minutes. Add potatoes, raisins and ¼ cup honey. Cover and cook an additional hour. Add prunes and more water, if needed. Cook another 20 minutes, then place in preheated 325° oven and bake for 2 to 3 hours. Do not stir. Add more honey, salt and pepper to taste.
✦ 4 main course servings; 8 side dish servings.

Note: Recipe can be prepared 2 days in advance, refrigerated and reheated before serving.

PASSOVER MEATLESS TZIMMES

Pareve Traditional Lighter

2 pounds sweet potatoes
1 pound carrots, peeled and cut into
   ¾-inch slices
½ cup pareve margarine
¼ cup firmly packed brown sugar
¼ cup honey
½ teaspoon cinnamon
¼ teaspoon nutmeg
½ cup orange juice
1 cup pitted prunes

✦ Bake potatoes until tender. Peel and dice into ¾-inch cubes. Place carrots in a saucepan, cover with water and boil until tender. Drain. Combine margarine, brown sugar, honey, cinnamon, nutmeg and orange juice in a large saucepan. Bring to a boil and add the sweet potatoes, carrots and prunes. Reduce heat and simmer until thick, 15 to 30 minutes.
✦ 8 servings.

Variation: Add matzo balls.
Note: Do not freeze. Recipe can be prepared 2 days in advance and reheated before serving.

P
A
S
S
O
V
E
R

✦ Nutritional information per serving

Calories: 399.3	Saturated Fat: 1.5g	Calories from Fat: 18.1%
Protein: 4.3g	Cholesterol: 0mg	Calories from Carbohydrate: ... 77.8%
Carbohydrate: 81.3g	Dietary Fiber: 8.9g	Calories from Protein: 4.1%
Total Fat: 8.4g	Sodium: 139mg	

DRUNKEN TZIMMES

3 large carrots, sliced
1½ cups sliced yams
10 pitted prunes
2 apples, sliced
½ cup raisins
½ cup chopped pecans
1 (8 ounce) can crushed pineapple,
    with juice
¾ cup firmly packed brown sugar
½ cup orange juice
¼ cup rum or sweet red wine
1 teaspoon cinnamon
½ teaspoon ground ginger
½ teaspoon allspice

✦ Combine all ingredients in a large bowl. Pour into a well-greased 2-quart casserole and bake, covered, in preheated 300° oven for 3 to 4 hours.
✦ 6 to 8 servings.

Note: Good for any holiday or Shabbat. Recipe can be made 2 days ahead and refrigerated.

It's five weeks before Passover, and today is my mother's 86th birthday. Next week she will begin her preparations for the holiday. First on her list of things to do is to make about 150 matzo balls and freeze them in packages of 15. That will be enough for the two seders — a package for each of my five daughters and their families, and some for other family and friends. A few days before the holiday she will make three gallons of wonderful chicken soup, two chopped liver molds, several marble cakes, chocolate cakes, Passover strudel, mandel bread, and at least four different kinds of cookies. My mom is truly a remarkable mother, grandmother and great-grandmother. She is adored by all of her family.

PASSOVER VEGETABLE CASSEROLE

6 matzos, crushed, or 3 cups matzo
  farfel
⅓ cup vegetable oil
1 large onion, diced
2 cloves garlic, crushed
1 red bell pepper, seeded and diced
2 small summer squash, diced
2 small zucchini, diced
1 small eggplant, diced
1 large carrot, grated
½ pound mushrooms, sliced
2 stalks celery, diced
2 teaspoons salt, divided
½ teaspoon pepper, divided
4 eggs

*Note: Can prepare 1 to 2 days in advance.
        Refrigerate uncooked.*

✦ Place matzo in a large bowl and add enough hot water to cover. Let sit 5 minutes, then drain in a colander. Heat oil over medium-high heat in a large skillet. Sauté onion 2 minutes and add garlic and remaining vegetables. Sauté 2 more minutes. Add 1 teaspoon salt and ¼ teaspoon pepper. Cover and simmer over medium heat until vegetables are soft, stirring frequently, about 15 minutes. Remove from heat and cool slightly. Beat eggs in a large bowl with remaining salt and pepper. Add matzo and vegetables and stir to combine. Turn into a well-greased 9 x 13-inch glass baking dish. Bake in preheated 350° oven until well browned, 45 minutes to 1 hour.
✦ 16 servings.

**P
A
S
S
O
V
E
R**

✦ Substitute two egg whites for each whole egg.

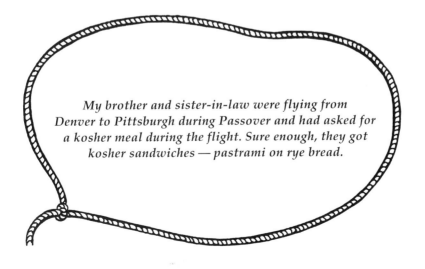

*My brother and sister-in-law were flying from
Denver to Pittsburgh during Passover and had asked for
a kosher meal during the flight. Sure enough, they got
kosher sandwiches — pastrami on rye bread.*

PINEAPPLE MATZO KUGEL

6 matzo, broken in pieces
4 eggs
1 cup sugar
1 teaspoon salt
½ teaspoon cinnamon
1 (8 ounce) can crushed pineapple, drained
¼ cup margarine, melted
1 (16 ounce) carton low-fat cottage cheese

✦ Place matzo in a colander and pour hot water over it until matzo softens. Combine eggs and sugar in a large mixing bowl and beat until light in color. Add salt and cinnamon. Stir in pineapple, margarine and cottage cheese. Add softened matzo and pour into a greased 9-inch square pan. Bake in preheated 350° oven until light brown, 50 to 60 minutes.

✦ 10 servings.

✡ See variation

Variations: *For an unsweetened kugel, omit sugar, cinnamon and pineapple. Add one large chopped onion and ½ pound sliced mushrooms which have been sautéed in oil.*

For a pareve apple kugel, omit cottage cheese, add 4 large peeled cubed apples or 2 (20 ounce) cans of pie-sliced apples packed in water and drained. Increase cinnamon to 2 teaspoons and add 3 tablespoons lemon juice. Substitute pareve margarine. Bake in a 9 x 13-inch pan.

✦ Nutritional information per serving

Calories: 327.1	Saturated Fat: 2.2g	Calories from Fat: 24.9%
Protein: 12.5g	Cholesterol: 109mg	Calories from Carbohydrate: ... 59.9%
Carbohydrate: 49.3g	Dietary Fiber: 0.9g	Calories from Protein: 15.2%
Total Fat: 9.1g	Sodium: 596mg	

PASSOVER BROCCOLI SOUFFLÉ

Pareve

1 (32 ounce) bag frozen cut broccoli
4 eggs
1 package onion soup mix
1 cup mayonnaise
salt and pepper
matzo meal for dusting baking dish
1 tablespoon matzo meal
paprika

✦ Cook broccoli according to package directions, drain and cool. Beat eggs, onion soup mix and mayonnaise in a medium bowl. Add broccoli and salt and pepper to taste and combine well. Pour into a greased 9-inch square glass baking dish which has been dusted with matzo meal. Sprinkle with 1 tablespoon matzo meal and paprika. Bake in preheated 350° oven for 30 to 45 minutes. Let rest 5 minutes before cutting.
✦ 9 servings.

CAULIFLOWER SOUFFLÉ

Pareve

2 medium heads cauliflower, washed
   and separated into small florets
¼ cup vegetable oil
2 medium onions, chopped
salt and pepper
2 eggs, beaten
¼ cup matzo meal

✦ Bring 4 cups water to boil in a large pot. Add cauliflower and salt to taste. Cook until very tender, about 25-30 minutes. Drain, return to pot and mash with a potato masher. Heat oil in a medium skillet and sauté onions until tender and lightly browned. Add to cauliflower. Season with salt and pepper to taste. Add eggs and matzo meal. Place in a greased 8-inch square pan. Bake in preheated 350° oven until golden, about 45 minutes.
✦ 8 servings.

ZUCCHINI POTATO LATKES

4 eggs
4 cups grated potatoes, with skins
⅔ cup grated onion
⅓ cup matzo meal
1 medium zucchini, grated
1 teaspoon salt
½ teaspoon pepper
1 teaspoon dried, minced parsley, optional
vegetable oil for frying
sour cream, optional

✦ Beat eggs in a large bowl until light and foamy. Add remaining ingredients except sour cream and stir until thoroughly blended. Heat about ¼ inch oil in a large heavy skillet or electric frying pan. Spoon a scant ¼ cup mixture into hot oil. Fry on both sides until golden brown. Repeat until all batter is used, adding oil as needed. Drain latkes on paper towels. Serve with sour cream, if desired.

✦ Yields 2 dozen latkes.

✡ See Pareve Food Preparation, page 30

PASSOVER CHEESE LORRAINE

2 tablespoons butter
1 medium onion, coarsely chopped
½ pound mushrooms, sliced
3 eggs
2 cups milk
4 matzos, broken into small pieces
½ pound grated cheddar cheese or mixed cheese
½ teaspoon salt
¼ teaspoon pepper

Variation: Add cooked, drained spinach.

✦ Melt butter in a medium skillet over medium-high heat. Sauté onion until soft. Add mushrooms and sauté until limp. Transfer to a quiche pan or 9-inch pie pan which has been coated with nonstick vegetable spray. Beat eggs in a large bowl. Add milk, matzo and cheese and stir to combine. Season with salt and pepper. Pour over mushroom mixture and bake in preheated 350° oven until set, about 45 minutes.

✦ 8 servings.

SEPHARDIC SPINACH TOMATO MATZO PIE

3 to 4 matzos, plain or whole wheat
2 tablespoons butter, margarine or
   vegetable oil
1 medium onion, finely chopped
2 cloves garlic, minced
1 (10 ounce) package frozen chopped
   spinach, thawed and squeezed dry
1 (16 ounce) can tomatoes, chopped
   with juice
½ teaspoon salt
½ teaspoon pepper
nutmeg, optional
2 eggs
6 ounces shredded cheese - any
   combination of mozzarella,
   Muenster, Swiss or American

✦ Place matzos in a large bowl and cover with warm water. Soak for 1½ minutes, then carefully place on paper towels to drain. Melt butter in a large skillet over medium heat. Sauté onion and garlic until tender but not browned. Add spinach, tomatoes and juice. Cook, stirring occasionally, until most of liquid has evaporated, about 5 minutes. Add salt and pepper and nutmeg, if desired. Remove from heat and cool slightly. Beat eggs in a large shallow dish. Add matzo and coat both sides. Place a single layer of matzo in an 8-inch square glass baking dish which has been coated with nonstick vegetable spray. Top with half of tomato mixture and sprinkle with a third of the cheese. Layer again with matzo, sauce and cheese. Cover with a final layer of matzo and the remaining cheese. Bake in preheated 375° oven until cheese is melted and casserole is bubbly, about 20 to 25 minutes. Remove from oven and let rest 5 minutes before cutting.
✦ 6 servings.

**P
A
S
S
O
V
E
R**

✦ Two cups of evaporated milk, beaten slowly,
will yield a pound of butter in a pinch.
Pour into a pan and chill.

MATZO LASAGNA

Meat

Basic Bolognese Sauce:
¼ cup pareve margarine
2 tablespoons olive oil
1 medium onion, finely chopped
1 carrot, finely chopped
1 stalk celery, finely chopped
1½ pounds ground beef or veal
salt and pepper to taste
1 cup dry white wine (Kosher for
   Passover)
1 (28 ounce) can Italian-style
   tomatoes, crushed

Lasagna:
¼ cup plus 1 tablespoon extra virgin
   olive oil
1 tablespoon chopped garlic
6 cups loosely packed spinach,
   washed and patted dry
4 to 5 matzos
3 tablespoons chopped fresh basil,
   divided

Note: Worth the effort.

✦ For the sauce, melt margarine with olive oil in a large saucepan. Add onion, carrot and celery and sauté over medium heat until lightly browned. Add meat. Cook and stir until meat is no longer pink. Season to taste with salt and pepper. Increase heat and stir in wine. Cook until wine has evaporated. Add tomatoes, cover and reduce heat. Simmer until sauce becomes medium thick, stirring occasionally, about 1 to 1½ hours.

✦ For the lasagna, heat ¼ cup olive oil in skillet over medium heat. Sauté garlic and spinach about 4 minutes. Spread bottom of a 7 x 11-inch casserole with remaining olive oil. Line dish with 1 layer of matzo. Top with a third of spinach mixture, a third of sauce and 1 tablespoon basil. Repeat layers twice, ending with a layer of sauce. Bake in preheated 375° oven until top is bubbly, about 35 minutes.

✦ 6 servings.

PASSOVER PANCAKES

2 eggs
½ cup matzo cake meal
½ cup water
2 tablespoons sugar
pinch of salt

Note: This recipe doubles or triples well.

✦ Whisk all ingredients together in a medium bowl. Drop by spoonfuls onto a greased griddle or skillet over medium-high heat. Turn when top is bubbly and brown on both sides.
✦ 3 servings.

> *As a very young boy on the West Side of Chicago, I was fascinated by an old man with a long white beard who sat on a folding chair on the sidewalk outside of the fish monger's. On a big wooden box, he had a hand grater that he used to grate fresh horseradish for customers. The strong aroma of freshly grated horseradish is always a reminder of my childhood.*

PASSOVER BAGELS

⅔ cup water
⅓ cup vegetable oil
1 teaspoon sugar
¼ teaspoon salt
1 cup matzo meal
3 eggs

✦ Bring water to a boil in a medium saucepan. Add oil, sugar and salt. Reduce heat to medium, add matzo meal and beat until smooth. Remove from heat and let cool 10 minutes. Add eggs one at a time, beating well after each addition. Drop batter onto a greased cookie sheet, dividing batter into 10 bagels, leaving 2 inches between each. Drop a little cold water in the middle of each bagel and press into the bagel to make the hole. Bake in preheated 375° oven until golden brown, about 45 minutes.
✦ Yields 10 bagels.

PASSOVER

PASSOVER ONION ROLLS

1½ cups boiling water
1½ cups matzo meal
½ cup vegetable oil
1 teaspoon salt
pinch pepper
2 tablespoons sugar
1 tablespoon potato starch
4 eggs
1 small onion, finely chopped

Variations: Add ½ teaspoon dried dill, grated Havarti cheese (Kosher for Passover), or Passover chopped, pitted green olives. Omit onion for plain rolls.

✦ Preheat oven to 400°. Pour boiling water over matzo meal in a large saucepan. Add oil, salt, pepper, sugar and potato starch. Stir well, cover and cool. When mixture has cooled, add eggs one at a time, beating well after each addition. Add onion and mix well. Fill greased muffin tins two-thirds full and bake until brown, about 50 minutes.
✦ Yields 16 rolls.

✿ See Pareve Food Preparation, page 30

PASSOVER BLUEBERRY MUFFINS

½ cup butter or pareve margarine, softened
1 cup sugar
3 eggs
¼ teaspoon salt
¼ cup potato starch
½ cup matzo cake meal
1 teaspoon lemon juice
1 heaping cup fresh or frozen blueberries, rinsed, drained and patted dry
cinnamon sugar

Variation: Substitute sliced strawberries or raspberries for blueberries.

✦ Preheat oven to 400°. Cream butter and sugar in a mixing bowl until light and fluffy. Add eggs one at a time, beating well after each addition. Fold in salt, potato starch and cake meal. Add lemon juice. Fold in blueberries carefully. Pour into 12 paper-lined or well-greased muffin cups and sprinkle with cinnamon sugar. Bake until lightly browned, about 20 minutes.
✦ Yields 1 dozen muffins.

✿ See Pareve Food Preparation, page 30

SPONGE CAKE OR JELLY ROLL WITH LEMON FILLING

Sponge Cake or Jelly Roll:
9 eggs, separated
1½ cups sugar
juice and grated rind of 1 medium lemon
⅓ cup orange juice
1 scant cup potato starch
¼ cup Passover powdered sugar (see page 269)

Lemon Filling:
2 eggs
¾ cup sugar
1½ tablespoons potato starch
juice and grated rind of 1 medium lemon
¾ cup water
1 tablespoon margarine or pareve margarine

Note: The lemon filling can be prepared 2 days in advance, then refrigerated.

✦ Beat egg whites until stiff. In another bowl, beat egg yolks until light. Gradually add granulated sugar and continue beating until thick and lemon-colored. Add remaining ingredients except powdered sugar. Fold whites into batter gently.

✦ For a cake, preheat oven to 350°. Pour batter into ungreased tube pan and bake for 1 hour. Remove from oven, invert and cool completely before removing cake from pan.

✦ For a jelly roll, preheat oven to 325°. Grease bottom and sides of a jelly roll pan with margarine. Line bottom with foil and grease foil well with margarine. Spread batter over foil and bake for 30 minutes. Invert onto a clean dish towel which has been sprinkled with powdered sugar. Remove pan and foil and roll cake in towel to cool.

✦ For lemon filling, beat eggs in top of a double boiler. Combine sugar and potato starch in a small bowl. Add to eggs. Add remaining ingredients and cook over hot water, stirring constantly, until thick. Cool.

✦ To assemble jelly roll, unroll in towel and spread filling on roll with a spatula. Roll back up (without the towel) and place on a serving tray, seam-side down. Sprinkle with additional powdered sugar and serve with whipped cream and strawberries, if desired.

✦ 12 servings.

✡ See Pareve Food Preparation, page 30

**P
A
S
S
O
V
E
R**

COCOA PASSOVER CAKE

Dairy or Pareve ✡

½ cup imported fine quality cocoa
⅔ cup cold water
9 eggs, separated
1½ cups sugar, divided
1 teaspoon vanilla
½ cup oil
½ cup matzo cake meal
½ cup potato starch

Topping:
1 cup whipping cream
1 tablespoon cocoa
1 tablespoon Passover powdered
    sugar (see page 269)

OR

1 cup pareve nondairy whipped
    topping
1 tablespoon cocoa

sliced fresh strawberries

✦ Preheat oven to 350°. Combine cocoa and water in a small saucepan. Bring to a boil over low heat and stir until thickened. Beat egg whites in a mixing bowl until frothy. Gradually add ¼ cup sugar and continue beating until stiff peaks form. Beat egg yolks with 1¼ cups sugar in another bowl. Add vanilla and oil and mix well. Sift together matzo cake meal and potato starch and add to yolk mixture alternately with cocoa mixture. Mix well. Fold in egg whites. Pour batter into ungreased tube pan and bake for 10 minutes. Reduce heat to 325° and bake 50 minutes longer. Cool cake for 20 minutes, then invert. When completely cool, remove from pan and cut in half horizontally. If using whipping cream, whip with cocoa and powdered sugar until stiff peaks form. If using nondairy topping, fold cocoa into topping. Spread half of topping of choice between cake halves and top with strawberries. Replace top of cake and frost with remaining topping. Garnish with strawberries.
✦ 12 servings.

✡ See Pareve Food Preparation, page 30

PASSOVER CHOCOLATE PUDDING CAKE

1 teaspoon instant coffee granules
1 cup hot water
2 packages Passover chocolate cake
    mix
1 package Passover chocolate
    pudding mix
4 eggs
½ cup vegetable oil

✦ Preheat oven to 350°. Dissolve coffee in hot water in a small bowl. Pour into a large bowl. Add remaining ingredients and beat for 2 minutes. Pour into a greased bundt or tube pan and bake for 40 to 55 minutes. Test with a toothpick after 40 minutes.
✦ 12 servings.

PASSOVER CHOCOLATE ROLL

5 eggs, separated
⅔ cup sugar
2½ tablespoons potato starch
⅓ cup sifted matzo cake meal
3 tablespoons cocoa
1 cup whipping cream
**¼ cup Passover powdered sugar
(see page 269)**

Note: Can be prepared 1 day in advance.

✦ Preheat oven to 375°. Beat egg yolks in a large bowl until light. Gradually add sugar and continue beating until lemon-colored. Add potato starch, matzo cake meal and cocoa. Beat egg whites in another bowl until stiff. Fold into chocolate mixture. Coat bottom of a 9 x 13-inch baking pan with non-stick vegetable spray. Line bottom of pan with waxed paper and coat paper with spray. Spread batter in pan and bake until cake springs back when touched, about 12 minutes. Invert cake onto a clean dish towel which has been sprinkled with powdered sugar. Remove waxed paper and trim hard edge off cake. Roll cake in towel from short end and let cool. Beat whipping cream with ¼ cup powdered sugar until stiff peaks form. Unroll cake and spread with cream. Reroll, without towel, and refrigerate.
✦ 10 servings.

PASSOVER CARROT NUT CAKE

1 cup sliced carrots
1 cup walnuts
6 eggs, separated
1 cup sugar
1 teaspoon cinnamon
1 teaspoon vanilla
¾ cup matzo cake meal
**Passover powdered sugar
(see page 269), optional**

Note: This cake can be frozen.

✦ Preheat oven to 350°. Place carrots and walnuts in a food processor and process until ground. Beat egg yolks in a large mixing bowl until light. Gradually add sugar and continue beating until thick and lemon-colored, about 5 minutes. Add carrots, walnuts, cinnamon and vanilla. Blend. Stir in matzo cake meal. Beat egg whites in another bowl until stiff peaks form. Fold some of whites into matzo mixture to lighten, then fold in remaining whites. Turn batter into ungreased 8-inch springform pan. Bake until a toothpick inserted in center comes out clean, about 50 minutes. Invert cake in pan and cool completely on wire rack before removing pan edge. Sprinkle with powdered sugar, if desired.
✦ 14 servings.

NOT-JUST-FOR-PASSOVER CHOCOLATE TORTE

 Dairy

1 pound semisweet chocolate chips
½ cup margarine or butter
5 large eggs, separated
1 tablespoon vanilla
¼ cup plus 2 tablespoons sugar, divided
cocoa
1 cup whipping cream
raspberries

✦ Preheat oven to 250°. Melt chocolate and margarine in a 2-quart saucepan over low heat. Beat egg yolks with vanilla in a large bowl. Slowly beat chocolate mixture into yolks until blended. Beat egg whites in another bowl with mixer at high speed, until soft peaks form. Gradually add ¼ cup sugar and continue beating until stiff peaks form. Fold into chocolate mixture a third at a time. Generously grease a 9-inch springform pan and line bottom with a circle cut from parchment or waxed paper. Generously grease paper and dust with cocoa. Spread batter evenly in pan and bake until toothpick inserted in center comes out almost clean, 1 hour to 1 hour, 15 minutes. Cool in pan, then remove side of pan. Remove torte from bottom of pan and discard paper. Place on serving dish and cut into 12 wedges. Beat whipping cream with remaining sugar until stiff. Top each torte slice with whipped cream and raspberries.
✦ 12 servings.

BITTERSWEET PASSOVER BROWNIES

 Dairy

7 ounces Elite bittersweet chocolate
½ cup margarine
4 eggs
¼ teaspoon salt
1⅓ cups sugar
1 cup matzo cake meal
½ cup chopped walnuts or pecans

✦ Preheat oven to 350°. Melt chocolate and margarine in top of double boiler over hot water. Cool. Beat eggs and salt in mixing bowl until thick and lemon-colored. Gradually beat in sugar. Add cooled chocolate mixture and blend. Add matzo cake meal and beat until well blended. Stir in nuts. Spread evenly in a well-greased 9 x 13-inch baking pan and bake for 30 to 35 minutes. Do not overbake.
✦ Yields 24 brownies.

PASSOVER MERINGUE TORTE

4 egg whites
¼ teaspoon salt
¾ cup plus 2 tablespoons sugar, divided
matzo cake meal
½ cup shaved semisweet chocolate, divided
1 cup whipping cream

Orange Filling:
4 egg yolks
⅓ cup sugar
1 teaspoon grated lemon peel
1 teaspoon grated orange peel
2 tablespoons orange juice
1 tablespoon lemon juice

✦ Preheat oven to 275°. Beat egg whites in a large bowl until frothy. Add salt and continue beating until stiff. Gradually add ¾ cup sugar, 2 tablespoons at a time, beating well after each addition. Spread in a well-greased 9-inch pie pan which has been dusted with matzo cake meal. Make edges slightly higher than center. Bake for 1 hour. Cool.

✦ For the orange filling, beat egg yolks in a small bowl until thick and lemon-colored. Gradually add ⅓ cup sugar. Add remaining ingredients and pour into top of a double boiler. Cook over hot water until thick, stirring constantly. Cool.

✦ Sprinkle ¼ cup shaved chocolate over meringue. Whip cream and 2 tablespoons sugar until stiff. Spread half of whipped cream over chocolate. Pour cooled filling over cream and gently spread. Top with remaining whipped cream and sprinkle with remaining chocolate.

✦ 10 servings.

CAKE-LIKE PASSOVER BROWNIES

½ cup butter or pareve margarine, softened
1½ cups sugar
4 eggs
7 tablespoons cocoa, sifted
½ cup milk or water
1 cup matzo cake meal
½ teaspoon salt
½ cup chopped pecans

Note: These brownies freeze well.

✦ Preheat oven to 350°. Cream butter and sugar in a medium mixing bowl until light and fluffy. Add eggs one at a time, blending well after each addition. Add cocoa and mix well. Combine matzo cake meal and salt and add to butter mixture alternately with milk. Beat until well blended. Fold in nuts. Pour into a greased 9-inch square baking pan. Bake until a toothpick inserted in center comes out clean, 35 to 40 minutes. Cool before cutting into squares.

✦ Yields 12 brownies.

✡ See Pareve Food Preparation, page 30

PASSOVER TRIFLE

Dairy

½ large Passover sponge cake,
   cut in ½-inch slices
cream red wine
1 (12 ounce) jar raspberry preserves
1 (3¾ ounce) package Passover instant
   vanilla pudding, prepared
   according to package directions
1 pint strawberries, sliced,
   or raspberries
1 banana, thinly sliced
1 cup whipping cream
1 teaspoon sugar
½ teaspoon vanilla
1 ounce semisweet chocolate, shaved
1 (3½ ounce) package sliced almonds,
   toasted

*Variation: Add Elberta peaches, canned or
   frozen and thawed, which have
   been well drained.*

✦ Quickly dip one-third cake in wine and line a trifle dish or glass bowl, bottom and sides, with a third of the slices, stopping 1½ inches from top of bowl. Spread with one-third of preserves. Spoon one-third of pudding into bowl, top with a layer of one-third of strawberries and one-third of bananas. Add another layer of cake which has been dipped in wine. Spread cake with preserves and top with layers of pudding, strawberries and bananas. Repeat until bowl is filled to 1½ inches from top. Whip cream with sugar and vanilla until stiff peaks form. Frost top of trifle with whipped cream and garnish with chocolate shavings and almonds. Refrigerate several hours before serving.

✦ 10 servings.

PASSOVER MANDEL "BREAD"

Dairy or Pareve ✡

1½ cups sugar
½ cup vegetable oil
½ cup margarine or pareve margarine,
   softened
6 eggs
2½ cups matzo cake meal
¾ cup potato starch
1 tablespoon orange juice
1 teaspoon vanilla
¾ cup chopped nuts
¼ cup sugar
½ teaspoon cinnamon

✦ Cream sugar, oil and margarine in a mixing bowl until light and fluffy. Add eggs, one at a time, beating well after each addition. Add matzo cake meal and potato starch and blend well. Add orange juice, vanilla and nuts and mix. Cover dough and refrigerate several hours. Divide dough into 4 logs, each about 2 inches wide. Place on 2 greased baking sheets. Bake in preheated 350° oven until brown, about 40 minutes. Remove from oven and cut into ½-inch slices. Place slices flat on baking sheets, cut-side down. Combine sugar and cinnamon and sprinkle half of mixture over slices. Return to oven and bake 10 minutes. Turn and sprinkle with remaining sugar and cinnamon mixture. Bake until crisp and brown, about 10 more minutes.

✡ See Pareve Food Preparation, page 30

FESTIVE PASSOVER MANDEL "BREAD"

3 eggs
1 cup sugar
¾ cup vegetable oil
½ teaspoon salt
2 cups matzo cake meal
½ cup potato starch
2 tablespoons matzo meal
2 tablespoons lemon juice
1 teaspoon vanilla or almond extract
1 cup chopped nuts
¼ cup sugar
½ teaspoon cinnamon

✦ Beat eggs in a mixing bowl until light. Add sugar, oil and salt and beat until thick and lemon-colored. Add matzo cake meal, potato starch and matzo meal. Blend well. Add juice, extract and nuts. Cover and refrigerate overnight.

✦ The following day, oil hands and divide dough into 6 logs. Place on 2 greased baking sheets and lightly score tops. Do not cut through. Bake in preheated 375° oven for 20 to 25 minutes. Remove from oven and cut into ½-inch slices. Place slices flat on baking sheets, cut-side down. Combine sugar and cinnamon and sprinkle lightly over each slice. Bake an additional 10 to 15 minutes, until slices are brown and crisp.

✦ Yields 4 to 5 dozen.

MAMA'S "OATMEAL" COOKIES

1 cup matzo farfel
1 cup matzo meal
¾ cup sugar
pinch of salt
grated rind of ½ lemon
1 teaspoon cinnamon
⅓ cup vegetable oil
2 eggs
1 egg white
¾ cup chopped nuts
¾ cup raisins

✦ Preheat oven to 350°. Place all ingredients in a large mixing bowl and blend with electric mixer until combined. Cover and refrigerate for 1 hour. Drop by heaping teaspoonfuls on greased baking sheet. Bake 15-20 minutes.

✦ Yields 3 dozen.

Variation: For chocolate chip "oatmeal" cookies, omit lemon peel, cinnamon and raisins. Add ¾ cup chocolate chips.

P
A
S
S
O
V
E
R

CHOCOLATE CHUNK MACAROONS

½ cup sugar
2½ cups shredded coconut
2 large egg whites
½ cup semisweet pareve chocolate
 chunks or chips
1 teaspoon vanilla
pinch of salt

✦ Preheat oven to 350°. Combine all ingredients in a large bowl, using hands to mix well. Dampen hands with cold water and form 1½ tablespoons of mixture into a loose haystack shape. Place on a well-greased or parchment paper-lined baking sheet. Repeat until all coconut mixture has been used, placing stacks 1 inch apart. Bake until golden brown, about 10 to 15 minutes. Cool slightly before removing from baking sheet.
✦ Yields 20 cookies.

COLORADO COCONUT CUPCAKES

4 egg whites
½ teaspoon lemon juice
½ teaspoon vanilla
1¼ cups sugar
1 (7 ounce) package coconut
1½ tablespoons matzo meal
1 tablespoon potato starch

Variation: Drizzle tops with melted semi-sweet chocolate.

✦ Preheat oven to 350°. In a large bowl, beat egg whites, lemon juice, vanilla and sugar until stiff, but not dry. Carefully fold in coconut, matzo meal and potato starch. Fill paper-lined muffin cups two-thirds full. Bake until light brown, 30 to 40 minutes. Do not overbake.
✦ Yields 15 cupcakes.

MATZO BRITTLE

1 cup butter or margarine
1 cup firmly packed light brown
   sugar
1 cup chopped pecans
6 matzos

Variation: Add 1 (6 ounce) package choco-
*   late chips to butter mixture,*
*   after boiling.*
Note: This brittle freezes well.

✦ Preheat oven to 325°. Place butter and brown sugar in a medium saucepan. Bring to a boil over medium-high heat and boil for 2 minutes. Stir in pecans. Grease sides and bottom of a jelly roll pan with butter or margarine. Completely cover pan with a single layer of matzo. Spoon butter mixture over matzo and spread evenly. Bake until very crisp, about 12 minutes. Cool in pan and break into pieces.
✦ Yields about 100 pieces.

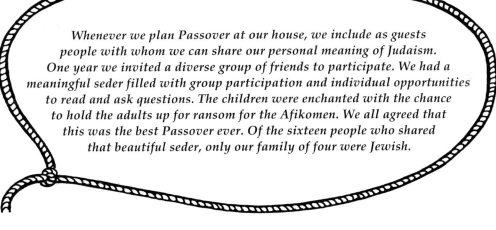

Whenever we plan Passover at our house, we include as guests people with whom we can share our personal meaning of Judaism. One year we invited a diverse group of friends to participate. We had a meaningful seder filled with group participation and individual opportunities to read and ask questions. The children were enchanted with the chance to hold the adults up for ransom for the Afikomen. We all agreed that this was the best Passover ever. Of the sixteen people who shared that beautiful seder, only our family of four were Jewish.

PASSOVER

DRIED FRUIT COMPOTE

1 cup large pitted prunes
1 cup dried apricots
1 cup dried pears
½ cup dried peaches
½ cup dried apple rings
½ cup raisins
¼ cup honey
⅓ cup firmly packed brown sugar
juice and grated peel of 1 medium
    lemon
juice and grated peel of 1 medium
    orange
5 whole cloves
1 cinnamon stick
toasted slivered blanched almonds,
    optional

✦ Place all fruit in a large non-aluminum saucepan. Add enough water to cover and stir in remaining ingredients except almonds. Bring to a boil, then reduce heat to low and simmer until fruit is plump and tender, about 20 minutes. Remove cloves and cinnamon stick with a slotted spoon. Cover and chill at least 4 hours or overnight. Garnish with almonds, if desired.

✦ 14 servings.

Note: This will keep in refrigerator for several weeks.

✦ **Nutritional information per serving**

Calories: 205.7	Saturated Fat: 0.1g	Calories from Fat: 3.1%
Protein: 2.0g	Cholesterol: 0mg	Calories from Carbohydrate: ... 93.5%
Carbohydrate: 54.1g	Dietary Fiber: 4.0g	Calories from Protein: 3.4%
Total Fat: 0.8g	Sodium: 15mg	

GLOSSARY OF TERMS

There are various spellings of the terms included in this Glossary. The "correct" spelling depends on the opinion of the "maven" you happen to ask. This version reflects some of the opinions among the Friends of Shalom Park.

Afikoman	The larger portion of the middle of the three ceremonial matzos served as the dessert to all at the Passover Seder.
Ashkenazic	Jews of Middle or Eastern European descent and their practices.
Ayer kichel	A plain egg cookie.
Babka	A yeast coffee cake with dried fruit.
Blintzes	Cheese or condiment filled crêpes.
Borscht	Cold beet or spinach soup; sometimes served hot when made with cabbage or meat.
Bubbie	Grandmother.
Challah	Braided egg bread for Shabbat and holidays.
Chametz	Any food item which contains leavening (not eaten during the Passover holiday).
Chanukah	The holiday celebrating the Maccabee's victory over the Syrians.
Chanukiyah	A nine-branched menorah (including the shamash) used only for Chanukah.
Charoset	Sweet apple, nut and wine mixture eaten at the Passover Seder.
Cholent	A bean, vegetable and meat casserole cooked overnight and eaten at Sabbath lunch.
Draydel	A four-sided top with Hebrew letters used in a Chanukah game.
Essen	Yiddish term meaning "to eat."
Farfel	A small round pasta (or crumbled matzo).
Feter	Uncle.
Fleishig	Made of, prepared with, or used for meat or meat products.

Fludin	A pastry similar to strudel.
Gedempte	Roasted.
Gefilte Fish	Ground and stewed fish usually made with carp or white fish.
Greggers	Noise makers used during the reading of the Megillah at the holiday of Purim.
Haggadah	The narrative relating the story of the Exodus, read at the Passover Seder.
Haimisheh	Unpretentious; friendly; warm.
Hamantashen	Traditional, three-cornered filled pastry eaten during the holiday of Purim.
Havdalah	The ceremony at the close of the Sabbath.
Kasha	Buckwheat groats.
Kishke	A casing stuffed with a meat or vegetable mixture, served as a side dish.
Knaidlach	A dumpling (matzo ball) made of matzo meal and served in soup.
Knish	A small, filled dumpling.
Kosher, Kasher	Terms used to designate food that is fit and proper to eat according to Kashrut Jewish law.
Kreplach	A dough mixture cut into squares, filled with shredded meat or chicken, folded into triangles and fried or cooked in soup.
Kugel	A casserole usually composed of rice, noodles or potatoes and served as a side dish.
Latkes	Potato pancakes.
Lokshen	Noodles.
Matzo	Unleavened bread.
Maven	Expert.
Megillah	A Biblical scroll, one of which contains the story of Esther read on Purim.

Menorah	A decorative seven-branched candle holder reminiscent of those used in the ancient Jerusalem Temple. (see *Chanukiyah*)
Milchig	Made of, derived from, or used for dairy products.
Mishloach Manot	Purim gifts.
Ner Tamid	A light which burns continuously.
Pareve	Food which contains no dairy or meat ingredients.
Pesach, Passover	Holiday commemorating the Jews' Exodus from Egypt.
Pirogen	Similar to kreplach filled with meat or cheese (never both).
Pletzel	A flat, crisp roll topped with poppy seeds and onion.
Purim	Holiday commemorating the Persian Jews' liberation from the evil Haman's decree of death.
Rosh Hashanah	The Jewish New Year.
Rugelach	Rolled cookie dough filled with cinnamon, nuts and preserves.
Sabbath, Shabbat	The seventh day of the week.
Schmaltz	Chicken fat.
Schnecken	A yeast roll, filled with raisins, nuts, cinnamon and sugar.
Sephardic	Jews of Spanish, Portugese or North African descent.
Shamash	The ninth candle on the Chanukah menorah used to light the other eight candles.
Shavuot	The summer harvest festival which commemorates the Jews' receiving the Ten Commandments and Torah at Mt. Sinai.
Shofar	A ram's horn blown to call the Jews to prayer at Rosh Hashanah, also sounded at the conclusion of Yom Kippur.
Simchat Torah	The last day of the joyous Sukkot festival which celebrates the fall harvest.
Strudel	A rolled pastry filled with sweet ingredients for dessert, or filled with meat or vegetables for a side dish.
Sufganiyot	Jelly-filled donut traditionally served at Chanukah.

Sukkah	Temporary hut built to commemorate the holiday of Sukkot.
Sukkot	Holiday celebrating the fall harvest.
Taiglach	Dessert made with honey and spices.
Tante	Aunt.
Torah	The Five books of Moses which compose the first section of the Jewish Bible.
Treif	Term designating food that is not kosher.
Tzimmes	A traditional holiday side dish combining carrots, sweet potatoes and prunes.
Varnishkes	A noodle side dish, often shaped like a bow tie.
Yom Kippur	The Jewish Day of Atonement.
Yom Tov	Hebrew expression for holiday, (also pronounced *"yuntif"*).
Zaidy	Grandfather.

LOWER FAT SUBSTITUTIONS

For:	Substitute:
Butter	Whipped butter
	Evaporated skim milk, beaten slowly (pour mixture into a pan and chill)
Cream	Evaporated skim milk
Cream cheese	Neufchâtel cheese
Cream Sauces	Lemon juice, herbs, spices
1 Egg	2 egg whites or egg substitutes (try this with muffins, cookies and puddings)
Evaporated milk	Evaporated skim milk
Mayonnaise	Nonfat or lowfat yogurt
	Lowfat buttermilk
Oil (for browning meat)	Brown meat in its own fat or use a non-stick spray
Oil (for sautéeing)	Chicken, beef or vegetable broth
	Pareve bouillon cubes
	Wine
	Tomato, lemon, apple or cranberry juice
Ricotta cheese	Nonfat or part skim ricotta cheese
Sour cream	Nonfat or lowfat yogurt or lowfat buttermilk
	Lowfat cottage cheese blended with skim milk and lemon juice
Swiss cheese	Part skim mozzarella cheese
Whole milk	Skim or lowfat milk

INDEX

300

C

I N D E X

301

I N D E X

INDEX

V

W

Y

Z

SHALOM ON THE RANGE

Friends of Shalom Park
14800 East Belleview Drive
Aurora, Colorado 80015-2258
(303) 680-5000 Ext. 2109
Fax (303) 699-4300

Please send me _____ *copies of:*

Shalom on The Range cookbook	@ $24.95 each $	_____
Postage and Handling for first book	@ $ 5.50 each $	_____
Each additional book (to the same address)	@ $ 2.00 each $	_____
Sales Tax (Colorado Residents only)	@ $ 1.80 each $	_____
	Total Enclosed $	_____

(Please print)

Name _____ Phone _____

Address _____

City, State, Zip _____

(If not shipping to above address, attach other shipping instructions.)

Please make checks payable to *Shalom Park*

Sorry, no credit cards accepted

Proceeds from **SHALOM ON THE RANGE** will benefit the residents
of Shalom Park, a continuum-of-care organization for the elderly.

Thank you for your order

- -

SHALOM ON THE RANGE

Friends of Shalom Park
14800 East Belleview Drive
Aurora, Colorado 80015-2258
(303) 680-5000 Ext. 2109
Fax (303) 699-4300

Please send me _____ *copies of:*

Shalom on The Range cookbook	@ $24.95 each $	_____
Postage and Handling for first book	@ $ 5.50 each $	_____
Each additional book (to the same address)	@ $ 2.00 each $	_____
Sales Tax (Colorado Residents only)	@ $ 1.80 each $	_____
	Total Enclosed $	_____

(Please print)

Name _____ Phone _____

Address _____

City, State, Zip _____

(If not shipping to above address, attach other shipping instructions.)

Please make checks payable to *Shalom Park*

Sorry, no credit cards accepted

Proceeds from **SHALOM ON THE RANGE** will benefit the residents
of Shalom Park, a continuum-of-care organization for the elderly.

Thank you for your order

Please PRINT Legibly

SHIPPING INFORMATION
FOR ADDITIONAL BOOKS ORDERED

Name _____

Address _____ Apt. # _____

City _____ State _____ Zip _____

Name _____

Address _____ Apt. # _____

City _____ State _____ Zip _____

Name _____

Address _____ Apt. # _____

City _____ State _____ Zip _____

- -

Please PRINT Legibly

SHIPPING INFORMATION
FOR ADDITIONAL BOOKS ORDERED

Name _____

Address _____ Apt. # _____

City _____ State _____ Zip _____

Name _____

Address _____ Apt. # _____

City _____ State _____ Zip _____

Name _____

Address _____ Apt. # _____

City _____ State _____ Zip _____